Coming Through the '60s
An American Rock 'n' Road Story

December 1969, High Park, Toronto

Coming Through the '60s
An American Rock 'n' Road Story

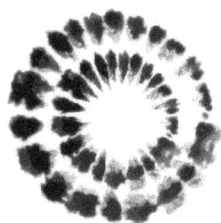

WILLIAM M. KING

7 ARTS PRESS

7ARTS PRESS

Published by 7 Arts Press
427 Christie Street Toronto, Ontario M6G 3C7 (647) 883-2919

ISBN 978-1-7771799-3-9 (pbk.)
ISBN 978-1-7771799-4-6 (EPUB)
SBN 978-1-7771799-5-3 (MOBI)

Editing by Kevin Wynne
Design and composition by Magdalene Carson / New Leaf Publication Design

To every child with a dream!

Contents

Acknowledgements

Over the past 40 years, I have been keeping notes, writing essays, and sharing recollections of my travels; the interactions and stage exploits, the thrills and mishaps, a fifty-year marriage, with friends, acquaintances, and readers of my weekly column at FYI Music News and Cashbox Magazine. I am often asked, "When are you writing that book?" "The book" is here. Not a book of celebrity run-ins, but a document of early life, ancestry, the anxiety and pressures of living with a decorated World War II veteran suffering PTSD; discovery, boyhood schemes, that first piano lesson, those early jazz concerts, education, leaving home, crossing America, homelessness, the flower generation, relationships, California, Greenwich Village, the army, and then Canada!

The good Lord has generously bestowed a near-photographic memory of places and events within me. At an age when past experiences commonly blur and fade, I've neatly stored a newsreel of occurrences that shaped my early life through the '60s — on the ground, near the highways, hitchhiking, sleeping in parks, begging for quarters, jamming the blues, and funking up the bandstand—the way I saw it! It is *Coming Through the '60s—An American Rock 'n' Road Story.*

During high school, Dad was diagnosed suffering from the trauma of war: Post-Traumatic Stress Disorder, PTSD. Instead of sidestepping the implications that took on my early life, I communicate the atmosphere in which the many children of veterans navigate survival lanes around the fear and anger and find forgiveness. Dad is that long thread between us that ties the love of music to our rocky history. The last decade-plus, Dad and I bonded through books, photography, and music, and spoke every week or so. I'd send him books—travel essays, war stories, biographies, all of which he consumed. We'd talk of others' experiences and our own.

The tone of this memoir may be difficult to comprehend at times, but I'll always honour the man who gave so much of himself in service of his country and jazzed up the home.

Coming Through the '60s—An American Rock 'n' Road Story never stalls in one place. It is my journey — one that packs serious mileage and countless adventures — written in the language as heard where the events occurred: the bandstand, streets, barracks and barrooms.

How do you thank those with whom you have crossed paths, who have enriched and challenged you? Let me try!

Military Ron (Silky) Sullivan, Craig (Scratch) Steffanides, Vic Bonndona, Jon Prano, Herb Abramson, Adam and Carolyn Mitchell, Vinne Fusco, Charlie Craig, John Cooper, Oscar Peterson, Ray Brown, Susan Oppenheim, Roger & Wendy, Don Barker, The Chateaus, Brad Campbell, Roy Markowitz, Andre the Street Hustler, Bob Slawson, Barbara Laszewski Garner, John Vaccaro, the Pines Hotel, the Jeffersonville High School Class of 1964 and the City of Jeffersonville, Eva Smith, Don Murray, Jamey Aebersold, The Michelones (Nellie, Linda, Chrissy, Uncle Ronnie, Jerry, Roger, and Medie), John Keskie, Linda Ronstadt, Chuck Berry, my aunts Margorie, Ann, Mildred and Maudie, Richard Quattrocchi, Kent Sprague, Pete Smith, Reginald Douglas, Kim Phuc, Susan Glickman, Eliza Clark, Gary Slaight, David Farrell, Kerry Doole, Derrick Ross, Billie Sue Smith, Jimmy Gales, and Jan Cooksey.

And to my editor Kevin C. Wynne, my profound gratitude and humble admiration. You took my story to heart and polished the rough edges into a brilliant sheen. This is our second run together — the first being *Talk! Conversations in All Keys* — and what a bond and mutual appreciation society. Visuals are also all part of making the words scripted on pages jump. As with Kevin this is a second run with the "A" Team and graphic designer Magdalene Carson of New Leaf Publication Design. The clarity and sleekness of *Talk!* carries over with this image of Kristine and me—late 1969, exactly when the story ends, captured in the timeless layout and design with reverence to the '60s. There was such a thing as "flower power" and we embraced. Cheers to Kevin and Magdalene. Most gracious! And lastly, to my print house CanamBooks and Jordan Dessertine. You folks are amazing. Quality, quality, quality. Service, service, service!

The big family love for dad Bill, mom Virginia, sister Karen, brother Wayne, my life partner Kristine, and my son Jesse—the latter two my life's purpose, brilliant sunlight, joy in the morning, peace as the night falls. My champions!

Mondo Jumbo

When the pandemic forced most of us indoors the projects began lining up. From March through August, I was able to complete a memoir, *Coming Through the '60s an American Rock & Road Story* and begin to lay the foundation for new music. When not locked to a computer keyboard, the other 88 keys roared. The J&B Kings were knocking out tracks—that's Dubmatix and yours truly while Dub was working on his own project—Bombastic. It is amazing what gets done when "time is on your side." With the J&B Kings, there came an overflow of new material—some more suited to my personal take on soul and funk. Jesse said, "Get going and get it down." Here we are near mid-November and what was meant to be two singles or maybe an EP is now a full-blown album of twelve tracks, *Mondo Jumbo*.

The deeper I got into the groove the more I began to think about the soulful players who most influence me and whose presence seems to be all around. *Mondo Jumbo* speaks wholeheartedly of those magnificent performers who have shaped my groove and keyboard prowess—Joe Zawinul, Bootsy Collins, Abdullah

Ibrahim, Miles Davis, Levon Helms, Rahsaan Roland Kirk, Fela Kuti, Roy Ayers, Leon Russell, and Ramsey Lewis. Since my teens, I have been mesmerized by the beat—that relentless pulse. Pop tunes have their place but a "down to the bone" popping chill rocks at my house.

Rhythm rules throughout *Mondo Jumbo* before dissolving into the finale, "Shadowland." I composed the solo piano piece in a moment of solitude—just me, my piano and a glass of fine wine. I keep coming back to this composition to reflect, pause, and think about the many faces and lives that have passed through my life cycle and speculate where they now reside. "Shadowland" is that illusory space where I imagine the dance continues into the afterlife and where loved ones patiently wait for our return.

● ● ●

Mondo Jumbo can be found at:
https://billkingpiano.bandcamp.com/album/mondo-jumbo

Preface

I have often thought about my heritage, that distant family, the ones near-forgotten in the mountains of the deep south, the class battles that run from birth to present day, the poverty and hardships that bound them together. They were "Jesus believers," whose faith in grifters put their souls in the hands of the "glory-makers" in a South teeming with charlatans, "funky-ass" preachers, rainmakers, unscrupulous bankers, and carnies of every persuasion. To understand my place on earth, I questioned if it led to a downed spacecraft and my arrival from a distant galaxy, a child, born of counterpoint, rhythm, melody, and harmony, in a solar system presumed lifeless.

Early on, the soundtrack to my life spanned 1,500 miles of the Appalachian Mountains. It was the blues, the hymns, the folk ballads, and spirituals haunting the region like ghosts hidden amongst the dust and rubble of a night wind carrying with it a mix of English, Scottish, Irish, Welsh, and African-American influence and history.

Each season we would pack the family station wagon and drive further south to visit aunts and uncles and, at times, search for a long-lost relative rumoured to be among the living, deep in the Tennessee woods. These detours were connected to father's upbringing in the border town of Hazel, Kentucky.

The Great Depression wiped the family out. Tobacco farming, the family business, the other, survival. The stock-market crash of 1929 left every family in peril. The farm was lost, and kids barely had enough food to encourage physical growth. There were decisions made who would attend school and who would work the fields, all based on necessity. For better or worse, confronting history and conditions in a region where thousands of lives were shed in conflicts over race and inequality.

Racism and poverty institutionalized, a genuine mistrust of government prevailed, and a belief that inequities could be resolved through resourcefulness and resistance. Beyond the hardships, it was a place where song, sound and the spoken word illuminated people's lives, echoing the joy, humility, aspirations, and conditions that obligated each family to stand for the other.

Along the riverbanks, there were baptisms, picnics, lovers' quarrels, and the occasional burial. The devil was everywhere, as witnessed by those Sunday "fire-breathing" preachers who ranted and raged against godless sinners. Further south "gator-land," a place where one never sank a foot into a pool of unclaimed water. Farther south, the smell of burning cane fields sweetened the midnight air as broken-bone slaves and itinerant workers planted and harvested the white man's cash crop.

Coal miners' strikes burst into all-out war. Near the rails, hobos rode boxcars through the lush countryside, begging for an occasional meal or handyman work. Along the way, there were juke joints, chicken shacks, unheeded plantations, overgrown antebellum castles, and a countless number of churches. The piano was the centrepiece, the recorder of history, the spokesman, the outlandish showman rarely contained. You boogied, you ragged, you waltzed, and danced pain away. It was a music born deep in the hills, languid small-town streets, and bustling seaports of the old South. Those same 88 keys have accompanied me from the bandstand to the studio to concert halls, nightclubs, through the hallways of power to the domain of the marginalized. *Coming Through the '60s—An American Rock 'n' Road Story* is my story, my family, and history.

Coming Through the '60s
An American Rock 'n' Road Story

1

The River's Edge

Most people are not the least bit curious about my birth-state, Indiana. There are territories situated on more appealing terrain with superior natural history. Still, not all states can boast a profound connection with adventurers Johnny Appleseed, Lewis and Clark, and luminaries such as: writer Kurt Vonnegut, comedian David Letterman, Mr. Basketballs, Oscar Robertson, Bobby Knight, Larry Bird and iconic jazz musicians Wes Montgomery, J.J. Johnson, Freddie Hubbard, and Leroy Vinnegar. Others, like composer Hoagy Carmichael of *Stardust* and *Georgia* fame, planned an early exit tailored to ambition. "Hoosierland," as they call it, is also a breeding ground for sanctimonious Republicans. A substantial cache of Republican embryos are hidden, freeze-dried, and stored in various undisclosed locations around the state. Democrats as rare as a three-toed sloth. During my third decade, the population of my hometown, Jeffersonville, was 19,000 — that is what the sign a few steps beyond the city limits guesstimated in 1960.

Founded in 1801, Jeffersonville, was briefly the *de facto* capital of Indiana Territory between 1813 and 1814. During the Civil War, its importance cannot be overstated as one of the principal bases for troops and supplies for the Union Army and an overland link to Louisville, Kentucky, and all roads leading to the deep South. During the 1920s, southern Indiana became a central gathering place for the Ku Klux Klan, and by the 1930s and into the '40s, Jeffersonville was nicknamed Little Las Vegas, rife with casinos, night clubs, betting parlours, and even a dog track.

Jeffersonville is still home to the Colgate-Palmolive Company. The buildings once served as the Indiana Reformatory South before being rehabilitated into a factory. The state eventually sold the property to Colgate in 1923. Toothpaste and soap suds. The other local industry? Boatbuilding. In 1819, Jeffersonville became the centre of steamboat building in America up until the Great Depression and World War II. Landing vessels were built at the Howard Shipyards, now the Jeffboats, which to this day is the lifeblood of the local economy, that history housed in the Howard Steamboat Museum. Most winters clouded in Gainsboro grey and summers overcast and scorching hot to near-suffocating.

Dad was honourably discharged from the army on December 11, 1945, bearing the emblems of service: a Bronze Star Medal, Purple Heart with one bronze oak leaf cluster, a Good Conduct Medal, an American Defense Service Medal, an American Campaign Medal, a European-African-Middle Eastern Campaign Medal, and a World War II Victory Medal. He then secured career-employment in plant protection at Colgate's. Along with those duties came the winding of a 40-ft.-diameter clock, a landmark that still faces south across the Ohio River towards Louisville, Kentucky. After a short stay on 10th Street, we settled two blocks north of the 981-mile-long Ohio River at 309 Pearl Street. On occasion, the family would hike along the Indiana side of the river, probing 390,000,000-year-old fossil beds near the falls (the oldest exposed fossil bed in the world) and rummage for souvenirs. Once fertile ground for woolly mammoths and every type of Paleozoic shallow carbonate seafloor invertebrate — brachiopods, bryozoans, crinoids — embedded and visible in the slate rock.

There is profound history along these river banks, hundreds of millions of years before I ever stepped anywhere near the mud-soaked coastline. There is always something pinched and floating amongst the currents. A constant deluge of driftwood crowds the water's edge and, over time, turns "bleached white" under a relentless Indiana sun. I have witnessed bundles of shredded trees and fractured homes and other weird objects whiz by unannounced. There is the loss of life, baptisms, picnics, murders, heavy industry, sex, drownings, and unexplained death all associated with river living. How you see it depends on one's association. I have snorkelled in deep waters three miles beyond the burning sands of the Caribbean Sea and held no fear. Any thought of leaping from a dock into the raging Ohio reeks of a quick death: the river, a swirling mass of improbable currents, unpredictable consequences, and the backdrop to my early life.

2

The Kings

William (Bill) King senior stood 6'4"— at times, a wild and scary, robust farm boy with a passion for sport fishing, music, radical right-wing politics, Methodist upbringing and raised on the limited acres of soil dividing Kentucky and Tennessee. As kids, we would straddle the imaginary line between the two states and predict on which side the other stood. Our early education in American history came through visiting Abraham Lincoln's first home, a small log cabin on Knob Creek Farm in Hodgenville, Kentucky. In 1811, the Lincolns worked 30 acres of land when young Abe was age two-and-a-half to eight years of age. It was here Lincoln first witnessed African-Americans transported along the old Cumberland Road sold as slaves, along with the birth and death of his brother. That land connected every doorstep throughout the south, and directly to our ancestors' tobacco fields. Running the backwoods of my Aunt Margorie's digs in Hazel, Kentucky, Pop's birthplace, I felt as if there were hands beneath the ground pulling me along. Each visit south was a three-day event, locked in time and steeped in history. A visit with Kentucky Lieutenant-Governor Harry Lee Warfield gave us a glimpse into Dad's early life, both childhood friends growing up in Calloway County. "Bill, do you remember when we ran wild through the backwoods, the crazy things we did, you the wildest of us all?" Dad said he rose to the rank of corporal, but lost rank after punching an officer over an argument. The other story: Dad, suffering from shell-shock, stole a motorcycle and drove across Europe until caught and busted.

Margorie Parrott Hankins could trace her and Dad's roots to South Wales, on to Ireland. In the 17th century, the Hankins immigrated to Virginia, on to North Carolina, then Kentucky, where they took up tobacco farming. Marjorie's sister, Era, Dad's birth mother, was a tough puritan woman. Dad said Era's side of the family had Native American blood and even encouraged me to do a bit of research. I could find no evidence of that.

Not long after World War II and tobacco farming long behind, Dad and Mom settled in Jeffersonville. Dad served four years, crammed down a foxhole in the Rhineland, Northern France, Normandy, Ardennes, and Central Europe, and witnessed numerous soldiers left for dead and wounded. War rarely returns the mind to its original state. Dad suffered many scars, some physical and a disproportionate number of them mental. It was near impossible to gauge his moods. At moments he would be playful and recall an incident from work or childhood he found humourous, and at other times, his hands would tremble, then he was violent. From a young child's perspective, living under these conditions made it near impossible to learn or own a moment of tranquillity. From my arrival on June 22, 1946, the first of four children, Dad and I began a peculiar, uncomfortable relationship. He could be demanding, overbearing, and at times, cruel; at others, with music in his heart, he could be the good humour man. It was if he was ransoming me penitence to rectify past misdeeds. I lived in a state of confused fear. It would take years to heal the severe physical and emotional scars.

Our house was a typical middle-American structure; white-shingled with a sizeable backyard and a flat pan or two, damp from fish gutting. All sides of the streets old folks played checkers and stitched together whatever needed mending. The silence was deafening, except for the wallpapered rooms where two adjacent cribs rocked and rumbled.

The first I realized a small person resided next to me, I was two years old and brother Wayne, one. We were in for the long run. Most days, we would gurgle, rattle cribs, and communicate the way small critters do when in a good mood or need of a diaper change. When left to play, Wayne and I crawled along the wooden floors past the "old man" and chart survival lanes beneath tables, along baseboards, and out the back door. A year later, sister Rhonda arrives, then a second sister, Karen, year ten. Our family now complete, and home, a prison by parental design.

I had little understanding that Dad's outbursts were linked to the battlefield. Some would say he was "shell-shocked." Dad was one of 21,000 infantry and tank soldiers landing on Utah Beach, Normandy D-day June 6, 1944. What he witnessed that day and in four years of infantry, scarred, frightened, and replayed as he slept. He would often say, "I have never had a peaceful sleep in my life. I still see the men dying." Dad was diagnosed with PTSD in his 70s.

The beatings began the moment I entered grade one. Until then, life was one long family adventure by station wagon up and down the east coast of America. The Lincoln Memorial, a stop at George Washington's home at Mt. Vernon, New York, Colonial Williamsburg, Virginia, two weeks spent each summer on Grandma Michelone's farm in Pennsylvania, summer days with the Curds—Edward, Darlene and son Tip, in Hazel, Kentucky. The Curds boarded my great-aunt Margorie Hankins and great-grandfather William.

I never met grandfather King; he passed long before memory. Dad's grandfather, William Sr. (Gramps), was present and born in 1865, a year after the Civil War ended, and lived in a small bungalow on the Curds' property. William looked much like those black-and-white photographs of men who rode the rails in the 1800s, clothes rumpled, intimidating, and reeking of pipe tobacco.

A cottage heated with kindling from a wood-burning stove provided all the warmth needed in the humid and bitter winters. Walls in the two-room cabin showcased remnants of the Civil War — medallions, rusty firearms, a broom made from straw and nearby, a spittoon. Gramps would stuff a pinch of chewing tobacco in the back of his jaw, slosh about, then launch a not-so-tidy stream of brown muck, intended for a tarnished metallic pot, and miss. The soggy gloop would veer right or left, miss, and strike a nearby wood-burning stove releasing a stomach-churning broth of putrid gas. The odour in the cottage, a memory I will never forget.

I would quiz Gramps about the Civil War, and when possible, play a game or two of checkers. I cannot say I remember much of these conversations other than it was said, Gramps murdered a man in a fistfight while riding the rails. On occasion, he would visit daughter-in-law Era, Dad's mother, and sisters Maudie, Ann, and Mildred. The tobacco habit and irritable behaviour got him banned from future journeys north.

Dad's sisters were as dissimilar as the continents. The aunts brought great relief and protection, intervening during Dad's most volatile breakdowns. The eldest, Maudie, was prim and proper, well-spoken, educated about the arts with a passion for birdwatching and children, although she never bore a child herself. Maudie married Doug, an employee of IBM and settled in Lexington, Kentucky, close to the racehorses and bluegrass estates. Late in life, she learned of Doug's extra-marital affairs, contracted hepatitis and died from what was perceived to be Doug's dalliances. Ann married and promptly divorced when discovered husband Bunk was a certified alcoholic. I would spot her ex most days in a neighbourhood bar or Jeff High football game standing back of the goalposts and nod. We rarely spoke. A year after the birth of daughter Vickie, Mildred lost her man, Johnny Ryan, to alcoholism. I have vivid memories watching the young man wither away in a barren upstairs apartment, Mildred nearby, racked by grief. All three aunts were my safehouse angels.

Often Dad was in and out of V.A. hospital either convalescing or facing surgery, and with that came long periods recuperating at home. These were the times we feared the most. Dad listened in on house conversation and reacted according to medication. These periods could last three or four months before he resumed shiftwork at Colgate's. Most times, surgeries occurred during the school year, twelve in total.

To understand the temperature and level of anxiety troubling our home, it came down to expectations. Education was a primary source of conflict in the household. Most days, Dad would pause and voice his demands, "There will be no girls, no dating only studies until the day you boys finish college. You will study, study and study and bring home good grades." Dad's decree came more as a threat than motivation.

Dad was a proud man, short on compassion and long on punishment for those who crossed him. He saw the world in strict black-and-white with no grey areas or regions of compromise, and money served a purpose, not for idle whims, or frivolous play. Retribution came swift without investigation or a judicial hearing. There would be no defense, no pleas for mercy or lesser discipline. Dad sanctioned whippings, usually with a hand-me-down razor strap like the one his father administered to his less than obedient children. Young people should never suffer the vengeful hand of those who deliver them to this world.

Mom was born in 1921, Virginia Isabelle Michelone in the southwestern hamlet of Williamsburg, Pennsylvania, nestled in the farm-belt of the Allegheny Mountains, barely a square kilometre in diameter and population of 1,300. Virginia was the first-born of 11 children, and as each arrived, they were assigned responsibility for the care of all newcomers. Mom experienced occasional lighthearted moments, absent of parental demands and family pressures. She spoke of the poverty, the long walks through waist-high snow back and forth to school, her studies, and the one prized possession, an upright piano she bought with her earnings.

Mom stood 5'2" — far down the ladder from Dad — but when on the same plane, fierce, determined, and at times distant. Her face carried the fractures and tributaries of premature ageing, the deep-set lines cutting north to south. Virginia shared the same genetic affliction as her brothers and sons: heart disease. Her hair — jet black, thick, and wavy, much to do with her Italian heritage. Mom spoke almost apologetically in a soft voice — the kitchen, command central; arts and crafts her specialty. She preached education and humility and carried herself much like a stern yet unassuming Catholic nun. I would not say she was religiously devout or tethered to scripture, however, she was civically responsible. Pride to her was as un-Christian as envy. She was part of a community of women who bonded as caregivers, caregivers by the '50s and '60s definition. They would visit hospitals, bring gifts and flowers to those in physical stress, and comfort the dying. Those moments she was not "on duty," she embroidered, stitched magnificent quilts, cut cloth, and sewed with exact precision. Most days, she moved about in the service of Dad.

Pinned to my studies and addressing Dad's ongoing health issues, I lost all confidence and the ability to concentrate. I could read with ease but could not recall the contents of the page. I tried word association, anything that would help in retaining facts or process meaning. I lived in constant fear. I borrowed library books, flipping chapter to chapter and attempt to memorize the printed word. At times I could retain, at others, confused and scatterbrained. I began to visually commit to memory the world around me, preserve a mental photograph of people and events. Through the arts, I began to make sense of my small, evolving world. I watched, listened and with a pencil, artfully drew everything.

From three to nine years old, I suffered from asthma. The attacks came in waves, breathing more difficult as Dad's violent outbursts intensified and every perceived indiscretion taken personally. We shared adjacent bedrooms, and asthmatic coughing kept him up at night. To suppress it, I would bury my head deep between the sheets. Dad would enter in a rage and interrogate, "Are you done yet? Why? When is this going to stop? I have to get up in three hours for work, stop now." I feared every visit and sensed his patience wither.

With asthma came night flying. Chronic coughing trapped me in an altered state. In 1952, air conditioning was a luxury and out of range of most families' earnings. Nights came with high humidity, blistering temperatures, dead wind, and epic phantasms. Past midnight, I would abandon my body and soar above the neighbourhood, glide about scraping fingertips tops of trees. I would calculate the distance between the ground below and above, then fly near the river's edge and watch the rapids spill over the falls carrying with it an undetermined mix of dark matter. I would then pull back and nose-dive back to earth, the getaway near impossible as hands and feet caught in a web of gummy substances. I never spoke to Dad or Mom of these incidents, knowing it would only confuse fact with fiction. The episodes continued for three years, then subsided when injections pushed the asthma into remission.

I first attended St. Augustine's elementary, the neighbourhood Catholic school, then transferred a month later to Wall Street public school, once Taylor High, a high school for black students. Singled out for one infraction or another, mostly drawing the alphabet outside the lines, I began to fear the nuns who would hover nearby, examine my work, scold, then demand I extend the top of my right hand and power-smack with a ruler. The "sister act" grew old when a hand swelled, lingered in that condition for ample time to show Mom and Dad, and justified placing me in public school. Dad long insisted that Catholicism and the Catholic church were a cult, and pressured Mom to convert from Catholicism to some other form of Christianity, which did not sit well with relatives in Pennsylvania, long-time parishioners at St. Joseph's Catholic Church. I was too young to grasp the religious tussle, although I felt the tension within the house. Grandma Nellie Michelone was certain Dad had robbed Mom of the "better life" and feared he was about to sever that sacred bond between church and family.

At eight-years-old, I imagined a world beyond family. I first saw the Rocky Mountains, the neon streets of Manhattan, the fall colours of Nova Scotia, the frozen lakes of Minnesota from the pages of Dad's collection of National Geographic magazines. I would beg Mom for a three-cent stamp, answer advertisements in the back pages and send for travel brochures. Over time, I filled a box deep in flyers, colourful brochures and hid it beneath my bed. Nighttime, I would shove schoolbooks aside and travel the world. I memorized the names of lakes, state and provincial capitals, landmarks, autoroutes, anything of interest in any given region. Then the unexpected. Dad enters, reaches under the bed, removes, and destroys. I was too paralyzed to speak. Two days later, he says: "You are spending to much time with this garbage—get back to your books." Although heartbroken, I was way too young to sense how impactful, valuable, and influential those travel brochures were on me as I grew into my teens.

3

Allegheny Moon

Each summer, we would journey east to Nellie and Albino Michelone's dairy farm in Williamsburg, Pennsylvania. For kids, it was a most excellent family adventure and a respite from tension.

Williamsburg, nestled in the Allegheny Mountains, was more storybook than otherworldly with big painterly landscapes and picturesque dairy farms at the heart of the community. Before the Etna-Sharpsburg bypass was completed in 1957, so to get to Williamsburg, we drove through downtown Pittsburgh, the home of Carnegie Steel. The sight of massive girders, orange-coloured sky, blast furnaces, and the hum of the pumping industry thrilled. The smell was overwhelming, as was the reality that freshwater flowing through the mountains and downstream was contaminated.

We would climb the hill above Williamsburg and marvel at the broad landscape below. I could see Grandma Michelone's two-story farmhouse and smoke sifting through a partially collapsed brick chimney in the far distance. Further down the valley, Uncle Ronnie's beagles howl at a full moon so grand and expansive only that big hill hindered it from owning the night sky. Hiking the back roads and across the broad fields with Grandpa Albino, I could be a shepherd watching over a flock or a warlord, master of an entire kingdom. Most days, I preferred running the woods with Wayne or alone, far away from Mom, Dad, uncles, aunts, and cousins — entirely possible from this vantage. What I believed a mountain was not a mountain at all, but a fair-size hill separating Nellie's property from elder sister Rose. Both arrived in Williamsburg in the early 1930s, lived on adjacent properties and rented farmland ripe with sweet corn, raspberries, yams and potatoes, carrots, lettuce, and tomatoes, just about any vegetable and a small vineyard south of the chicken coop.

The acreage from Grandma's garden over the hill to the Figurellas' was thick with vegetation. Wild turkey, small fox, pheasant, raccoons, grouse, quail, deer, and the occasional skunk lingered outside the back door, just a few of the apparent wild animals. The domestic ones — pigs, cows, and chickens — did not share the same aura but kept everyone fed and clothed. It seemed most in the community had Italian roots. After the first wave of immigrants, word spread quickly of this private enclave, which shared comparable soil and weather conditions with central Italy.

Nellie came from Poggio Picenze in the Abruzzi region. Williamsburg, a dream world where English was a second language mostly spoken when showing a prized sow at the state fair, or negotiating with a local bank manager. Nellie knew her future husband, Albino, lived in her father's boarding house in Calderone Hollow, Williamsburg, and married him at age 15. Albino, 23, worked at Mason Mine.

At best, farming was a stressful, all-consuming occupation. Nellie's father and grandfather owned several in Italy. Most males held second jobs to pay off car loans, feed and clothe families. For the first sixty years, the farm was a primary source of income and stability. As brothers and sisters married and relocated to nearby communities; others moved as far away as California, Delaware, and Virginia. After every wedding, it seemed another artery connecting the hamlet was severed — the only constant, the Catholic church, erected with Nellie's blessings.

There were not many things that happened out of the ordinary, mostly the birth of a calf or a dramatic weather change, the occasional automobile crack-up or a draft notice leaving a male or two absent for an extended period. The infirmed and dying received traditional Catholic care at St. Jude's Hospital, everyone on a first-name basis with nurses and Catholic sisters.

4

Gloryland

Dad enjoyed driving the long, winding roads through the back-country. He would recall the trails and hidden regions where relatives distilled moonshine. Before the last great war, Dad ran moonshine in a souped-up black Ford sedan across the back roads of Kentucky and Tennessee. "That's Golden Pond," he would say. "During prohibition, feds would come with plenty of firepower and chase folks up through those woods; this was *big poverty living*." Something to which he grew accustomed.

We attended bi-racial schools from kindergarten through high school. Across the row were kids of colour: bright, intelligent, athletic, engaged, at times stand-offish, who often scored superior grades. I sincerely believe this was the beginning of the long-term disconnect between father and son, lasting well into Dad's '70s. He could not shake history, his history, prejudice, and poverty. When "dirt poor" is the measuring stick? Find someone in far deeper economic stress to rail against. "They can't even afford shoes. Look at them. They eat canned food. Bet they all livin' off the government. I pay taxes, you know, and they don't," Dad would say. In the early '50s, during a family vacation and drive through downtown Memphis, I got my first taste of institutionalized racism.

Dad stopped for a refrigerated cola. Most times, he would buy one for himself while the family swallowed from a water fountain. Across the road, a water faucet. I bent down to sip from a spigot when a troubled white woman marched over and scolded Dad. "Can't your boy read? It says coloureds only!" I stepped back, and caught the long view and discovered two fountains, words scribbled above: Whites Only and Blacks Only.

The farther south one drove, the greater the prejudice and hate. Dad loved weaving his way through Kentucky, Tennessee, Georgia, Arkansas, Alabama, and his second home, bug-infested Florida. He loved to camp, fish, and talk with like-minded men. In the early '60s, we made the "Grapes of Wrath" stopover in Big Sandy, Tennessee, Dad in search of lost relatives believed living amongst the surrounding forest.

Dad located a distant uncle, George King, who insisted Wayne, Dad, and I climb in the back of a flat-board wagon and travel 13 miles into the backcountry. This shit was real — the poorest of the poor. Upon arrival and from every direction an assortment of families emerge from the shadows of a treelined forest, then circled George. George reassured kinfolk there was nothing to fear from our presence. All the warmth available came from a fired-up hollowed-out tree-stump encircled by kids in torn apparel, teeth missing, barely capable of mouthing vowels, sounding more grunts than yes and no, as if time-travelling refugees from another dimension. To this day, the scene resides in my head like a slow-moving black-and-white picture show; nothing friendly about this encounter.

On the drive home, Dad visited Minerva, a black woman who reared us the first years of our lives and had a connection to Dad's upbringing. Minerva tended to us while Mom worked at a parachute factory and Dad did shift work at Colgate's. Minerva's humble abode burned hotter than a blast furnace. Confined by health issues to a rustic recliner, Minerva snuggled in a blanket next to a wood-burning stove. She recalled Dad's early life—his sense of humour and the fact that she loved caring for his boys. Trapped in ghosted memory, I remembered her familiar embrace and soft words.

Deep in the spikes and further down an isolated side road, Dad located an aunt dwelling in a small trailer/camper, "bandage-wrapped" in tentacled vines — face spoiled by all sizes of protuberances and lips stained from chewing tobacco. Throughout the conversation, she coughed, spit, reached for a tin of snuff, pinch powder, and stuffed up a nostril, then inhaled. "Bill, you remember how hard we worked pulling tobacco? Wasn't it backbreaking, and your father was so hard on you? So sad your daddy lost the farm and died so young," she says.

Dad owned a hectare of land across from an amusement park on Blackiston Mill Road in Clarksville, Indiana. Throughout the day, kids played and leaped from the stone walls of the Black-iston Mill into six-feet of creek-water and splashed about for a small fee. An assortment of miniature rides and campers filled the grounds. Music blasted from morning to midnight. Dad's rental property, at the height of the market, brought in a good 40 dollars a month, just enough to pay for upkeep. The grounds concealed a minefield of muddy crayfish burrows, all linked to nearby Silver Creek. Every year or so, the creek would rise then flood Dad's prized two-bedroom stucco bungalow and uneven grounds. There were seasons when the flooding submerged the cottage in a foot or so of water. It was up to brother Wayne, sister Rhonda and me, to scrub mud from the walls, strip paint and yank rotting fish from the toilet. It was a nasty gig. Then mid-summer, the Holy Rollers arrive like something from the pages of that *Elmer Gantry* novel, except we had plenty of rain and sweltering humidity.

Early morning, a Pentecostal preacher clutching a bible pitched his tent, then approached Dad, and begged him to let them camp on "God's acre," save souls, all for a negotiated fee. Caravans of religious zealots, many left behind from the dust bowl and Great Depression, criss-crossed state lines in search of worshippers. Most bartered for seasonal work to buy land and re-establish roots. Dad found it amusing, him a weekend Christian himself.

Holy Rollers conjured spirits, much like the voodoo queens of the bayou. An upright piano was unloaded and placed centre stage, then the big tent lit, and testifying, singing, and praising the Lord began. Then the occasional pause, arms raised and waved overhead as if chasing the devil from the grounds; the passing of the collection plate — not two or three times, but in rapid succession. It was always about the dollars. Preacher man prospered from the "Jesus" business. The more fearful, the higher the donation. "Lord Jesus be with us tonight as we drive the devil from the hearts of Sister Emma and brother Clement," he would say. "You can feel the Lord's spirit all around—thank you, Jesus." Has anything changed today?

The faithful, situated in metal seats, echo-answered as preacher man shouted, "There he goes." Heads spun, eyes rolled to the back of the skull, only the whites exposed, wailing and testifying. As if choreographed, the good folks rose, hands clapping, plunging to the ground and wedging themselves between the metal chairs. "We must drive Satan from our hearts and out of your homes," the grifter sermonizes. "Dear Jesus, take the devil from us now, chase him down the crimson road, and restore our goodness for we have all sinned," preacher man persists.

Amongst a few invited work pals, Dad distributed a handful of lawn chairs. As the show commenced, we watched in astonishment — mesmerizing and highly entertaining. Preacher man yelled, "Don't look back, don't look over there! The devil is in that park, and gonna make those sinful kids do Satan's business." It was the weirdest blend: a raucous mix of exuberant kids at play, screeching rides, circus music, down-tuned piano, wailing souls, and preacher man speaking in tongues, a mini "off-Broadway" production; surreal and confusing. One could not help being fascinated, that great divide between religion and entertainment, a mishmash of sonic misunderstanding.

The day after, the preacher man disappeared and avoided paying the lot rental. Dad tracked him down the next town over and cornered him, "Come by early tomorrow morning for your money, I had some bills to settle," the preacher said in a sincere, yet mawkish tone. Dad did just that, and discovered the caravan, big tent, and most evidence of the revival gone. Poof! It was like a spaceship airlifted and whisked off to another scam-site.

I was puzzled by the lack of musical instrumentals in our religious family hang, the Church of Christ. Some Bible freak uncovered a verse in the King James edition declaring instrumental music a sin or even graver. Only the voice in play. Sundays, locked to the radio, I hear "black gospel" music beamed across the Ohio, and question how I got hooked up with the wrong crowd. There was big joy circling above the agitated river amongst those energized gatherings. It was that "call and response" thing that caught my attention: "How do you feel tonight, brothers and sisters?" Everyone responded in unison, "Uh-hum. We feel real fine reverend." I wanted the same for us, a good taste of righteousness.

We lived in evangelical lockdown. The wives of church deacons and elders camped down the front, gobbled every song and reduced to a dirge, not that celebratory "second line" New Orleans stuff. These folks nailed us to the "Old Rugged Cross." A good day for them was all about pain and suffering, even though their hands were lily-white and absent any marking of rusted nails or heads trimmed in bloody thorns. That said, many believed if you sang about it, the Lord would intervene and deliver us all to white-people heaven.

5

Death Near the Falls

Early morning heat pushed the harmful vapours from the river's belly beyond the flood wall through the trees into neighbouring eyes and noses — an intoxicating blend of dirt, industry, decay, petrol, nature, and raw sewage all along the river's bank. The river had a way of churning unwanted elements mixed with clay and silt, stirred into a sizzling broth, passed through light and wind, the remains thrust back into the air stream. Some days the smell of rotting fish was more potent as trade winds blew between toxic, neutral, sometimes organic. I grew to admire the strength and beauty of the Ohio River. Waters rose during spring thaw and regularly flooded low-lying communities. The last major torrent struck in 1937, doing an estimated $250,000,000 in damage, leaving the whole town submerged, except for a church steeple or two. Then floodwalls were erected.

I would pack a knapsack and small pickaxe and walk the lunar surface and, at times, chip a fossil from the roof of a small lime-stone cave. I imagined a king-size prehistoric cave-beetle lurking inside spew a paralytic preservative at me, disable, then stash me in his meat cubbyhole. I determined my best defense was to come in blasting with my plastic "ray gun," zap and rescue civilization, then commemorate my bravery with a long swig of Kool-Aid from a Boy Scout canteen.

A first view of life along the river proved to be much more intriguing than imagined. Dad docked his "low-rent" cabin cruiser on the Indiana shoreline. River water seeped unabated through the wood shell flooding the interior. Any excursion up or down the river assured brother Wayne and me of coffee-can detail, dipping, scooping, and tossing overboard. On return, we occasionally steered the well-travelled craft ourselves as Dad played with hooks and fishing lines. On the cruise downstream, we'd lose sight of the industrial outfits and palatial estates behind thick vegetation and woodlands on both sides of the river — playing imagination as if Tarzan camped with an entourage of noble animals hiding amongst the swollen bushes. One could only hope.

Steering through the shallow waters separating the mainland from Six Mile Island, I would catch sight of smoke billowing above a patch of weeds, camouflaging what seemed a makeshift campsite. The dense foliage gave way to open ground, jagged ferns, concealing the private lives of the mysterious "river people." As we slowly cruised past, I would run forward and position myself much like a hood ornament from a used Chevy. Through the trees I could see frayed blankets and damp cotton sheets secured to trees serving as a cover and underneath, people of various ages suspicious of our intent. I had seen those expressions visiting Dad's relatives deep in the backwoods of Tennessee and knew to keep a distance. These were folks with survival knowledge of the river, the inlets, outlets, and hiding places.

Under a blistering sun, Wayne and I would bike along the banks of the falls, roam amongst the reeds, and inhale the scent of the decomposing landscape; this a "fisherman's habitat." Below the falls, a path of connecting rocks led to pools of trapped fish, casualties from the rapids above. These small enclaves housed the fattest game. Near the falls, the fishermen, mostly African-Americans; the grounds, a source of food and reliable company.

My first impression of the falls came through the "fight game," and a man near the top of the welterweight division from Louisville, Kentucky, named Rudell Stitch, ranked second in the world. Stitch, a Kentucky State amateur champion 1951, '52, '53, '55, and '56 occasionally sparred with another amateur, Cassius Clay and at times appeared on *The Fight of the Week*. As the months passed, he began to fill out the local sports pages. My affection for the man grew: a decent person in a nasty sport.

One late June afternoon in 1960, Stitch and a friend were

fishing near McAlpine Locks and Dam on a rock shelf. The friend slipped, grabbed Stitch's jacket and pulled both into the rampaging waters. Stitch rescued himself, heard his friend cry out, and jumped back in. Stitch couldn't save his fishing buddy as they both struggled to reach the slippery rocks. The weight of water-heavy hip waders dragged the men into the swirling vortex. Stitch drowned that night, as did any hope for a boxing champion from our area. Rudell Stitch was later named a Carnegie hero.

The river was not so kind to third-grade classmate Wesley White, who sat across from me. Wesley was black, loud, and much bigger than the rest of our classmates. After school, White fished with an uncle late into the night. One fateful occasion, returning from an evening's catch, the two encountered a barge, were quickly swept under, sucked into the rotating blades, and carved to bits. The horror of that incident haunted me. I imagined my friend pulled below the surface, twisting, and rolling, flesh ripped, pools of splattered blood and body parts lost in the river's undercurrents. In the days that followed, there were few words shared about Wesley amongst the students, an event that severely traumatized classmates.

We usually gauge our commitment to sports heroes through the influential men around us. Dad loved the Boston Celtics' Bob Cousy, the Boston Red Soxes' Ted Williams, and the Yankees' Mickey Mantle. Uncles in Pennsylvania worshipped the Pirates, Penn State, and the Steelers, and near us, the Cincinnati Reds. Basketball, baseball, and collegiate football were — and still are — huge draws. Boxing was on the periphery, yet it was a right-of-passage in tenth-grade gym class. I, for one, was not prepared for this. Though sports were ingrained in us as much as music, we were not allowed to play in organized situations. Why? To protect our hands, Dad would say.

I arrived on earth physically equipped with an endless source of renewable energy, and aware that the only way to wear me down was to keep me in motion. Speed eluded me; endurance, my greatest strength. There were times I would encounter a large open field, park my bike, run the broad terrain like a wild deer, then collapse.

During a Grade 10 gym class, we were divided according to weight, and ordered to lace on a pair of oversized boxing gloves and slug it out. I remember absorbing more punches than my opponents. Admittedly, I had zero tolerance for physical violence and never attacked or fist-harmed another. It must be genetic, dating back generations, maybe Mom's side of the family. Too many boys around me seemed to delight in "bringing the hurt." I never felt the urge, or held that level of rage.

Early 1960, a new face rose from the pain and sorrow of Stitch's departure. Another young boxing hopeful emerged from Louisville: Cassius Clay. Clay had just won the Olympic Heavyweight Boxing title in Rome and recently returned home. He was loud, proud, and boisterous. Cassius beat all-comers, and would soon become a symbol of black resistance and coming change, the son of a river city, divided. It was a time when white establishments refused to serve black customers, and were legally free to do so up until 1965.

Like his white pals from Colgate's, Dad anticipated Clay would be "knocked cold," yet it never happened. Here is the contradiction. Pops loved many things black: music, the athletes, and good relationships with folks from the black community, but there was a side of him that could not expel the seeds of prejudice planted in his belly. He was a battle-scarred man thrust into modern times who failed to acknowledge the bigotry imprinted on his soul.

I can point back to a time when my father parked his 6'4" frame Friday evenings in front of the old Admiral black-and-white television and watched the *Gillette Cavalcade of Sports*—*Friday Night Fights*. Wayne and I never got much "kick-back" time during the season. There was always a catch to these all-male social gatherings — antenna duty.

Television reception in the late '50s was a constant challenge, absent of cable and satellite dishes — just a pair of bent rabbit ears. It was all about the "reception" — keeping the ghost images at a minimum and pulling down a definable picture, never dull, especially with punches thrown in flurries. Baseball required long hours holding a signal. The drawback? Teen boys do wear down much like knuckle down-dummies.

As Clay began to work his way up the professional ranks, whipping every opponent with clever footwork and swift hands, whites pleaded for his demise. The more deep-seated the hatred, the more "in your face" he got. Clay stuck it to them. The poetry, round predictions, the speed at which he delivered blows, all frustrated his detractors. Dad despised and envied him! He would recite and garble Clay's poetry and predict the next fighter would shut him up.

Early on, the fights came fast and ended just as swiftly. Dad, hunched over his bedroom radio, called the "play-by-play" action, the round-by-round projections: "Clay is getting his butt whupped," Dad cheered with delight. Twenty minutes in, the fight was over, and the room stilled. Humbled, Dad would take a short walk through the neighbourhood, return to his bedroom, and grieve in silence. That hush was more than golden and most welcomed.

One glorious day on the way to school, Wayne and I strolled near Bales Motors, a combination car lot and showroom for new and used vehicles. Bales was also a prime location to beg for a plastic model promo car. Occasionally, a salesman would slip us a "not-so-cool" lime-green late-model '50s-style Plymouth sedan or Edsel 2-door hardtop. During one of our disruptions, we spotted a pink Cadillac parked in the driveway, outside the showroom, the striking figure of a large black man conversing with an equally tailored black man clasping the steering wheel of a pink Caddy. Wayne freaked out. "That's Cassius Clay—it's him," he said. That was our cue to stalk the champ.

Once Clay was inside, we cracked the front door of Bales Motors and began taunting, "Over here, champ; we can whip you, big man." Almost everyone ignored us. I resumed: "Hey Cassius, I can kick your butt. You ain't fought nobody until you fight the both of us." Those may not have been the exact words, but they sure come close. "Bam!"—Clay spun around, spotted us, then ran towards the front door as if in "chase," watched as we scattered like cockroaches, laughed, then shouted, "Come back here and say that again!" We fled, regrouped, slithered out of hiding, then snuck back to the front door, slightly cracked, and shouted, "I can whip your butt, Clay—everyone knows I can." "Bam!"—Clay returned with wallet in hand. "I have 10 dollars here that says you boys won't step in this room." He was right. We raced down the road to a remote observation post and surveyed as the school clock ran out on us.

The civil-rights movement was expanding and targeting the unrepentant segregated white establishments. Louisville was a progressive city with kinship and respect for the arts, yet a sordid history when it came to civil rights. Black leaders challenged Jim Crow laws beginning with sit-ins and protests, demanding an end to segregation culminating in a two-year fight (1961-1963) when a civil-rights ordinance forbidding discrimination by race in public accommodations took hold. It became the first such law in a southern state. That conflict expanded when Dr. Martin Luther King spoke at a massive rally in Lexington, and the urgent inspirational tone of his message spread throughout the country.

There were restaurants around Louisville that banned blacks and advertised whites-only. Clay would find this an affront to his growing popularity and core beliefs. Not long before, he beat the best athletes in the world and brought the heavyweight championship back home, yet he was considered less than human by some in the white community. The Olympic celebration ended when a local eatery refused to serve him, and asked him to leave. This appalling act ignited an all-out battle. It was rumoured Clay packed his Olympic medal, walked "dead centre" of the Clark Memorial Bridge connecting Louisville and Jeffersonville, Indiana and tossed it in the raging Ohio waters. Weeks later, I rode my bike to where I understood it lay submerged, staring down between the steel girders for any evidence of the prized medallion on the river's bed. I, like so many young people, were getting a feel for American justice, the inequities, and the scourge of systemic racism.

High school proved to be the tipping point in race relations. Whatever Pops would say, I spoke the contrary. In the early years of high school, there was racial discord in the classrooms, and scheduled confrontations between blacks and whites announced through rumour. "There's going to be a gang fight on the court-house lawn after school," word came. A few combatants would show and "jaw" at each other. Then one day, the epic confrontation, blacks and whites facing off, and the slugging began. After school I watch as punches were thrown, avoided it myself, and ran the back alleys home. The following day there was talk of knives and chains — and arrests.

6

Mongoose in a Box

Dad harboured an unpredictable mix of emotions. Bouts of cold silence, impatience with those he stamped as undesirables, moments of fierce rage, and weeks playing the Good Humor man. We never knew which Dad was present at the dinner table. Outside family hours, he was a hit with men who appreciated his sporting attitude, folksy politics, straightforward talk, and rock-solid positions on politics. Dad regarded people on the left of the political landscape the enemy, deadbeats living in drug-infested squalor, and himself to the right of Goldwater. He lived by his definition and appraisal of others in a world he saw squeezing white men farther to the edge, which brings me to a lighthearted episode.

While driving the back roads from Cincinnati, Ohio, to Jeffersonville and after spending the day at the Cincinnati Zoo, we stopped for gas. Family time could be big fun unless you asked for a chilled Dr. Pepper. Let us just say the request was like asking for a down payment on a seaside estate in Malibu. Most times, Dad would buy one for himself—drink, then look over at his boys, "You know that cost a nickel." Occasionally, he would offer us a shared bottle or move on.

We pulled into one of those classic old-time service stations where a shabby dog lay biting fleas near a patch of crude oil and discarded fan belts, an old Packard on racks, and a grease monkey hobbling underneath. While paying for gas, Dad detected a mysterious wooden box atop a counter near the cash register. The rectangular chest looked out of place as if something alien was trapped inside and captured for top-secret government inspection. Dad inquired, "You've got an animal in there or something?" The attendant looked down, rubbed his chin, lifted his ball cap, smeared a blend of toxic oil and sweat around his eyes, and swiped upwards into his hair. "The only animal that can kill a King Cobra, mister!" "How's that?" Dad inquired.

Brother Wayne and I closed in, hovering, peering through a layer of chicken wire, and inspected the interior. Below, a bed of sweet grass, partially eaten carrots, and protruding from a hole in the back of the box, the tail of a small animal. "This boy kills deadly snakes — it's a mongoose. You only find them in India," the man said. "How'd you get it?" Dad inquired. "It's complicated. There was this circus train come close by, jumped the rails, crashed, and a bunch of wild animals escaped. We caught it near the back of the garage. We're just keeping it until the folks from the zoo collect it." My thoughts were now in adventurer Marlin Perkins' knapsack. I am thinking of *Wild Kingdom*, cobras, deadly snakes spurting venom in the eyes of the curious. I questioned Dad's familiarity with India, and curious if he thought the man meant Indiana. I knew he watched plenty of television, and had a passion for animals and shows that featured lions tasting antelope. "Boys, come in here, that lion just killed himself a cape buffalo and is dragging into the bush. Just awful!" I often wondered if it was the meds.

"Why don't you folks step over here and have a good look; I'll coax him out of his hiding place," says the man. We fixate on a clump of animal hair snaking in and out of a small mouse-like hole. "Whap!" — the tail of the invisible animal smacks Dad in the middle of the face. Wayne and I run screaming for help. Dad high-jumps, trips over himself, bounces off the counter, mumbles a few words, looks around, then 360 scans the neighbourhood and asks, "Where'd he go?" Mr. Texaco burst into laughter, nearly banging his head on a row of mason jars loaded with bolts and screws from above, and howled as if he had just told the funniest joke ever heard. Wayne and I slid around back, and discovered the killer mongoose was no more than a tuft of fake fur tethered to a string. We watched as Dad reset his balance and eased back into the garage. Then the laughter, the gut-busting hollers. After the "punking," we hung around as Dad recalled the incident with emphasis on every minute detail. For his part, he was not leaving until he mentally blueprinted the construction of the gag box. Dad had a dozen or so technical questions, all measured in inches and decimal points.

The next hundred miles were a celebration as Dad regurgitated every detail from start to finish, then rewound the story. Twenty miles outside Jeffersonville, the boys swore an oath of secrecy — valued at two Dr. Peppers!

Late evening, I caught pops with tools in hand and a pile of wood, cutting and hammering, and by morning applying the finishing touches. Dad invented tactics to distract Mom. He would send her on errands and ask for the impossible. I suspected he was contemplating dropping this on her first, before summoning a wider audience. Two days passed when I heard the old man yell, "Everybody in the kitchen, I've caught a mongoose." I'm sure Mom had not a clue what the prankster was up to. As far as *Wild Kingdom*, she watched Dad watch television. He would say, "Cover your head, they're going into a bat cave." Mom would say, "Bill, Wayne, cover your head, they're going into a bat cave."

Pops positioned Mom around the box. Guardedly she asked, "This is what you've been doing the past two days on the back porch?" Dad ignored her and began the con: "It's a mongoose, and we're looking after it for a few days. This animal kills cobras: people die all the time in India from a snake bite." Mom scanned the box, then looked back at Dad, mostly disinterested, yet loyal enough to entertain his quirks and peculiar hobbies. "What's it doing in my house," she asked. "You have to move in closer," Dad said. Mom stepped about cautiously. "Plap!"—The funky snip of tail uncoiled, and struck Mom in the centre of her face. Pops howled. Mom paralyzed by fear, collapsed, then raced into the living room. "I don't want that animal messing in my home. Bill, Wayne, catch it and get it out of here." Petite, with plenty of ice in her veins, Mom was pliable and gagworthy.

That evening, the magic box sat dead centre of the kitchen table near a bowl of plastic fruit. Wayne and I toyed with the string, manipulated the tail, and tried to perfect authentic-creature movement. We dared not flip the latch without adult supervision, for fear the spring-loaded door accidentally cracked a nose or busted a jaw.

The following day, Dad invited some good folks from the church in for a bit of socializing and Jesus talk. After a little church banter and a few "aw, hecks," Dad strolled in with the "box of laughs," placed it in the middle of the living-room coffee table, and went into this long dissertation on Indian culture, notably the ceremonial role poisonous snakes and flutes play in their lives. The religious folks, soft-spoken and gently white, nodded respectfully. Before summoning, Dad warned, "This animal is lightning fast, and kills venomous snakes." "Does it eat a lot? Do you feed it mice? I see a lot of green stuff in there — is it hiding under there? Does it bite people?" asked the minister. Dad waved the good folks closer. "Bam!"—Bodies flew. One couple leaped backwards on the couch, two folks dashed from the room screaming — heaps of eye-popping terror. Pops loved it. "Mr. King, you scared the daylights out of us — I think we need to get home." Gone in a flash. Dad could not stop laughing. The boys stood around basking in the "old man's" jollies.

In the coming days, Dad ramped up the terror tour. The mundane for him revolved around plant protection and security. He walked Colgate's from building to building, locking and unlocking, a good 30 years, then chased the occasional thief from the Colgate-Palmolive dump. I don't think we ever purchased a box of detergent or bar of soap; the back porch jammed with an infinite supply of both. Palmolive soap and its sister Camay were much like applying aromatic sandpaper to skin.

Dad arrived just past 3:30 p.m. with a tale to top all tales he would say. "I sprang the mongoose on the black men down by the dump; you should have seen their eyes pop out, big as cannonballs, I tell you." They said: "King, you are crazy, why don't you hang around until Hubert gets here; he'll shit his drawers." Dad does just that. Hubert jumped a fence and wasn't seen for days.

Dad could not wait to spring the magic box on the Michelones in Pennsylvania. Just outside Pittsburgh, Dad made a pit stop for gas. Inside, a genial black man behind the counter. The two exchanged pleasantries, shared a few men yarns; then Dad lured the man to the mongoose-in-the-box "crime scene." Pops walked him back of his duotone Ford Fairlane station wagon, shoved luggage aside, lowered the back door, and yanked the box to the edge. He then narrated the ever-evolving tale of cobras, flutes, deadly encounters, killings, and capture. Dad, well prepared, again hooked them with the all-too-familiar suspenseful saga, "Just get down where you can see it," he said. "What have you got in there, a rabbit? You feed it, what, mice?" asked the man. "No, he likes snakes and stuff like that," replied Dad. "But he will eat a small deer." "Snakes? I don't like snakes; he can have them," said the attendant. As the last vowel was about to abandon his lips, Dad popped the lever and "Bang!"—the tail flipped and smacked the man atop his ball cap. Off he ran, into the area where tires and oil were changed. No escape. Pops bent over from laughter. We stood back, giggled and speculated where this was leading. "Mister, you crazy, and you can take your joke box and fake snake killer and move on. I may need to see a doctor 'cause of you." Dad calmed him, and explained how to build it — the essential facts behind staging an epic moment of mayhem. The man pondered, then decided he should construct one for himself, something he could spring on passing tourists.

The drive through the mountains beyond Altoona, Hollidaysburg, and past Canoe Creek into Williamsburg were thrilling. You knew 20 miles or so out from town we were closing in, the stinking smell of the paper mill a first hint. The other? The sight of dairy farms. Parked outside Nellie's house, Dad wasted little time uncrating the magic laugh box. It was noon, and the basement of grandma's house crammed with family: Uncles Joe, Medie, Roger, and Jerry, all football players, boisterous and chatting with one another. One could pay a hefty admission to experience first-hand the earth-rocking fun these brothers brought each time together. Dad mostly supplied the entertainment. He'd draw from his bag of tricks; some learned as a set-up man for magician Harry Blackstone in the '30s.

Nellie's basement looked much like a farmer's market, delicious Italian foodstuffs everywhere. She would hand-cut the pasta into strips, grind the meats, fold the ravioli to a precise form, then cook. The smell was identifiable for hours on end. Aunts provided an assortment of cakes, cookies and cupcakes, and fresh-baked pies; on this occasion, grandma's pies left cooling on the basement stove. Nellie's back porch, an open area with much family history and long windows stretching to the concrete floor, a couple of deep freezers, picnic benches, and hanging above, Vapona pest strips. Flies, flies, dead flies. An ancient wine cellar and storage area stocked with jars of preservatives gave the room the aroma of a fermenting plant. It was a recognizable fragrance, one that comforted and challenged. Adults claimed the best seats, kids got the small tables near a washing machine. Wayne and I were of age to join aunts and uncles. A walk past assured a big hug, a squeeze, and scrape of chin whiskers. These were big-muscle arms; the kind of bulging biceps farmers earn repairing heavy machinery and tossing bales of hay.

On this occasion, a best friend of Roger "Junior" Michelone, a certified football star, was in the house—Galen "Butch" Hall. Hall was born in Altoona and, after the death of his father, raised by grandparents in Williamsburg. Hall played quarterback under Rip Engle's Penn State Nittany Lions 1960-61 and quarterbacked victories in the Liberty Bowl and Gator Bowl. Hall would later join the Washington Redskins then New York Jets in the newly formed American Football league. Dad had an audience with big star talent!

Dad planted the magic laugh box on the kitchen table just out of sight of the dining area. He then calculated the precise angle for maximum impact, within range of the stove and the three cooling pies. "Gather 'round. I'm looking after a deadly snake killer," Dad announces. "It comes from India, the only animal in the world that can kill a cobra and eat it as well." You could see the look of horror on my aunts' faces. The men overheard, dropped napkins, slid chairs in close, and looked on attentively; four uncles, Joe, Medie, Jerry, Roger, and family friend Galen. Dad started his pitch. "They ran around the backside of the cobra, attacked, and sank those sharp teeth into the rear of its neck." The attentive men close in as Dad tugs gingerly at the string. "You know, the bite of a cobra will kill you in seconds, but this little guy has blinding speed. He's so fast you won't see it happen, but when he's got you, he never lets loose, come a little closer." Dad seduces much like those Pentecostal ministers back in Indiana, "Dear Jesus, these are good men, please watch over as I go about blowing their hearts out of the roof of their mouths." "Bill, where did you get this animal, and why did you bring it here," asks an aunt. It escaped from a circus train and got caught by a service-station manager who saw it eating garbage," says Dad. "Bam!"—Dad popped the lever, the tailpiece soared through the air, and smacked Uncle Joe down the middle of his John Deere hat. Tables crashed as chairs fall over, uncles bounced off walls, and big flesh charged in four directions. Roger exited and returned with a stick. "Where'd it go? Let's surround it," he insisted. Joe remained in place, tottering from the head slap. A confused Hall panicked, then leaped backwards and crash-landed on top of Nellie's pies. The house exploded with laughter. Speaking in broken English, Nellie ran about chattering something indistinguishable and crying tears of laughter. "You're sitting on my pies, my pies," she said. Galen smiled, much like a child caught in a playground mishap. Somewhere there is a photo.

Men with this kind of energy rattle stone walls. The story is told and retold. Dad kept the box in motion for three or four additional uneventful episodes, yet nothing rivalled the big show. The ringmaster, the conductor, performed before the best audience on earth and made them laugh.

7

Eva Smith and Piano Lessons

Any free time after school was spent shooting hoops and playing one on one; then the big announcement: "The boys are taking up the piano." Not long after, Wayne and I were driven up Utica Pike and introduced to septuagenarian Eva Smith, a sophisticated black woman in her early seventies. Diminutive cheekbones masked in scarlet rouge smeared in circular patterns, an extra layer of cold cream made her appear a descendant of African royalty, Queen of a Nubian ancestry. Physically compact and immaculately dressed, Eva insisted on proper manners and spoke with moral clarity. She addressed Wayne and me by name and quickly put us at ease, charging fifty cents a lesson.

After Eva's husband passed, we were told a stillness consumed the house, and with that came the markings of time. The edifice had the scent of ancient sweetness, age-cured furniture, antique books, and well-worn cologne. For companionship, Eva kept a succession of black cats named Boogaboo. During lessons, "Boog" stealthily strolled the house and, for no apparent reason, shifted into high gear, spread claws, speed-skated across the kitchen floor, and crashed headfirst into the cabinets below the sink.

Eva was serious about teaching the basics. Her system included memorizing the notes of both treble and bass clefs, all key signatures, and musical notations, before any interaction with the well-worn ivories. I anticipated playing her piano, and when that day arrived, what resonated was disquieting. The upright sounded far worse than anything imagined. It was as if the piano had been dredged from the bowels of Eva's frog pond, rescued, and granted clemency. Every note echoed five or six discordant tones beyond sonic description. Only once during the two years of weekly lessons did Eva have the piano tuned, far too late to rescue the gasping relic.

Eva was proud of her personal history boasting that the "Father of the Blues," John Handy, hired her during her early '20s to play piano in his band. To verify that claim, Eva reached deep into a wooden trunk and removed an embroidered hand-stitched pillow with her name sewed in golden threads, gratitude for her service.

Eva Smith had a fair sum of money safely deposited in the bank, affording her a satisfactory degree of comfort. Friends and relatives insisted she spend a portion while she could still enjoy herself — advice she generally ignored. After months of consideration, Eva withdrew $8,000, and, with cash in hand, purchased a shiny, black 1957 Cadillac sedan, an item of status and opulent beauty. Then driving lessons.

Eva centred her small frame on a pillow under the oversized steering wheel and sat for hours heartened by the posh interior. With the minimum lessons necessary and now a licensed driver, and with the aid of a friend, Eva drove up, then down the interstate past her house, and parked the Caddy. The experience distressed her. Over time, the prized Cadillac was abandoned and left to gather dust.

During lessons, Dad sat mostly silent. Eva owned a set of Encyclopedia Britannicas he would browse, intrigued by the Lutheran theology of Martin Luther and consumed all he could on the subject. He would listen to Eva's instructions and recite them with precision the following day. As the weeks passed, and we progressed beyond the rudiments, Dad's presence in the room became a source of undue tension. Dad wanted instant results, and Eva was not moving us in a direction he anticipated. We continued with Eva two years as she taught us basic practice technique, reading skills, and inspired me to search beyond exercise pieces and novelty songs and pursue music in long-form. Then came the time to move on.

Uptown Jeffersonville, I would routinely spot Eva dressed in red plastic boots, umbrella at her side, and thin white scarf neatly wrapped around her head waiting for the Utica bus north. One college summer, Eva was gone. She died of natural causes.

8

Love Me Tender

The spinet piano rumbled and raged in our house. I looted the downtown Carnegie Library, arms thick with piano transcriptions and recordings, and soon after, symphonic scores. Wayne and I practiced chromatic and keyed scales: Czerny, new music, Rachmaninoff, and whatever was buried in the piano bench or within hands' reach.

During the first three years of piano studies, I spent long hours building piano technique, and revisit the compositions of the masters. Wayne and I made decent progress until the day arrived, and we were handcuffed to "weapons of mass destruction," second instruments, clarinets. It was then we settled into junior-high and high-school band programs. Keep in mind: this is big marching-band territory — bold, foot-drubbing, half-time bands. Honestly, I preferred playing sitting down. The 8 a.m. to noon, "hot-shoe pavement" action wore me down. The brothers were more focused on sports; marching robbed us of basketball and ball-diamond time.

Dad genuinely loved music. He entertained on radio, in minstrel shows, and at church outings dipping into a songbook replete with a colourful assortment of "Depression-era" hardship sagas. Strumming the gut-strings of his guitar, he would "talk-sing" for dramatic effect. Evenings, Dad would unpack his Gibson guitar and beat a few bars of less than memorable Tin Pan Alley fare. He would lecture us about the 12 lessons it took to master a handful of basic chords. Dad conjured up a composite of three-chord wonders tossed in the dustbin of music's past. Coincidentally, the picture he portrayed always seemed to resemble

Elvis Presley, who was by no means renowned for his command of the six-string instrument. We were impressed! Someone had taken lessons in the family.

The monotony of middle-American life had been interrupted when folks first heard *Heartbreak Hotel*. That young singing sensation far-south nudged recording stars Nat Cole, Patti Page, and Perry Como to the sidelines, and everyone in our Meigs Avenue congregation was worried. Who is this guy Elvis? What kind of name is that? Men laughed, women gossiped, and teenagers rage-worshipped. Everyone had an opinion, and everyone watched, the "good" church folks always the first to condemn. It seems whenever there's change on the horizon, those in the "Jesus know" pre-judge and denounce. Those fire-breathing evangelists were everywhere, even in our community.

"Take those Elvis records to the dump and burn 'em—wait, let's do it in the church parking lot and make an offering to our Lord God and saviour," they'd insist. Most men scratched their heads, tapped shoulders, and laughed. To them, Elvis was just a silly country boy whose popularity would soon pass, much like that corny Davy Crockett Alamo record. Schoolgirls fainted as main-street boys greased up. That sound: a mix of country blues, gospel, and rhythm & blues poked some white folks in uneasy places. Most never bought into the "rough-edged" street blues of black Americans with those suggestive lyrics. A white makeover was acceptable. It was that "fat-back" beat that simultaneously rocked and swung, that inspired innovative ways to dance around a pulse, rattling bodies out of their safety zone. You had to sculpt a sexy dance move to join the club.

Elvis Presley was the chief salesman, sweet-faced, soft-spoken, humble, and thoughtful—a boy every momma would love to nurture and marry off. Some church folks could not get past the sex part. You knew everyone was doing it because "assembly-line" babies kept popping out at a rapid pace, yet talk of such things engendered morbid guilt. The good folks knew *Playboy* magazine had been around since 1953, and mostly read by curious men in boardrooms, neighbourhood bars, backs of barnyards, men's washrooms, and at frat parties. To them, society was falling apart. Morality? There were a few notable liberal-leaning families in our community where the man of the house proudly exhibited the "girly" pages in his man-cave.

Elvis was the big talk in our house. Dad could not wrap his head around a Major 7th chord but was sure he out-flanked Elvis. He knew jazz guitar great Jimmy Raney personally, and there was no way Elvis could rival his venerated jazz idol. I had no opinion. I was too young and mostly trapped and conditioned by Grandma Eva's hymns. Then one day, the big announcement, *Love Me Tender*, Elvis's film debut was coming to the Grand Theater in New Albany, Indiana. I would never assume such stern and dismissive parents would add this to their calendar of "must-do" events, but they did.

It's the first showing, and as the curtain parts, Dad begins talking nonsense to everyone within earshot. Looking for affirmation, Dad sounds off, glances around, hoping to make eye contact with other working-class men, hoping they would agree and return an approving nod. Mom remained fixated on Dad. If Dad said, "that was awful," she'd respond, "that was awful" — the world of women in the '50s.

Love Me Tender caught fire, and most locals made repeat visits to watch an attractive momma's boy shake, rattle, and roll. September 9, 1956, as Elvis "jigged and jagged," as the Kings witnessed along with millions a television camera amputate Presley at the waist on *The Ed Sullivan Show*, guitar bouncing at his side to *Don't Be Cruel*, while young girls screamed in wonderment. Black-and-white film makes every entertainer look credible. Elvis pulled it off.

The title song was so rich and textured, and Elvis so sensual; young and old talked about it for weeks to come. Most local record stores could not keep vinyl in stock. Nearly every teenage girl papered her bedroom walls with Elvis's boyish face as white boys imitated his slick hairstyle, short-legged pants, and underwent a cosmetic change. Elvis not only conquered vinyl culture, but he was also about to assert influence over international fashion and lifestyle. Rock 'n' roll was here to stay! The soggy sounds of yesterday seemed distant overnight. Boys toughened up;

girls got mouthy. Kids began to punk-out in school. James Dean, Brando, rebellion, retaliation, the impending cultural uprising is about to play to the same beat. Meanwhile, the young man who started it all was just a plain-old country boy who loved his momma and a good song.

Night after night, brother Wayne and I toiled under pop's five beat-per-bar guitar strumming and piano-bench repertoire. Oh, did he try our patience! Dad never gave up on back-dated songs: *It's a Sin to Tell a Lie*, or *Jada*. His war-ravaged hands trembled, as his body shook. You could sense the anger and frustration when he was engaged in one of those internal scraps. We never interrupted, and let the night unfold as it should, then slip quietly back into our bedrooms and hibernate until morning.

Pops had a passion for jazz: Woody Herman, Buddy Rich, Count Basie, and Duke Ellington excited him. Wes Montgomery and Herb Ellis sent him over the top. By his estimation, country and rock music were played by "mentally flawed three-chord wonders." Classical music and jazz, the music of the educated and cultured. A victim of poor eyesight and no resource for obtaining corrective eyewear, Dad got as far as the tenth grade before dropping out of school. There was little money for medical concerns with a father whose "taste" for alcohol and gambling condemned the King clan to menial, back-breaking work. Even during early piano lessons, Dad was always talking jazz to us. I was not curious at the least. I was all about Mozart, Chopin, Rachmaninoff, Tchaikovsky, Beethoven, Rimsky-Korsakov, Bach, and Haydn. Nothing could deter me from exploring that music.

Dad eventually located a second teacher who had a better grasp of popular music than Eva Smith. He wanted us to gain a proficient knowledge of sheet music, enough ability so that the men of the family could gather instruments, read, and play together. A second teacher came highly recommended grounded in the "popular" movie themes of the time: *Theme from The Apartment*, *Warsaw Concerto*, *Lover's Concerto*. Music of a gentle nature. I enjoyed the rhapsodic movements, but in a few short months, I technically outdistanced my instructor and yearned for music with substance, a diet rich in the classics. Eva introduced me to the masters, and nothing short of that would satisfy. I would rummage through the Carnegie Library in Warder Park and borrow orchestral scores of Stravinsky, Beethoven, and Mozart. I would bring home and listen intensely for hours, study the harmonic complexities and melodic fantasies each composer scripted for piano and orchestra.

9

The Marching Red Devils

Mom enters, then Dad, and calls a meeting around the kitchen table. "Bill, you are now in high school, Wayne next year. There will be no more lashings. You know what we expect from you: good grades, practice your instruments and stay out of trouble," says Dad. A momentary sigh of relief gushed through me. Was this a set-up? What is happening with the old man?

The next four years were routine. Dad worked the morning shift, 7 a.m. to 3 p.m., then the night shift from 11 p.m. to 7 a.m. Most days after work, he spent packing fishing gear, collecting lures, and driving to his favourite fishing hole. Wayne, sister Karen, and I kept it light, giving Mom much needed comic relief, each day much the same — school, ball, practice, books, and bed.

Wayne and I joined the junior-high band when I was thirteen, and Wayne twelve. We put the clarinets to good use practising long hours blowing long tones and sight-reading. When high school approached, the two of us auditioned for the school band, both concert and marching. In a short period, both of us moved from third-chair clarinet to second, then first. With advancement came the offer to play in the high-school dance band. I jumped at the opportunity when the piano chair opened. Not long after, Wayne and I began playing in a variety of dance bands and small combos and now inhabiting the outside world; musicians a far different community than church and home — where "real life" began for the brothers, setting up our eventual escape.

My first paid engagement came when I was 14, and arranged through my high-school band instructor, Hugh Scott. Scott supplied the dance band sounds of the day for prom nights, mostly society fare before the rock 'n' rollers took over. Scott approached each social affair with serious intent. Wayne and I were much like the comedy duo, Martin and Lewis: Dean Martin and Jerry Lewis. Laughter and practical jokes were our trade. We would mess with Scott in the most creative ways. During band practice, we would hide Scott's conductor's baton, or start a "laugh wave" that would loop the room and suspend the moment.

Prom night 1960, we restrained ourselves, knowing there were dollars involved, "mucho" dollars three hours down the line. Observing the school "lovelies" from the stage was the bigger payoff. We knew Dad and Mom would never allow us to date or even catch the scent of a young woman. The folks were guided by a strict religious code of their own making that forbade contact between the sexes, which could have messed us up for life, yet made us more craven and girl crazy. I collected my $2.45 pay from prom #1 and deposited it in my money-stash, next to my bed — cold hard cash.

High-school band was not only a front-row seat for basketball tournaments and football games, but the only way to meet girls. Girls *did* hold "band boys" in high regard if they didn't blow a French horn or bassoon. A shortlist of players was drawn from the marching band for the high-level seats behind the backboards in the Field House gymnasium, with an unobstructed view of the best basketball teams in the state of Indiana, that being our Red Devils and visitors. The only downside — wearing those prickly, woolly band uniforms, much like creeping inside a dead animal skin. Down below, history made. The Indianapolis Van Arsdale brothers, Southport High School all-star Louie Dampier, powerhouse basketball at its best.

Scott took a liking to the King boys, and cut us a fair amount of disciplinary slack. He made sure that Wayne and I entered regional and state competitions in classical music. Both of us brought home numerous first- and second-place medals on clarinet and me a few additional ones on piano.

Humour was my best defense to combat family dread. Each moment outside of home laid the foundation for the "Great King Escape." The kids at ball games, at dances, going and coming from school, seemed to reside in a world far looser and distant from ours. Most seemed genuinely happy with a larger say over their lives. We had our neighbourhood pals, the Kelton brothers (Greg and Reggie), the Campbells, Barry and Mike, Donnie and sister Nancy Brown, and our sisters as constant companions. It was impossible to stray too far or do anything out of the ordinary with the Orwellian eye of Mom focused on us. Mom saw no grey areas, there was right, and there was not-right and nothing in-between. With bookings coming and Wayne and I absent a football game or two, Scott, fed up, purged us from the band program.

10

John F. Kennedy

Before John Kennedy was elected, Dad went about preaching to the walls that it would be the fall of America if a Catholic became president. He was certain we'd all be required to spin rosaries and take communion, and the Pope would be calling the shots. Camelot, as it was described through America's love affair with the Kennedys, was cover for a secret Opus Dei takeover.

With music racing through my veins, the war was starting to beat a path to our door. Night after night, Vietnam played like a scary B-grade movie with no end. Walter Cronkite and Dan Rather gave us the big picture, and got me thinking about the future, and then in late November, President John F. Kennedy was assassinated. It was just after lunch, and students were walking from class to class when word came of JFK's murder. Some students laughed, thinking it was a practical joke, but when confirmation came, every student wept and felt as if their lives were shattered. I remember a numbness come over me, disbelief, and tears — then sent home early to watch on television. There was this atmosphere of doubt. Was it because Kennedy was Catholic? Maybe retribution for the Bay of Pigs invasion? It was the first time the family sat together and watched tragedy unfold on television and looked on in horror. We bounced from radio to TV, looking for any tidbit of additional information. How could this happen? Who could have done this?

That Saturday, we watched Lee Harvey Oswald's capture, arraignment, called friends, and speculated about who else could be arrested. I'm up early Sunday morning and beg Mom to cancel plans for worship, which she doesn't want to know about. Church breaks up just before noon, we return home, and I lock eyes on the tube, Dad still sleeping from an overnight shift, waiting for Oswald to be transported to the Dallas police headquarters. Then it happens: New Orleans club-owner Jack Ruby pushes down front of cameras and fatally wounds Oswald with one shot to him while facing the entire world. Holy shit! I run upstairs and shake Dad out of his sleep, as the family gathers downstairs. Dad saw communists behind the killing—American agitators. I knew from that moment on that we would never be the same. My classmates shared the same sense of doom and dread. A nation watched in horror as both Kennedy's killing and Oswald's murder replayed right up until JFK's funeral procession.

11

Don Murray

Dad's best friend at Colgate's was a guitarist named Morris "Twid" Austin, who, much like him, admired jazz guitarist Herb Ellis. Austin recommended a pianist in Louisville who played in society bandleader Ralph Marteri's orchestra, and had a solid reputation as a brilliant teacher and musicologist. An audition was arranged in an old Victorian-style house transformed into a music academy on Ormsby Avenue not far from Louisville's downtown core. I was apprehensive, but inwardly hopeful; the audition would bring me closer to the music of the great composers.

Don Murray was an academically-schooled pianist whose knowledge surpassed most high-school and university teachers. He understood the mechanics of 20th-century harmony, counterpoint, composition, and application to contemporary music, right down to the mathematics and science between the bar lines. Don had a ravenous appetite for music and a more than affable exterior.

On the first view of the spacious studio, my eyes fixated on a beautiful, 6-foot, black Baldwin grand piano facing the back wall. I'd never seen a piano of such quality and beauty up close. Don quizzed, calmed my nerves, and punctuated the hour with anecdotes about consequential artists. I was already a voracious sight-reader, yet weak, perfecting the nuances bridging the written page to hands. Well into the audition, Murray's head raises, turns in my direction, then offers a grin of reassurance. I had passed the test. Not only passed the test, but caught the interest and attention of a master pianist.

Murray's features looked as if sketched from the pages of a "far-out" comic book—smooth, wavy, salt-and-pepper hair, the look of jazzman Dave Brubeck, and the physique of a twisted vine. When engaged in laughter, the oversized head bobbed side to side. In the years that followed, our relationship would be one of total immersion, intense admiration, and dedication. Don pushed me as swiftly as I could absorb. I became a serious student of music theory, repertoire, and performance. I learned to play a composition in its fullness sensitive to the originator's intent. I memorized extended classical recital pieces, and performed only when comfortable and competent.

The weighty emphasis on classical music tried Dad's patience. He was expecting a practical song list, something we could communally share. I was disinterested in pop tunes, the ones he favoured from the '40s and '50s. I felt there was a limited shape to the melodies and a sameness to the beat. After practicing the minimum daily hours, the family jam sessions were always there to consider. Wayne played bass, Dad was on guitar, and I would doze at the piano. Whether before or after these sessions, we would still practice woodwinds ahead of retiring. Occasionally, during piano lessons, Dad would interject and suggest Murray push me towards jazz and less classical. Murray would not budge.

Back home, tempers flared. I was adamant about staying the course. Jazz was being forced on me by someone who had enormous control over my life. I stood firm in my resistance. There were days of conflict and spent tears. I remained optimistic Dad would stop interfering and allow me to study privately, absent retribution. It did not go as planned. I would break down during lessons and lose the ability to concentrate, Dad only feet away. Eventually, I would collapse in tears, privately confide in Don that I could no longer manage the sustained pressure. Don supported me, and asked Dad to take a seat in the hallway. Dad left, never to return, hurt, angry, but not defeated. Dad found other methods to apply pressure. Unexpectedly, jazz piano books surfaced. Who was this guy Dave Brubeck, and what the hell is

Themes & Improvisations and Variations and songs like *The Duke* and In Your Own Sweet Way? Who is Teddy Wilson and why *Piano Patterns*? Errol Garner's *Five Original Piano Solos*? George Shearing's *Conception*?

Over time, Don exposed me to pianist Oscar Peterson, jazz, and blues. The relationship between these great jazz pianists and the classical virtuosos I most revered came to light during theory classes. We studied both genres, music passages from both fields and how jazz and classical forged a mutual kinship. I heard "the now" and developed a willingness to explore beyond the scripted page. The brothers were now learning Bach chorales, Debussy, Scarlatti, Miles Davis, Bill Evans, everything of interest with big smarts. Murray never said much about rock 'n' roll. He left those lectures to Dad and drilled us in music theory, taught us to read orchestral scores, and write out the parts.

The silence that mostly deadened our home gave way to 60 or 70 new occupants — violins, violas, brass instruments, tympani blasting from the family stereo: Shostakovich's *Symphony No. 1*, Stravinsky's *Rite of Spring*, Bartok, Ravel, Prokofiev. My hunger for music, dense harmonies and romantic undertones came with a twist of a knob on that less-than-hi-fi record console.

Murray escorted Wayne and me into the socialized world of jazz through Monday-night rehearsal bands. Wayne was learning to play jazz bass from the *Ray Brown Bass Method*, and I was hanging on to every morsel of information Murray implanted in my brain. Monday nights were salvation, a time when adult players with an abundance of jazz knowledge and road mileage jammed with young guys itching to play those precious charts and solo. Wayne and I studied, worked hard, and absorbed every style of music presented to us.

12

A Real Gig

My first decent-paying gig was a drive up the road to Corydon, Indiana, at one of those country-club settings: suits and ties, and music to soothe. My repertoire consisted of approximately 10 memorized songs, with the rest from sheet music. The gig was "call standards on the spot in any key" and play. By "standards" I mean songs scripted by masters of the 32-bar romantic, refined, lyric-based songs, the Gershwins, Jerome Kern, Harold Arlen, Cole Porter, Irving Berlin, Johnny Mercer, Richard Rodgers, Lorenz Hart, Duke Ellington, Hoagy Carmichael and others — way out of my comfort zone and beyond my capabilities.

The evening came absent sheet music. Big fear sets in. The elder, a one-armed trumpeter, Floyd Myles, took note and guided me through chord changes he would call as we played. Lovely, lovely, lovely. He then asked, "Do you know a blues?" Unexpectedly, we found common ground. I thought about the many listens to pianist Don Shirley and those folk-blues passages I committed to memory, and knocked out a few down-schooled blues riffs. Myles smiles, then counts in a medium swing beat, looks over and smiles again. I dig in. The evening resumes with patrons requesting one blues number after another: "Do you know *Blues in the Night*? *St. Louis Blues*?" I found my comfort zone. The night turned on a dime. No longer fearful, I pounded and stomped the blues. By night's end, Myles graciously hands me $15 and welcomes my return anytime I could free myself. Week after week, he would call, but Dad was not up to the drive.

It was a short time between Floyd Myles and hooking up with Don Krekel and the Stardusters, a 17-piece big band that played a good many society balls, Catholic functions, and proms. I'm now 15, and sharing the bandstand with men in their thirties. On drums, another 15-year-old, Charlie Craig. Weekends pay $9 to $15 a night.

Krekel carried with him two leather cases, one with band charts arranged for the evening, the other requests. Don always fulfilled obligations, even if he had to stall 20 minutes between songs to locate and distribute additional parts. Krekel's charts, a good 10 to 12 pages in length, spread the width of the piano. I could play a hundred measures before stumbling on a three-note piano interlude, mostly written in the upper register. Most hours spent hammering basic chords on beats two and four, plenty of room for clowning and ample time to humour myself. I would flip hands, then play upside down and play like a sea otter for laughs, my best Chico Marx impression. I competed for laughs behind Krekel's back, knowing there was an assortment of like-minded clowns in the band, but none as reckless as me. Playing with adults pushed my maturity button, and forced me to "get my head on straight," something I sorely needed. Standing 6'2" and weighing 185 pounds, I was still a mid-teenager capable of reading any music dropped down in front of me, yet a bandstand clown.

Bassist Joe Goff enjoyed a beer or two, and could be incorrigible after a few pints. After a few too many, and for the sake of the gig, and over the limit, Krekel would lock Joe in his vw bus then ask me to fake upright bass, of which I knew nothing. I would pluck the strings as if I were Ray Brown, Oscar Peterson's bassist. On one occasion, Goff breaks free and returns fully loaded, sights me playing his bass, and becomes irate. I rest the bass on the floor, and slide back on the piano bench. Goff picks the bass up, stares wild-eyed at me, lifts, then swings. Holy shit! Krekel and sidemen corral and drag Goff away, and lock him back in the van. Two years in, my time with the Stardusters would soon end. As a prank, I planted a bottle of Jim Beam down the throat of Krekel's baritone sax. He a non-drinker, gets caught by his wife, and fires me in a fit of rage. I grew a few more inches that night!

13

Radioland

Summers, the night-blooming air of an uncompromising July heat hung over the fossil-emblazoned banks of Jeffersonville, blistered bedroom walls, yielding layers of half-baked wallpaper. You could run fingers up and down and peel away a soggy patch, maybe uncover a memo from a past ancestor. Sleep came when it came, never when most needed. Air conditioning was something that few had, and most could not afford. All hours of those oppressive nights, an ever-present transistor radio reached out to the starlit heavens pulling down the most astonishing sounds. When scanning, I would catch shades of rhythm & blues and jazz. It could be Little Anthony and the Imperials and *Hurt So Bad*, or the Contours' *Do You Love Me*. It was those Sunday nights tuned in to WKLO where I first heard a brave new world of jazz artists.

With schoolwork done, I would plant myself bedside next to the radio and listen to anything transmitted. There were plenty my ears did not agree with and more than enough sounds to nourish a growing habit. Not long after that first jazz fix, I began to soften. There was Little Anthony's *Hurt So Bad*. Damn! I heard jazz chords in those tracks, rhythm & blues, and I am in. There was something in those recordings that took a bite out of my brain. For me to admit I was falling for music built on an odd assortment of chords with few rough edges stood against home indoctrination and current music schooling.

Around that time, a new breed of British jocks was spinning The Pretty Things. A good many American jocks were storytellers, big hype men, some anti-Vietnam War, curbside preachers, and night swinging DJs part of that big radio explosion. Wolfman Jack, with that back-country howl leapt from the transistor radio like a big dog barking at a full moon. 6 p.m. it was television and the national news holding court. To us, CBS, ABC, and NBC news were interludes between baseball and basketball, those Cincinnati Reds and Jeffersonville Red Devils. Daytime was about school and high school sports. Late-night was when you tuned in to the rest of the universe.

It was a bike ride midtown to Woolworth's Department Store where inside I found a world of discovery, and sudden addiction to '45s, those 7" recordings with a donut hole in the middle. Woolworth's was Mom's favourite hang. She liked the bargain clothing, pens, pencils, school supplies, dish rags, or whatever.

Woolworth's began as a "great five-cent" retail store on June 21, 1879, in Amish country: Lancaster, PA. What caught my attention were those wire lines streaming high above that cut across the upper regions of the store, hauling a brass canister of dollar bills and coins from cashier to an unmarked room high above. I watched in awe and imagined a bespectacled "money-miser" hidden in a crawlspace gobbling up those coins and dollar bills. Down below, the wood floors creaked and buckled under the heavy drag of bowed legs jostling for discounted kitchenware, mops, and buckets. Magically, I spot a bin jammed with '45s.

My first purchase, was a three-song EP I mistook for a '45, three jazz songs pressed and ready to play: *Livery Stable Blues* by the Original Jass Band, jazzman, pianist Oscar Peterson's take on" The Sheik of Araby" the third cut still a mystery? I could not blow past Peterson. Peterson did the impossible; he played boogie-woogie like Franz Liszt played *Hungarian Rhapsodies*.

On another visit, I uncover an orange disc labelled, *Little Stevie Wonder Fingertips Pt.1* on the Tamla Records label. Honestly, I could feel greatness in my hands. I knew this was epic — something beyond my snobbish classical and jazz mindset — music that'd spin the head 180 degrees and bring me closer to the blue edge of a song. I heard organist Jimmy Smith and Cannonball Adderley playing the crossover stuff: *Back to the Chicken Shack* and *Work Song*, Ray Charles marrying both worlds, creating his epic, *Genius + Soul = Jazz* recording. Oh, the power of radio. Then comes *Fingertips*, a magic moment that brought it all home to me.

I had little understanding of what was cooking in those grooves. There was a *Part 1* and *Part 2* on the flipside. I soon became disinterested in A-sides, much like when I flipped The Who's *I Can't Explain*, and lost my head in the reverse side with *Bald Headed Woman*, a cantankerous blues, packed with grinding guitar rumoured to be the work of Yardbird Jimmy Page.

I would wait until the folks abandoned the house and get far down the street, then pick the right time to pop *Fingertips* on the family hi-fi console. It was a rare and magical moment, one never lost. Bongos cracked at the drop of the needle. An improvised beat wrapped in an effervescent jazz-swing pattern. The prelude? Little Stevie's first words: "Clap your hands!" Loved it!

Stevie's speaking voice resonated like most teenage kids from the neighbourhood. When I heard him enter blowing "blues-worthy" jazz on his harmonica, I knew it was coming from a real place—not that campfire harp playing heard at a community pig roast, but something radically different: soul-jazz out front, and layered above a popping drum beat supported by a great big brass band in shout mode. Then it was over. Next play, the flip side, *Pt.2*, and more of the same. "Little Stevie Wonder"! I had not a clue this big soul music was coming from a 12-year-old. It would be weeks before I would learn it was a live broadcast from the Regal Theater in Chicago, part of the Motown Revue and Wonder's first #1 album: *Recorded Live: The 12-Year-Old Genius*. As more and more English bands arrived, Little Stevie's popularity waned. Even the folkies began to push Wonder from the headlines. Folk and rock music quickly became the soundtrack to the era.

I did not appreciate the hypnotic power of radio until I spun to the right, and the buzz and hiss turned to conversation and music. The hi-fi played like an aural photograph of life for me soon. I programmed the masters of a bygone era, their symphonies on the house system by day, but it was a radio that spun the living by night. The '60s were ripe for change, not only politically and musically, but the way radio sounded. I can still hear that bridge between the '50s and '60s, the light chatter, sweet and goofy songs: Perry Como, Andy Williams, Nat Cole, Patti Page, the *How Much Is That Doggy in the Window* stuff.

Dad hooked into the local jazz scene, mostly jazz concerts taking place at the Brown Theater in Louisville. It was 1962, and our second year in the high school band when he whisks us off to catch the Modern Jazz Quartet. What I heard that night did not move me. Rhythm & blues were all around and punching at my gut and starting to make sense — all twelve bars and more. That night, the Modern Jazz Quartet lulled me to sleep with "classical jazz" chamber music, absent the fire overheard from the home hi-fi. It would be years before I made any sense of their music.

It was a first hearing of pianist George Shearing when my ears stood up and assessed jazz harmony. It was all there, and coming from behind a curtain. Shearing was in town with his famous quintet playing the Brown Theatre and warming up before curtain call. I heard the most mystifying chord sequences and dense harmonics before recognizing the song *I'll Be Around*, but could not pin down the key. Shearing's playing was otherworldly gorgeous, the tonal colours, brilliant and at other times, muted. That moment, I wished I could sneak backstage and sit next to the master and spy on his hand positions. It was decades later when I interviewed Shearing that I asked him about that night. Shearing responds as if the night had occurred only moments earlier: "Oh yes, I played that in F#. Sometimes I move the keys around to play a song differently; so many possibilities." Wow!

It must have been 1963, and Duke Ellington and Orchestra played the coliseum, this was the primo ensemble featuring tenor saxophonist Paul Gonsalves, known for his elongated solos, and star alto sax man, Johnny Hodges. The band was magnificent, Ellington, eloquent and mannered. I was an evolving listener and had not fully adjusted to hearing the past in the present day. There were moments the music sounded dated. I remained mostly fixated on Ellington and the almost coded movement of his conducting hand. Reed and brass sections seemed to claw at each other, overlap, then merge in the same lane. It was all about the sophisticated arrangements, the bleed from one instrument onto another above the wails, cries of muted trumpets, and wide vibrato coming from the reed section and steady rhythm.

Stan Kenton arrived with his massive orchestra and performed his most notable orchestration, *Artistry in Rhythm*, another one of those long-flowing pieces that caught the imagination and then lulled. Kenton and crew were nothing less than spectacular in performance. My comprehension and hearing were still less than mature.

Both heart and mind caught fire the moment Miles Davis arrived along with bassist Paul Chambers, drummer Jimmy Cobb, saxophonist Hank Mobley, and pianist Wynton Kelly. Here was something to get worked up for. I had been transcribing the "pedal point" sequence of chord changes over the intro to Miles's *Someday My Prince Will Come* and struggling in the process. Kelly incorporated harmonic voicings I had only heard pianist Bill Evans integrate. The intro appeared to cover the same distance as a typical solo, and with each harmonic superimposition, Kelly elevated the tension. The right hand danced about lyrically, punctuating each tonal shift and chordal sequence before segueing to Miles playing the melody. The effect was breathtaking. From that moment, Miles grabbed my attention, held, and squeezed more emotion from me than any sonata in Chopin's repertoire. I sat, trance-like, the rest of the evening, as the band spun through an array of Miles collectibles. Songs like *So What*, *Green Dolphin Street*, *Joshua*, *All Blues*, and so on.

Miles would soon introduce his second *great* quintet in the spring of 1963 in New York City, an even more delectable unit, propelled by 17-year-old drummer Tony Williams, and a sonic blast when he returned to Louisville in 1963. Those situated around me at the Brown Theater commented on the seemingly radical personnel changes and the group's heated interplay. Even tunes like *My Funny Valentine* had a newfound tension. Pianist Herbie Hancock's harmonies were dark, dissonant patterns, allowing Davis superior options. As the final cymbal crash faded, you could sense the relief and contentment in the room.

On two separate occasions, saxophonist Cannonball Adderley arrived with his quintet, once with pianist Joe Zawinul, the next with saxophonist Yusef Lateef. The first concert, a definitive reading of the blues, *Sack O' Woe*. The second? More exploratory and painted in Middle Eastern colours. On both occasions, I sat transfixed by the hard swing, blistering bebop tempos, and understated funk.

Not long after, Wayne and I got word the Count Basie Orchestra was playing the annual Musicians Union New Year's ball in Louisville — both of us underage, in a hotel ballroom, and permitted to hang out side stage. I dreamt of this moment: Basie's banging rhythm section, sparse piano musings, and tight horn section.

We arrive in a festive mood and quickly learn the evening was about couples and dancing. It was evident this was a social gathering, and every song played mid-dance tempo as if the Glenn Miller Orchestra hijacked the occasion. Mid-set, someone must have alerted the band a good portion of us was there for the robust swing. The group then cued up *Whirlybird*, the kind of hard swing for which Basie was known. Three minutes later, the pace drops, and the dancers are back in place. Enough! We split.

A year or so later, Basie returns, this time to the coliseum with the Jamey Aebersold Sextet opening, and far different. Aebersold and band were at the top of their game. Quick tempos and Aebersold is blowing somewhere in the range of an Art Pepper and Cannonball Adderley. Aebersold had won the Best Combo/ Composition, and Alto Sax awards at the 1964 Collegiate Jazz Festival held at the University of Notre Dame before a judging panel of jazz luminaries: Julian "Cannonball" Adderley, Oliver Nelson, arrangers Gary McFarland, George Russell, and others.

The Basie band was in full-flight, complete with the magnificent drum work of Sonny Payne. Payne twirled the sticks, smacked the cymbals from underneath, and drove the group like an expensive German-made automobile, bellowing top speed down the Autobahn.

One of the strangest and most embarrassing concerts was that of organist Jimmy Smith. Smith was beyond tardy, and the Brown Theatre packed. I was more than a thoughtful fan; I was a Jimmy Smith advocate, owner of two of the organ man's great albums: *Walk on the Wild Side* and *Got My Mojo Workin.'* Before the concert, and at various intervals, an emcee arrived centre stage, stalled for time, and spouted some story about the flight being late and Smith on his way. A temporary plea for patience worked, but 45 minutes in, Dad gets impatient and starts clapping. Not the applause of an appreciative fan but one meant to rile paying customers — the clapping hastening the emcee's return. "Sorry to keep you folks waiting. Mr. Smith is here in his dressing room and relaxing a moment or so before the show. Please bear with us," he pleads. Dad grits his teeth and holds tight. Behind, an older black man starts bantering with Dad. "Those your boys?" he asks. "Yes, they are," Dad says with a hint of pride. "They like this music," the man asks? Dad responds: "They are musicians." The middle-aged black man says, "Well, there's a pretty girl down there your older boy should meet. She keeps looking back at him." Dad's face sours. He promptly turns and scolds the man, "My boys will have nothing to do with girls until they graduate college." Holy fuck! Did he say that?

Outfitted in a duck hunting vest with a dozen or so slots where shotgun shells fit, Dad and garment rise, as he yells, "We ain't taking anymore of this crap from Smith. We know you are stalling everybody, your plane ain't late, you've been wasting our time. I know this for a fact." The room applauds. Wayne and I slither down the row, out and resettle in the upper balcony. We could see pops squirm, pontificate, and look around for more agreeable patrons. Smith eventually walks out as Dad sermonizes, yells something at Smith, the room falls silent. Smith and trio ignore, turn to their instruments, and fire up the hall with a smoking take on *Back at the Chicken Shack, Walk on the Wild Side, Mojo* — a feast of glorious soul-jazz.

After the show, we encounter pops in the lobby. "Where'd you boys go?" he asks. "We met some classmates from school and sat with them." He pauses, then says in a victor's tone, "Get in the truck, I showed that Smith guy."

Early teens, Dave Brubeck's *Take Five* was one of the most requested pop/jazz songs of the day, and the biggest-selling jazz single of all time. That popularity stretched over two gigging seasons. I don't know if learning the song attracted many girls, but it sure earned Wayne and me respect amongst musicians. We even made the pilgrimage to the Brown Theater in nearby Louisville, Kentucky, for the sole purpose of watching our heroes, and the night did not disappoint. The unit played *Take Five*, featuring drummer Joe Morello's iconic elongated and lyrical drum solo. I can still hear the kit reverberate in the hall: Do bap a dap, boom bam — do bap a dap, boom bam, a swinging 5/4 beat.

Not long after, Wayne and I were summoned to play *Take Five* on WHAS-TV as part of the *Crusade for Children* charity show, which also meant we had to teach the house drummer to play in 5/4. Wayne on alto sax and I on piano scuffled our way through rehearsal before the main event. "Ladies and gentlemen, from across the river in Jeffersonville, Indiana, here to perform the Dave Brubeck Quartet's hit recording, *Take Five*, the King brothers, Bill and Wayne. Take it, boys." I count the tempo in, and the quartet hits the downbeat spot on, then something unusual happens, beats one to four fall in sequence, absent beat five. Suddenly, the brothers find themselves in the weirdest bandstand crossfire imaginable trying to squeeze melody and rhythm into a squared measure. I glance at the drummer and notice he is swinging a metre of his choosing — one fit for a perky dance band. The miscue virtually transports the "stress" brothers to the emergency room of downtown Norton Hospital. I try to hand-signal beat five, but the staff drummer misreads the cue and smiles back. I then cram Paul Desmond's glorious melody into four-bar cycles, to no avail. From the corner of an eye, I see cameras glide about the room, one close in on my hands and almost panic and thought, what if viewers catch me fumble and falter on TV? I am too young to flunk a fundraiser. I read Wayne's eyes, the anxiety on his face as if dodging an oncoming bus.

At the song's end, we were clapped off and praised as child prodigies. The brothers had little understanding that most folks watching at home through those 12-inch Philco television screens were more focused on a receptive black-and-white picture, not junior jazz, especially with Mr. Tennessee Waltz, Pee Wee King, waiting in the wings. It was a close call. Hours later, in a worried state of mind, I imagined us sentenced to jazz prison, hard labour and charged with "botched jazz time."

Take Five is the centrepiece for Brubeck's top-selling jazz side, *Time Out*. It was the first jazz album to sell over a million copies, and in 2011, the RIAA certified at over 2,000,000 sales worldwide. Miles Davis's *Kind of Blue* is still the top-selling jazz album of all time, surpassing four times platinum. *Time Out* is all about experiments with time. My favourite, *Blue Rondo à la Turk*, which Brubeck wrote after hearing a group of street musicians playing a traditional Turkish folk song in 9/8 during a tour of Eurasia, starts in 9/8, swings 4/4, then fluctuates between Turkish and western rhythms. In the composition *Three to Get Ready*, Brubeck alternates between 3/4 and 4/4. *Everybody's Jumpin'* and *Pick Up Sticks* are situated in a 6/4 rhythm zone. All of this in a short 30-plus-minute, long-playing album.

Decades later, Brubeck said this to me in an interview: "When *Take Five* first came out, there were many guys who were fantastic musicians who couldn't play it. Locally, a few jazz snobs got impatient with me. You can't play jazz in 5/4, they said. In fact, at the time, there was a meeting of some outstanding musicians like members of The Modern Jazz Quartet, Ornette Coleman, Gunther Schuller, and others discussing various musical matters. Some of them said I should not play jazz in these odd time signatures. A black doctor in the crowd named Willis James stood up and started singing in some African tribal language. When he finished, he asked if anybody knew what time signature he had just sung in. It was so complicated that nobody responded. He said that it was in 5/4. 'African music is very complex. Why are you condemning Dave for experimenting with this when he's on the right track?' I could not have asked for a better endorsement."

14

The Summer of 1963, Oscar and Me

In 1963, other than a few albums, *Downbeat Magazine* was my sole connection to the world of jazz. I purchased a subscription for an inside view of jazz musicians and the music they were creating. The following year, a free Pacific Jazz recording of the Gil Evans Orchestra (*Pacific Standard Time*) came with renewal. Individual faces: Miles, Monk, Sonny, Dizzy, Bill Evans, and my hero, Oscar Peterson. Familiar fixtures in a genre deep in superior artisans and staggering creativity graced the pages.

While savouring an issue, I came across an advertisement: "Win A Scholarship to Study with Oscar Peterson." My heart pumped insanely; a chill passed the length of my body. It's Oscar Peterson, the fastest hands east of El Paso, the heir apparent to Art Tatum. I imagined standing close enough to observe those piano hands roar. Perhaps even coax Mr. Peterson to reveal the secrets to what made him such a formidable pianist. The mind teased. There must be a jazz god? I imagined my thin frame loom above Oscar's imposing presence and a 40-foot-long ebony grand piano, and Peterson's oversized fingers strike those deluxe harmonies I could never comprehend. I envisioned saying "Freeze!" and Oscar would pause, sustain a "fat" 10-finger chord, one that resonated with me, one I had heard him play so many times before revealing all that mystery. I then wished Oscar would invite me to slip my fingers under his, and allow enough time to trace those enigmatic solo flourishes, and then commit them to memory. It was all wishful thinking.

I enlisted Wayne on bass, and good buddy John Cooper on drums to record a demo tape. Two songs, the standard *Sometimes*

I'm Happy, the other, The Beatles' *Ticket to Ride*, and mailed them to the Advanced School of Contemporary Music, 21 Park Road, Toronto, Canada. Weeks later, I receive a Western Union telegram announcing the awarding of a partial scholarship, half the tuition paid. One can never underestimate the delight and inner joy a teenager feels the moment something of this magnitude intercedes in the humdrum of life. Mom and Dad agree to let me follow through with the journey north if I secured lodging with Christian-minded individuals in Toronto. Negotiations between Meigs Avenue Church of Christ and an east-end Church of Christ in Toronto guaranteed accommodations for me with an elderly couple living off Coxwell Avenue on Currie Avenue for a fee. I had been saving my earnings with The Don Krekel Orchestra and banked $700 from weekend gigs. Schooling and admission to Peterson's summer camp, $125, lodgings, $120, and a $20 bill tucked away into my wallet for six weeks of nickel and dime rationing, the remainder in my bank account destined for future education.

Crossing the border into Canada, Dad began acting as if he had entered *The Twilight Zone*. Cars zipped by at a rapid clip. "Right on red" screwed with his sense of law and order. Downtown Toronto, bustling with trolleys and pedestrians, confused and unnerved him. Dad swore he would never return, other than to snag his self-absorbed son.

My surrogate guardians resembled an English take on the famed middle-American TV show, *Andy of Mayberry*. I now had my own Aunt Bea to upset. Breakfast was appalling. Never assume a 17-year-old mid-western boy can get by on marmalade toast and a half-baked, extra-terrestrial egg. My palette was hitched to a Kentucky spread: country sausage, farm eggs, white toast. Not survival rations.

I was extremely fearful of entering Peterson's brick schoolhouse at 21 Park Road. The Advanced School of Contemporary Music stood across from where the Hudson's Bay Store now resides. To me, it was an address of mythic proportions, the house Oscar held court, where bassist Ray Brown and drummer Ed Thigpen would soon tutor me, and jazz icon, Dizzy Gillespie, would drop by for an impromptu hang; a place where the "hip" community of Toronto stored those secret jazz codes.

After checking in, I'm greeted by receptionist Geordie McDonald, walked down a hallway and guided to a chalkboard, read the necessary qualifications, told we'd be divided into groups A, B, C, and D, and then informed I would have to submit to a terrifying ear-training exam. As the test begins, chord changes jet by, making note-chasing near impossible. Only when a medium-tempo blues slow-walked, was I able to identify the form. Oscar later admitted the opening salvo was no more than basic rhythm changes. A thorough grounding in theory and proper piano technique earned me a placement in the C group. At 17, I was the second-youngest student on the premises.

The long days were devoted to lessons in ear training and theory, with Ray Brown and Ed Thigpen as my constant companions. I became so immersed in jazz; I would practise eight hours a day, drag my tired legs across town to Aunt Bea, who, after my long absences, was less than enamoured with my erratic schedule.

I did not see Oscar again until week two, when a stunning navy-blue Mercedes convertible pulls up and parks alongside the school. I had bonded with a 16-year-old drummer from Minneapolis, and together the two of us slip around back and examine the master's ride. Both awestruck. The interior of Oscar's Mercedes convertible hinted of European luxury. I had never seen such plush, soft-brown leather interior in an automobile, especially up against Dad's International Harvester wagon.

Week two, Oscar arrives, and class begins. I'm mindful of the questions I want to ask; I sit mute, much like a whispering pine. I recall the hours I had spent dissecting those elegant harmonies Peterson scripted for the trio's *West Side Story* album, those glorious arrangements! I longed to inspect the manuscripts, but how could I ask? More than anything, I wanted to see precisely where Peterson's fingers rested as they travelled the length of the keyboard and the positions where such magnificent ideas originated.

Oscar sits, places his enormous hands across the piano keys and plays a short passage from a standard. I recognized the touch of the lyrical right hand and dense harmonies then ask myself, why is he pausing? Oscar then speaks in generalities, the lesson an overview of piano jazz, peppered with thoughts on Art Tatum, Teddy Wilson and others, nothing specific. It was more about his physical presence and stature. Oscar, a jazz celebrity.

As the days begin to mirror the previous, I trap my hero in his ground-floor office. I speak to Oscar of my heartfelt admiration and ask about new music, anything that would enlighten and expand my universe. Oscar graciously pulls out a recording of pianist Claire Fischer, *Surging Ahead*. He draws from above another, pianist Junior Mance's, *Live at The Village Gate*. Peterson insists Mance plays the blues like no other, and Fischer was onto something he found enthralling. He also circled Mance's *Smokey Blues*, and said, "All you need to know about playing blues piano is in those grooves." That was all I wanted to hear. Peterson's inspired words were sufficient to launch me full tilt into jazz and blues.

As the summer in Toronto wore on, I began walking to and from school. Although trolley fare was merely fourteen-and-a-half cents if you owned a book of tickets, I had blown most of my wallet stash on restaurants, something I had had little experience with back home. I would sip the occasional lemonade, then a late-evening prowl through the barren Toronto streets, through the folk- and jazz-crazed haunts of Yorkville Avenue, and order a hot chocolate or cola.

Across the road from the school stood a farmhouse-style structure I would soon learn was a well-liked jazz haunt, the First Floor Club at 33 Asquith Avenue. With strict liquor laws, the fire escape was the only vantage point I could catch a glimpse of the world inside. One glorious evening, Minnesota and I hang on the fire escape and watch from an open window be-bop pianist Lennie Tristano serve up what seemed like Bach playing jazz. Another Sunday afternoon, I dared slip inside for a jam session where local drummer Archie Alleyne and saxophonist Kenny Baldwin played the opening strains of some unidentifiable song. Decades later, both musicians would become central players in my life. Another walk took me up Avenue Road to 169, The

Cellar Jazz Club. I watched from the street a young man I would learn was the same age, but far more advanced. Tony Collacutt was playing a scorching bebop solo on an upright piano.

I lived and loved studying jazz on Park Road. I also relished my private third-floor study. It was July, and humidity peaking, now and then bassist Ray Brown would unexpectedly knock, slide in with acoustic bass in hand and attempt to subdue my scattershot tendencies. Brown knew I was searching for the cagy sounds the "great one" served up, and advised me to lower my expectations and work with what I knew and about to learn. His patience and advice paid off. Upon leaving summer school, I heard those intervals and complicated harmonies that all but alluded me. Four years later, at Local 49 Los Angeles Musicians Union, I walked up to Ray Brown, and introduced myself. Brown was then the bassist for the Merv Griffin Show. As he sipped from a drink, he mumbled something. I feared I stepped on sacred ground. As I walked away, Brown turns and asks, "What did they call you back then?" "They called me Louisville." Brown pauses and then says, "I remember you. You don't look the same. Keep it up." I hope not. Back then, I was a borderline nerd-boy, much like most other teenage musicians my age. With Brown, every student identified by the city of their origin: Denver, Chicago, Minneapolis, Louisville.

In my final week, I ran out of money and walked the long stretch from 11 Currie Avenue to 21 Park Road and back, exhausted and fed up and facing a school bully. The age difference between me and the others was boy to man, and at times, frustrations boiled over into near punch-ups. It was drummer/adult Bruce Styles who pushed my button, and never missed a moment to ridicule or demean. Even in an environment as assured and creative as this, confrontations took place between players. Styles had it all; a beautiful girlfriend, freedom, and me as tag-along baggage. He also had mini-battles with Thigpen and other staff; a fixture, and not going anywhere. I had more opinions than options. Styles would throw them back at me then laugh. Teenage anger knows no bounds. Eventually, it all came to a head when Bruce verbally abused his girlfriend as we drove around in a taxi. I saw her as a

European screen beauty, not deserving of abuse; all women precious in my young eyes, never to be demeaned or intimidated. It was a hallway run-in resulting in a shoving match then separation by staff, both of us warned to avoid the other or face expulsion. Our paths would cross again seven years later, 1970, at 851 Hallam Street, an eight-room apartment complex housing musicians. Bruce dropped in to meet a friend and introduced himself to me. I looked on in astonishment and returned the greeting, pause, recognize, laugh, and we hug. Bruce was now a martial arts expert. Indeed, a sense of relief and far better memory than that of an imagined boyhood menace.

The family arrives on the final day to retrieve their eldest son. I packed everything but my monaural Ampro reel-to-reel tape recorder, with taped evidence of my progress and set to "play" position. Upstairs at Auntie Bea's, Mom greets me as I pack a few clothes. I then ask her to sit on the edge of my bed and listen. I turn the lever to play. Mom quickly rises and shouts, "Turn that down; you're bothering people." Emotions thundered in me between anger and sadness. I packed the machine and swore it was last time I would ask her to listen to anything musical of me. I learned early; Mom had no interest or curiosity about music, only the fear of offending or interrupting the outside world. So be it.

15

Jazz Up My World

Pianist Don Murray moved his studio from the classical confines of the Ormsby Avenue mansion to a barn-like structure called the Arts in Louisville, a foremost jazz club with Playboy style bunnies serving drinks. Murray's downstairs space served not only for teaching but Monday-night jam sessions. My instruction time with Don ended a year before, but we kept up the jam sessions. I would also drop by the waiting area of Don's facility to inspect the latest jazz records on display.

I have no recollection of how I landed my first jazz piano trio gig in the Arts, other than those six weeks studying with Oscar Peterson in Canada. Then the call came, opening act for the Wes Montgomery Trio. Damn! A sixty-minute set and our trio with a good half-hour of material. There would be a lot of blues in play.

We arrive early, set up, and I tap a few notes on the baby grand piano, which was not an instrument a pianist could take to heart, but passable. I then situate myself at the bar, look above and notice the upper perimeter of the room lined with empty liquor bottles, a decorative consideration. The Arts was massive, cut in rough timber, and covered in wall posters of 19th-century Parisian life, jazz clubs, jazz musicians and other destinations. Playing in the background, newcomer Nancy Wilson's dynamic *Guess Who I Saw Today?* Those five words hit me like a keg of dynamite. I was down for a cola and ask the bartender who's singing. "That's Nancy Wilson," he says. I had heard her sing *Happy Talk* and *Sleepin' Bee* on WKLO Sunday nights, one of the rare times I didn't switch the dial in favour of an instrumentalist. Wilson debuted with the Cannonball Adderley Quintet in 1961 on Capitol Records: *Nancy Wilson / Cannonball Adderley*. Then I hear, "I was born in a bunk, my momma died, and my daddy got drunk." Lord help me. "Who's that?" I ask. "That's Lou Rawls and his trio — Lou Rawls Live!" the bartender says. It was like a bomb went off in my head introducing me to the world of great jazz singers. Vocalists I had mostly ignored.

Content to drink cola after cola, I beg the bartender to replay the recordings. Then the most stunning woman I had ever observed, barmaid Jackie Myles takes my order. Jackie "Myles" Brengle, as she was known then, was the daughter of my first paid employer, trumpeter Floyd Myles, and married to the local bassist, Jack Brengle. Lovely from head to toe and every boy's dream pin-up girl. It was a challenge at this age to even have a conversation with a mature woman, especially one this attractive and a good seven or eight years older. For a shy Indiana boy, just conversing took greater courage.

A few jazz heads sat down front of our opening set. We jam away but didn't perform anything that advanced or challenging, just a righteous groove and kept it modest. At set's end, the three of us are awarded a polite, complimentary round of applause. Enter Wes Montgomery! Big star time, and the room reacts. As quickly as we exit the stage, the barn fills up. Organist Melvin Rhyne extends a few drawbars on the Hammond organ; Montgomery taps the strings, the trio now in motion. As the trio play, I ask myself, when is the organist going to squeal like Jimmy Smith? It never happened. Someone next to me says, "He's not very exciting, is he?" I had to listen and shed any preconceptions I had about the Hammond B-3. This was from the head and heart, absent that gospel dynamic or expected blues intent of purist jazz. The trio played the groove with precision whatever the style, from Ellington's *Satin Doll* to Ann Ronell's *Willow Weep for Me*. In passing, I said something to Montgomery, of which I will never recall, and he smiled back. I stood close to the man and thought to myself, this is the same guy I had read about, when at 19 he would fall asleep with the guitar in his hands and practice 16 hours a day. It all happened that fast!

16

Jamey Aebersold

We hit gold with educator Jamey Aebersold. Jamey was graduating from Indiana University with a degree in alto saxophone and became our trusted mentor. Aebersold is still an astounding musician who lives one town over in New Albany, Indiana. Jamie taught us how to compose and hear jazz. We spent hours listening to the bebop grooves of Sonny Rollins (*Saxophone Colossus*), Hank Mobley (*Poppin'*), Bud Powell (*The Amazing Bud Powell*), Kenny Dorham (*Una Mas*), and the like.

Aebersold's method was a far different instruction style than my studies under pianist/composer Don Murray. Jamey was straight to the meat of the matter. Improvisation and research. Murray — Bach, Beethoven, then Bill Evans. Both solidified and grounded me in music. Where Don took an interest in the emotional well-being of his students, Jamey brought much-needed levity and humour to each session.

Occasionally, Jamie would hire me for a park concert or casual gig. Teaching was his priority and getting out and playing with his quintet a necessity. Aebersold was already somewhat of a local hero — a no-nonsense, passionate, and, at most times, an understated funny man. He walked a different path than most players and inspired us by doing so. Jamey's presence was a lesson in grounding, commitment, and possibilities. Aebersold was not only an award-winning alto saxophonist but an excellent traditional jazz bassist and bebop pianist. It was those rumpled and sometimes discarded pieces of manuscript paper, improvised lessons that blossomed into a series of universally embraced educational play-along books. Jamey was not the sort of person who surrounded himself in opulence, but a man of great humility and character. Aebersold, to this day, is noted for his "quiet" charity, commitment, and humility.

One of the most memorable gigs with Aebersold occurred in a ballroom in a swanky Indianapolis hotel and way beyond description. The gig? The Teddy Phillips Orchestra and his "Laughing Saxophone" featuring Daisy Mae.

Phillips was a staple of social circles in Chicago playing the Aragon Ballroom with two radio hits in the bag: *Melancholy Mood* and *Don't Call Me Sweetheart Anymore*. In the early '60s, Phillips modified his act to become the Mexicana Brass, with wife Coleen "play-acting" at half-time a weird blonde bombshell character, Daisy Mae, from Dogpatch, USA, based on the newspaper comic *Li'l Abner* from cartoonist Al Capp. Throughout the gig, Aebersold played it mostly straight until the slurpy novelty tune, *Josephine*. Jamey exaggerated the melody with a wide comedic vibrato. When called on to solo, Aebersold would play with amusing determination. I laughed so hard that my stomach cramped. Phillips took note and scolded me, oblivious to Aebersold's liberties with the song.

Half time, I hung for the floor show and the blondie act, near impossible to watch. The heavy breathing, fake Marilyn Monroe farm-girl muttering, barnyard squeals, all hideous and laugh-inducing. Phillips spots me chuckling, and backslapping another player, calls a meeting backstage with Jamey and me, "I want to fire you," he says. "You made fun of my wife. You are just a boy with much to learn." Jamey intercedes and lowers the temperature. Then Coleen goes off on me, swears, growls and hisses. Next set, I tone it down and ready to ride the evening to a subdued conclusion when I spot a massive bouquet of balloons floating near the piano, helium-filled and bundled. During a tacit section of another insipid Phillips medley, I swipe a patch from the air and hook to my Sammy Davis style broad-rim glasses, and release, thinking the grouping would linger around the piano. The unexpected happens, the balloons catch a breeze and float out of range. I am unable to leave my position, sit and watch as the horn-rims glide past the bass player then stall in front of

Phillips. Phillips spots them, snatches them in one desperate swipe, then yells, "Whose the fuck are these?" I meekly wave back. Phillips goes ballistic, flings the glasses and balloons my way, walks over and unleashes a dozen or so profanities. The balloons barely moved a foot beyond Phillips's music stand. He then scoops, curses, hands them to me and walks away. Afterwards, I let Jamey settle the pay thing, and politely disappear.

17

Hard Day's Night

That ever-present transistor radio twisted my head up, as well, the evening news documenting a massive cultural shift and a progressive youth movement. Straddling the landscape between jazz and rock, was simple for me as Wayne and I decide to push in a direction more in tune with the times. A good many Americans viewed England as either the Queen's property or a place where a disobedient band of scavengers led by Robin Hood ambushed the wealthy from their Sherwood Forest hideout. Most did not know the exact location of Sherwood Forest, yet it seemed overly crowded with bandits in perpetual conflict, compared to the untapped Smoky Mountains of Tennessee and occasional hillbilly shoot-out.

Stateside, hairstyles for men ran the gamut between military to Princeton cut. Either you adopted a flat-top, both sides of the head skinned and seared like a freshly braised lamb chop, or the JFK look, lightly cropped along the sides, parted, and side-combed. I never gave it much thought until the arrival of the great British Invasion.

Young Americans were in a foul mood, still ailing from the death of a beloved president. Then something suddenly happened: the British Invasion. The Beatles arrive, John, George, Paul, and Ringo. Even more so: an optimistic, triumphant single called *I Want to Hold Your Hand* finds its way into the pulsating hearts of America's pre-teens.

In school I channelled the Beatles and bad boy Rolling Stones, even pencilled their names across my textbooks. To me, the Beatles where mildly entertaining compared to the roadhouse blues and coarse guitar work of Keith Richards and Brian Jones. How could one blow past a band which named themselves after a Muddy Waters song? What the hell was a Beatle anyway? While the world is firmly in the grip of rock 'n' roll, I'm under the growing influence of Memphis soul. Elvis reigned supreme while Jerry Lee Lewis raised hell around the perimeter. Chuck Berry still had a hold on the naughty girls, but that was about to snap after a fling with an underage child. Suddenly, one small 7" 45-rpm single was about to transform AM radio.

Few recognized the coming upheaval. At first, it seemed almost comical. Four young men from Liverpool, England, a place so not on the world map. Not a birthplace of cultural significance like Chicago, Kansas City, or New Orleans, but a city of negligible interest. Four boys — sporting long hair, short bangs, outfitted in custom-made suits, and pointy boots — threw light on a depressing world clock, and shook us out of a '50s coma.

December 10, 1963, CBS Evening News ran a five-minute special on The Beatles. Within moments request lines lit up across America. In less than three weeks *I Want to Hold Your Hand* sold nearly a million-and-a-half copies, America about to be blanketed in Beatles paraphernalia. Five-million posters of the handsome boys with a peculiar dialect papered the landscape. Most of us did not realize there was a decade in age separating the Liverpool quartet from young admirers. The screaming begins. Oh, those shrieks and happy tears!

From a teenage boy's perspective, change came way too fast and with consequence. Like so many young men of the time, keeping pace with The Beatles meant growing hair down below the ears and dressing apart from the crowd. Suddenly, our house becomes a battlefield, Dad offended by non-conformists. He assumed they were a threat to his position in the community and an embarrassment to the King family. A good portion of America was not accepting; by this, I mean The Beatles seemed like a harmless diversion, yet poking at middle America brought with it a long-term conflict. That struggle played out from home to home, depending on family values. Athletes and war personalities were the measures of a man. Musicians and artists were way too radical, unemployable, and unacceptable in the eyes of a good many conservative families.

I remember crossing paths with Mom at Kroger's Supermarket in downtown Jeffersonville, and a woman approached and said, "How can you live in the same house with that Beatle?" The interloper fixated on my hair, no more than an inch or two in length. Mom's face reddens, she turns to me, scolds, then insists I get a proper haircut, something collegiate or military in style. "I don't want to walk around town with all these women coming up to me and talking about you like that," she says. These daily altercations began to multiply. Keep in mind, we are traversing territory where few whites embraced their black counterparts, lived side by side, but kept a distance. On another occasion, I was waiting for a bus to Louisville when a woman walked up and spit on me, saying, "You look like a Beatle. You should be ashamed of yourself." "You can't be spitting on girls, ma'am." These words spoken by a skeptical bus driver.

The first wave of Beatlemania charmed and uplifted Americans. The rest of the biosphere had already embraced the Beatles, most without reservation. The band was eloquent, stylish, and confident trendsetters and, above all, big fun and made for television. Ed Sullivan took a fancy to the group absent the kind of criticism Sullivan endured showing a sexually charged Elvis doing the infamous "leg-tremble."

The Beatles went a step farther than Elvis, and enlisted art-film maker Richard Lester to make a riotous Beatles "run-about" film: *A Hard Day's Night*. Lester chose to craft a comedy integrating each personality, starring John Lennon, Paul McCartney, Ringo Star, and George Harrison splendidly shot in black-and-white and loaded with great songs; singles ripe for top-40 airplay. Lester and writer Alun Owen tapped into an evolving film genre channelling the rhythm of the new wave of British filmmaking and allowing the individualities of the Beatles dominate. *A Hard Day's Night* follows two days in the life of the band. And yes, plenty of screaming.

Wayne and I catch the film at the Rialto Theatre on 4th Street, just south of Chestnut in Louisville, Kentucky. Even Elvis's films played there in 1955. I realized nothing this carefree and blissful existed in our home, willing to believe anything was achievable. As the curtain rose, the screams rocked the theatre from its foundation. Tears, more tears, squeals of joy overwhelmed, then the crying. It was easy to transpose oneself onto the big screen and imagine that what was happening to these four musicians could happen to you. Wayne and I would return multiple times to view the Beatles follow-up film, *Help!* The Beatles, a welcome fantasy in our world, far removed from the claustrophobic melodramas playing out at home and in high school. Where Elvis came across as shy and coy, the Beatles fired on all cylinders, much like the Marx Brothers in *A Night at the Opera*. I, for one, drawn to the sound of the band, each recording original and imaginative, marvelled at the extraordinary interplay between players.

Over dinner, I would try my parents' patience playing everything from Stravinsky's *Firebird Suite* to John Coltrane's long-winded *India*, both pieces surpassing the duration of a "sit-down" dinner lingering into study time. I tested Dad's preference for jazz with Coltrane's "bag-of-snakes" sound, as he called it — the ferocious energy and biting soprano saxophone. I would drop the needle just as Mom was plating chicken, fried steak and mash potatoes, Coltrane improvising 14 heroic minutes through the main course. I could read the dread on their faces. Other times, I would serve up The Beatles' *I Feel Fine*, clocking in at two minutes and ten seconds, necessitating multiple plays to complete the first course, me enamoured with Ringo Starr's drumming. Ringo played a jazz-rumba shape I was familiar with, playing it with authority throughout. Near song's end, the band does this breakdown section leaving Ringo to complete a few syncopated strokes on the toms and snare drum. I'd spin the single time and time again in awe of those loose mini-flourishes. With me, Ringo earned the same enthusiastic reaction as when listening to Coltrane.

Around the home area, the casualties of Beatlemania were the local disc jockeys. The older jocks who spoke with a sweet Southern drawl or "brain-challenged teenybopper cadence" were tossed aside in favour of younger men with forged British accents. Not only did DJs modulate tone, but they were also now expected to talk publicly in a manner unheard, ushering in an age of gimmicky British-style promotions.

The fake radio jocks rode around Louisville in horse and carriage, mimicking what Americans perceived to be British mod style, and speaking in a cockney accent while draped in Carnaby Street chic. Those sock-hops featuring 10-piece cover bands playing the latest top-40 hits gave way to four-piece units acquainted with the current Beatles catalogue and a game-changer.

The Beatles wrecked our home. As the war in Vietnam escalated, and the youth movement became politicized, The Beatles began playing their age and committed to numerous social causes. The band experimented with mind-altering drugs and flirted with mystical shamans in step with the seasons. The times they were a-changing, and so was I, and those around me. However naïve we may have been, we now stepped at a different tempo, as if awoken from a long sleep. I, for one, embraced it. The Vietnam War loomed just beyond my upstairs bedroom window, and I now had allies in the coming struggle.

18

The Chateaus

Occasionally, the mind will resurrect an image or two from the moments when the brain began to collect and compute the world around. I have this memory photo of Wayne and me when we first lived on 13th Street, sitting on a curb and playing with a toy rake. For reasons unknown to me, I whacked my brother upside the head, drew blood and the wrath of Dad. Why kids do shit like this is beyond asking. A second image was that of the older boy living next door who I would track along the backyard fence. Only months in this world, and barely able to stand or comprehend my surroundings, I became fascinated with the boy next door. His sweetness and gentle demeanour eased the tension quaking every blade of grass and plant in our backyard.

Donnie Barker was a few years older and quickly out of my life. We moved to the centre of downtown Jeffersonville, 309 Pearl Street, and lost all connection with the folks from the old neighbourhood. Barker was two years ahead of me in junior high and high school and mostly out of view, except for the occasional cordial exchange. I knew Don had a love for music yet did not know where this would lead. Then the call came. It's 1964, and Donnie invites me to audition for his rock band, The Shadows. I had a basic understanding of rock, mostly listening to the radio and scribbling the names of my favourite bands on the front and the back of notebooks and had surface-learned a few rock tunes omitting the essentials. I passed the audition, and found myself playing weekends in the top Midwest teen venues in the towns up and down Indiana and Kentucky, and soon discover that Donnie was still the same kind, level-headed person I had spied through the backyard fence. The Shadows: vocalist Donnie Barker, Tinsley Stuart, Gary "Squeaks" Harrod, Bill Garrett, Frank Bugbee on guitar, Bobby Webb on bass, Gary King, Bill Rowe on sax, and Johnny Coffman on drums were a band of mixed personalities. Two horns, four rhythm and four lead singers and plenty of teenage testosterone playing a mix of R&B and pop.

Early on, The Shadows were booked to play the R.J. Reynolds mansion for the tobacco/aluminum king, at a party celebrating the 15th birthday of a son. The band sets up on the family's ornate wood veranda near where I catch a glimpse of teenagers partying around the family pool. An hour into the festivities amid heavy drinking, a teenager trips and falls in the pool, then chaos erupts when an adult dives in and rescues them. While on a band break, I spot a young black man wander nearby, gripping hedge clippers, trim a bit, peek around the bushes and spy on the festivities. The closer he gets, I recognize the features: square-cut hair, muscular arms, and workman's outfit. Under a soft porch light, a familiar face shone through: it was Cassius Clay! I wanted to jump the railing and hug the big guy and wish him well and beg him to drop by my gym class and beat the snot out of one of my dreaded sparring opponents. Clay was financed and practically owned by a consortium of 11 high-end Kentucky investors. The cutting of hedges was no more than an assigned chore on the Reynolds property — a training-camp routine and all part of the contract.

1964, and The Shadows had a regional hit with a cover version of the Contours' *Shake Sherry*. The band would soon undergo a name change when it came to the attention of the record label, and a copyright issue surfaced. Great Britain already had a highly popular and successful group with numerous #1 hits—Cliff Richards and The Shadows. As we morphed into The Chateaus, Wayne joined the band, and we released an instrumental, *Moanin'*, in May 1965 on the Soundstage 7 label, written by jazz pianist Bobby Timmons. It was a gospel-tinged rock/jazz single. The track opens with Wayne on alto sax, giving a spiritual read of the melody; I then restate the theme establishing the tempo, drummer Johnny Coffman rocks the beat, and near song's end Frank Bugbee knocks out a wicked electrified rockabilly guitar solo. *Moanin'* would climb to #49 on the Billboard Magazine Top 100.

A month before the release, we played before 30,000 screaming teens at Freedom Hall in Louisville opening for Cincinnati rockabilly great, Lonnie Mack, pop artist Billy Joe Royal, and country giant Tex Williams at the annual *Toys for Tots* fund drive. Lonnie Mack's band was far more rooted in country blues and significantly more popular than we were. *Shake Sherry* gave us traction and fans. Onstage, Mack and company, Bill McIntosh, David Waddell, and Dennis O'Neal were thrilling; tremolo guitar, soul-jazz organ blasts, big-footed drumming and insatiable drive as the band's stage persona. With a few prominent dates behind us, we were promptly booked as an opening act for a band whose popularity would soon blanket the universe — The Beach Boys.

July 16, 1964, with the temperature hovering in the low 90s, we find ourselves situated in the dugout of the Louisville Colonels minor league baseball team near a stage erected along the third baseline in front of thousands of screaming fans there to witness the first appearance of The Beach Boys. The band was riding a wave of Southern California surf-crazed hits, and laying the groundwork for tours to come. Approachable, and ready to claim a patch of America, the Boys were in high spirits.

The finale of The Chateaus' opening set was an impromptu pie fight. Drummer Coffman loaded up the tin plates with Crazy Foam, and let it rip during *Summertime*. Coffman thought it would set us apart from the other acts on the bill. The zaniness caught the eye of Beach Boys lead singer Mike Love, who grabbed a handful of paper dishes then plated with Crazy Foam, and goaded The Beach Boys in an onstage battle. The crowd went wild!

Before the band's set, chaos erupts in the staging area leading to the men's dressing room. Guitarist Al Jardine was in a grand mood and in for the hang, but drummer Dennis Wilson recoiled from stomach cramps and insisted on being left alone in a toilet stall. Security did not read it that way and tried to drag Wilson from the booth. Wilson goes ballistic. Then a security guard attempts to strong-arm him, and yanks Wilson from the toilet as brother Carl intercedes. Panic and profanities marred the pre-show happenings. Backstage, musician Glen Campbell, filling in for lead singer/bassist Brian Wilson, was the brunt of all jokes. A constant source of amusement, Campbell was a graduate of the hillbilly school of road charm. Founder and bassist Brian Wilson was also on hand for the good times, but Campbell did the singing and playing on this occasion.

Campbell exited the band in April 1965, going solo, then replaced by Bruce Johnston, who himself had a run at producing surf records. To complicate and add a bit of hilarity to the moment, brother Wayne decides timing was perfect to beg for a celebrity autograph. Wayne shoves a slip of paper down in front of a groaning Wilson. Wilson grabs the pencil and stabs a hole dead-center.

I later transcribe the stunning melody and vocal harmonies of Brian Wilson/Gary Usher's gorgeous pop ballad, *In My Room*, that appears on *Surfer Girl*, a song written late at night in the Wilson family home. Wilson said every time he heard it played, it reminded him of the nights Dennis, Carl, and he lived in Hawthorne, California, and slept in the same room where he taught them to sing harmony. *In My Room* is a trademark Beach Boy vocal — sweet, sophisticated, angelic, and spot-on.

December 30, 1964, we were again part of a bill with The Beach Boys, Jay and the Americans, backing The Newbeats, a popular music trio, touring behind their hit *Bread and Butter*. The song reached #2 on Billboard's Top 100 Hundred chart. Then a final encounter with The Beach Boys, August 26, 1965, a shared bill with the Shangri-Las and Sir Douglas Quintet. What a glorious concert. First backing The Newbeats, and then the Shangri-Las' *Leader of the Pack*, *Remember (Walking in the Sand)*, and *Give Him a Great Big Kiss*. Afterwards, the hang backstage, short on conversation with the Shangri-Las' Mary Weiss and the Ganser sisters. The fantastic set flew by.

The Chateaus' ultimate onstage music moments came when

we performed those big epic instrumental production numbers: James Bond's *Goldfinger*, guitar-laden instrumentals, Chuck Berry's *Memphis*, Lonnie Mack's *Chicken Pickin'* and vocalized on Motown covers, *Shake Sherry* and A-side *Do You Love Me*. The band was also much loved on the black circuit, frequently playing Club Cherry in Lebanon, Kentucky. We travelled the back roads leading to the Flame Club and The Whiteland Barn in Indianapolis, Indiana, down to the Golden Horseshoe, Club 68 and Club Cherry in Lebanon and a whole lot of school functions in between.

Club Cherry—more memorable the day The Chateaus added 16-year-old soul singer Sherry Chenault. Sherry had that mighty, big blues voice and loved to rip it up on stage, keeping the crowds focused on the band. The big-voiced redhead brought the fire gone missing as band members exited and moved on to other concerns. The group was very protective of their new member, especially the time when a much older *Palisades Park* Freddy Cannon took a liking to our front person. Drummer Johnny Coffman fired a drumstick his way in jest as college fanboys down front pelted him with ice cubes.

Located near a set of railroad tracks on Water Street in Lebanon, Kentucky, Club Cherry was under the thumb of a corrupt mayor, Hyleme Salem George, with its wide-open liquor policies and robust nightlife. George was an immigrant from Lebanon and the owner of Club 68 and Club Cherry. There were seven clubs in a town with a population of 5,000: Club 68, The Golden Horseshoe, Kitty Kat Club, Club Cherry, Jane Todd Inn, and Ben's Discotheque, along with The Plantation Club featuring performers like Tina Turner, Nat King Cole, Lloyd Price, Jerry Lee Lewis, Rufus Thomas, Creedence Clearwater Revival, Steppenwolf, The Platters, Amazing Rhythm Aces, Otis Redding, Jimi Hendrix, Little Richard, Clyde McPhatter, Bo Diddley, Jackie Wilson, The Supremes, Ray Charles, James Brown, Chuck Berry, Fats Domino, Sam and Dave, Wilson Pickett, B.B. King, Percy Sledge, Hank Ballard, Junior Parker, Joe Tex, Laverne Baker, The Coasters, Shirelles, Bobby Blue Bland, Dinah Washington and Count Basie. Weekends, the population of Lebanon would expand to between 4,000 and 6,000 teenagers. Club Cherry was called, the "Sweetest Stop on the Chitlin' Circuit" and managed by Obie Slater, an entrepreneur with an eye for talent.

First indoors, Wayne and I fixated on two jugs of animal parts preserved in what looked like formaldehyde. One contained a floating pig snout, the other, pig's feet. Neither Wayne nor I could fathom why anyone would keep body parts in a jar, let alone nibble on them. "You boys hungry or something?" the desk clerk asks, our first introduction to the "world of black," a universe beyond any landscape we had previously walked. The venue was awash in chrome kitchen chairs, '50s style, built to seat 300 patrons. The nights B.B. King and crew were in town, Slater could cram 1,000 partygoers in the room.

We requested a dressing room, and what we got doubled as Slater's office and "love den." The aroma of pomade, spent cigarettes and rough sex shrouded the room in a pungent odour. Club Cherry came bedecked in posters of the giants of jazz, blues and rhythm & blues, from Otis Redding, Count Basie, Sam & Dave to Etta James. The Chateaus, with Chenault, built a repertoire deep in blues classics mixed in with a few soulful organ landmarks.

Men loved Sherry, and hung close to the stage and sweet-talked as the crowd went about socializing and slow dancing. One occasion, a fight breaks out. I catch the silhouette of a chair raised then smashed down the backside of an unsuspecting man. Alcohol and single women will light a fire under the seemingly jilted. From there, a brawl ensues. The Chateaus play on as if it's nothing out of the ordinary. At gig's end, we go about loading the band equipment in the back of the U-Haul trailer after the gig, Wayne appointed guardian of the band property. We take turns retrieving amps, organ, and sound system. I return for pick-up, and catch a view of this heavy-set black woman chatting Wayne up. Next trip, I notice the door to the U-Haul shut tight. I tap and wait, no answer, then I hear, "Bill, is that you?" Wayne's voice: "Is she gone?' I assure Wayne all is safe, and wait until he unlocks. He then cracks the door, looks me in the eye and says, "You shouldn't have left me with that woman. Do you know what she asked me? Have you ever made love to a black woman?" She was twice my size, maybe more. I'm scared, brother Bill, I'm scared!" Never short of laughs with Wayne. Drummer Johnny Coffman thought it wise to forego return visits with Sherry fronting the band.

The Chateaus came to play the Whiteland Barns in Indianapolis the same night Jerry Lee Lewis played just a floor above us. Whiteland was a two-story concert venue, Saturday nights, all about country music; Sundays, rock 'n' roll. Jerry Lee arrives in a sport sedan and is immediately confronted by autograph seekers. Lewis slaps a couple of pen strokes on a promo photo or two, then hustles through a side door and out of sight. It was one of those mob scenes when security insist the star quickly disappear.

The Chateaus' set was nothing spectacular, yet one designed to grow an upstate following, not reshape the world. As we go about performing, we could hear the roar of applause for the The Killer's entrance a floor above. Lewis was the reigning champ of the barrelhouse piano, and from the downbeat of Lewis's performance, I knew the night was over for us. You could feel the weight of his heavy boot, the time-stomping, the slamming of the piano keys, the bouncing off and on the piano stool and enthusiastic cheers of fans. With each hardwood floor shuffle-dance and Lewis's big-footed stomp, dirt between the wood beams loosened and rained dust and debris down on us. Although we rocked, we did with less authority.

That summer, I bought a copy of The Byrds' recording, *Mr. Tambourine Man*. Always interested in change, a new sound, or rhythm or style, The Byrds struck a chord with me. It was that blend of six- and twelve-string guitars and I was amazed to discover the band covering a Bob Dylan song. I drove to Chateaus guitarist Frank Bugbee's parents' home and urged Frank to place the vinyl on the family stereo. Bugbee examines the cover, smiles, seizes the moment, digs in, plays, and replays, each time shifting left to right to catch the stereo separation. We both marvelled not only at the electric twang of twelve strings, but also the stereo split between instruments. In the coming weeks, it is decided The Chateaus had to adapt and record a track or two with this new electric sound. I pored through recording after recording of

Bob Dylan and settled on a song called *The Bells of Rhymney* as a potential new single. Boss Records, our label, owned by Floyd Lewellyn and Hardy Martin, auditioned songs and came up with a tune called *I'm the One* for the A-side. Frank and I worked the arrangements to make it as contemporary as possible, and not long after release, it started climbing the charts. After modest success, Wayne and I were sacked by the band, no room for keyboards or sax in a guitar-based unit. Sometimes discovery is a better-kept secret.

19

Derby Eve, 1964

The Kentucky Derby Festival originated in 1935 with a parade, a riverfront festival and orchestra, even the formal crowning of the king and queen. The first director was Olympic gold medalist Arnold Jackson. For local musicians, the two-week period brought full employment, higher wages, and one big roaring derby-eve party. Step back 55 years—1965, Derby Eve in Louisville, Kentucky, the Patio Lounge on Shelbyville Road, Wayne and me on stage with Cosmo & the Counts, Tom "Cosmo" Cosdon, the reigning king of blue-eyed soul with a stream of regional hits and a nose for racehorses. Not long after, Cosdon retired the band and spent the next four decades or so at the racetracks. If you were without a derby gig then, you were an outlier.

One memorable derby eve, Babe's Patio Lounge in Mid City Mall Bardstown Road Shopping Centre, seat capacity of 300, overflowed with suits, sports maniacs and beautiful women, the smell of greenbacks, Chanel No. 5, jocks, and horse-wagers. You must understand sporting events and Louisville. If the Louisville Cardinals basketball team is on the tube, the band unplugs. You still get paid for watching the game and high-fiving patrons.

The front door of the Patio Lounge swings open, and a big persona enters: Paul Hornung, All-American triple threat, Notre Dame football star, Heisman Trophy recipient, and Green Packers ace running back and kicker and eventual Hall of Famer. Not a hi-I'm-here-style entrance but a drama parade of low-cut dresses and dashing young women, followed by Mr. Desirable. Legendary coach Vince Lombardi called Hornung "the most versatile man who ever played the game." Women trailed behind as if Hornung was 215 pounds of handsome money. Suspended a season for betting on NFL games, Hornung was still living large. Baseball great Pete Rose died 10 deaths for doing the same, and could never make amends. Gorgeous Paul survived untarnished. The man was just too good-looking and untouchable. Then again, Rose's mug was more suited for "Wanted" posters. I have been around men who congregate around women wearing that "money glow," like former Louisiana governor Edwin Edwards. I caught his act in Las Vegas, and it was as if someone applied a third coat of varnish and polished skin to an eye-dazzling sheen. Even his perfectly coiffed grey hair glowed like the Queen's silverware.

Behind Hornung came Packer greats and offensive guards, Ron Kramer and Fuzzy Thurston. There is no way any combination of these three is going to leave the band out. Moments in, Thurston muscles his way on stage and shouts, "Play *High Ho Silver*," as Hornung and posse congregate around the bar. Brother Wayne, in a playful tone, orders Thurston off the stage. Just before Derby Eve, Thurston, Hornung, and Kramer appeared on *The Ed Sullivan Show* and gave the nation a bit of Sunday night silliness performing *High Ho Silver*. As part of an agreement with the NFL, Hornung was warned to avoid the Derby, or face reprisal. The man had no fear.

Thurston stared Wayne down, then awkwardly counted the band in. Wayne then eyeballs. You must get with Wayne's stage outfit. Diving goggles, rubber fins, a workman's helmet with Hell's Angels written dead centre, and hanging from the waist, a machete. Wayne's stage ensemble was that of an aquatic miscreant. Brother Bill was not amused, and focused on the band's set. I am thinking, let's make an impression, and maybe the Packers whisk us off to Green Bay for a half-time appearance in seven feet of snow, and frigid, -35°C temperatures. Not the case. With Thurston howling away and Wayne egging him on, I take leave of the bandstand and slip behind Hornung and scrutinize the beauties lining the bar. A ravishing blonde, streamlined brunette, two or three starlets and another seven in waiting. I considered an impromptu dash back to the keyboard, and a flashy Rachmaninoff arpeggio — a seductive blast of virtuosity possibly netting a fence-sitting football groupie. Nope, this night belonged to Wayne and his crew of celebrity muscle.

Things were in full swing when Packers offensive guard, Ron Kramer, hoists Wayne above his head, and rests him on his shoulders. In doing so, someone offers to take Wayne's sax from him. Wayne obliges, then counters by beating Kramer's head like an oversized bongo. Wayne bongo-pounds Kramer's skull until the ring on his middle finger opens a wound, causing Kramer to bleed. Not amused, Kramer passes Wayne over to Thurston. Thurston dances about, bouncing Wayne up and down on his massive shoulders, Wayne still in full bongo head-smacking mode. Near the bandstand, Thurston spots a woman situated at a café-style table with a heavy-set man dressed in a grubby white T-shirt, dances over, grabs her by the hand, pulls her to the dance floor and starts doing the twist. The partner takes offence, the dancing thing way out of bounds, and moves on Thurston. Thurston spins, points to a chair, and orders the guy to sit back down. The guy obeys, and the girl dances on.

Dripping blood, Thurston turns on Wayne and dumps him like 100 pounds of bird feed. Wayne signals both Thurston and Kramer to step outside. Without hesitating, both Kramer and Thurston drag Wayne across the room to where Hornung and entourage are holed up and shove his head down atop the bar counter. Through all of this, Wayne has not cracked a smile. En route, the goggles fall off, flippers crumple around Wayne's feet. Kramer bends over and rests his massive arm across Wayne's throat and presses downward. Both Thurston and Kramer drop a few harsh words on him. Wayne struggles, and just as circumstances are about to turn raw, Wayne says four words: "You guys had enough?" The place explodes in laughter. Both release, and Wayne falls to the floor like a half-eaten melon. The rest of the night was one crazy party, with killer laughs.

Hornung played pro football from 1957-1966, and won four championships and the first Super Bowl. Kramer played seven seasons with Green Bay, and three with Detroit Lions, known for his fierce blocking and tackling abilities. He died in September of

2010. Thurston claimed he drank 10 vodkas before the infamous Ice Bowl, played in 1967 in 13°F temperatures between the Dallas Cowboys and the Packers at Lambeau Field. He was first an All-American offensive lineman with the Baltimore Colts, then the Packers.

Wayne and I laugh our way back home and are promptly intercepted by Mom who unlatches the front door before we can plug a key in, a chore not of necessity but of suspicion. Most times, I'd barely twist, and the door would spring open, and hit with the same question, "It's late, where have you been?" Gig to gig, I was always aware of the time. As the months passed, the interrogations rang false. The boys did not drink, do anything malicious, and often arrived home at a reasonable hour.

The following morning, I heard big footsteps shuffling our way and an argument brewing a floor below. I'm about to open my eyes when I see Dad empty a bag on my bed, raise the machete and slash down the middle of a white oval-shaped object. "No son of mine is joining the Hell's Angels, do you hear me?" Dad screams, then a follow-up chop. I leap back of the bed and watch as Dad slashes the scuba fins, goggles, and workman's helmet to bits. I gather myself and say, "This is not my property — this is Wayne's." Dad pauses, then slowly walks into Wayne's room. Words passed between the two, then over. Dad and Wayne had a far different relationship than Dad and me. Wayne was mostly spared punishment. Mom knew Dad overreached — rarely comforted or apologized, just stayed in her corner.

I don't know what prompted Dad to assign Wayne the task of driving him to work early mornings in his International Harvester Travelall. I was told it was so Wayne could cart Mom around town for groceries; whatever appointments come her way, the wagon was the only source of transportation. One near-fatal morning, the police arrived just before breakfast and ask me to accompany them to Colgate's. I was taken to a visitor's area then told a half-sleeping Wayne accidentally drives up an off-ramp of the Indiana interstate and is instantly hit head-on by a dirt hauling semi, leaving 40 yards of guardrail destroyed, littering the highway much like trees uprooted from a tornado, and Wayne in shock. Shaken, half laughing, and half traumatized, Wayne cries out, "What will Dad say, what will Dad do?" I'm thinking, bro, you could have been killed. Dad will figure this out.

Before dropping us home, one officer says, "Son, you are one lucky boy. Maybe not so lucky when your Dad gets home, but you're still alive." We waited for the wrath of God to bring the pain, but Dad said nothing. He did not utter a word for two weeks. And when he did, it was over dinner. "Wayne, I've thought about this and how we could have lost you. In some ways, I should have never made you get up that early after school and music lessons the day before, but I have to do something; you won't drive a car for a year, so give me your licence." That was it! No fighting, no screaming, no all-out war. A moment of clarity.

20

Working Man

When I first heard Bob Dylan, I was sure he fell off a chuckwagon somewhere between Wichita, Kansas, and Cheyenne, Wyoming. Dylan sounded like the guy who made up songs around a camp-fire — a lonesome cowboy or travelling medicine-man. I would soon learn Dylan was a folk-singing Jewish boy from Hibbing, Minnesota. When I thought of Minnesota, the first thing that came to mind was those Thousand Lakes promos; winter so harsh it could rival Yellowknife, NWT, and stories of caravans of 18th century Swedes there to populate the new land.

I was 19 and hooked up with an internship at U.S. Steel in southern Indiana, a 90-day trial period before induction into the steelworkers' union. I met this guy at one of our gigs, who was a fan of Cosmo & the Counts who liked to "frat party." He also worked at the plant, and would stop by and pick me up early mornings — the ride, insane "bad-boy" patter. First pick-up, he asks if I had heard of Bob Dylan and insists I listen to the record-ing, *The Freewheelin' Bob Dylan*. The following morning, he brings the album and allows me to devour the liner notes and cover art. The cover carried an image of a young, vagabond walking with his love (Suzie Rotolo) along the frigid ice-covered streets of Greenwich Village. In the background, a Volkswagen van, which to me, represented the coolest escape vehicle imaginable, the complete package and story of a small-town American guy, living his art, precisely what I wanted to do.

When my pal first dropped the needle on Dylan, I thought to myself this is some sad singing. Yet, there was something about the acoustic instrumentation and roots harmonica and lyrics that set Dylan far apart from other strumming minstrels. I could visualize the places and events Dylan was recounting. I knew of them. We were mid-westerners/southerners whose roots extended from Missouri down through Tennessee back up through Kentucky and Indiana and across to Pennsylvania. We had relatives farther south but rarely seen. Dylan captured the poetry of life; the words forged with melody, easily understood.

During the morning drive, my good pal would sing to me the Dylan passages that spoke to alienation and coming of age. We felt the pressure to conform, enlist and fight the war in Vietnam, but Dylan offered us an alternative to war closing in. I was angry, confused, and restless. Even the morning drives were manifestations of recklessness. We would plow the backroads over residential lawns, leaving deep tread marks, smash mailboxes, and scream nonsense at the countryside. These adrenaline-filled sprees came to a crashing halt when I observe a pile of October leaves roadside and situated in the middle, a cardboard box. The urge was to drive through and over and crush, but for some unknown reason, I chose to bypass. That instant proved monumental in my life. As we pass, I spot two young children climb from a box. I shivered and cried to myself, "My God, what was I about to do? What stopped me?" I felt sickened, overcome with guilt, then relief. From the top of my head to the depths of my soul, I wept inside. Ashen-faced and subdued, my friend looked at me as if spared a trip to hell. I told myself, there would never be another moment of childish recklessness in my life. I will freely live, but I will never push the odds. That moment, I saved myself from myself.

Two weeks later, I am in a rush to school and driving a good 80-mph in blinding rain across the John F. Kennedy Memorial Bridge connecting Jeffersonville with Louisville. I spin out of control. All around me, traffic slows to a cautious tempo. I continue to turn around three or four more times, halting only inches from a guardrail and saved from toppling over and into the frigid Ohio River. I pause, catch a breath, straighten up the car and slowly re-enter a traffic lane. It was as if time stopped. Through the rear-view mirror, I see several vehicles, some resting at a full stop, and others a safe distance begin to slowly pass: two episodes which were the most instructive moments of youth. I had grown up!

I had never heard words crunched together like Dylan's. "Listen to this," my pal says as he recites the lyrics. "Masters of war, build to destroy. You play with my world like it is your little toy. All the money you made will never buy back your soul." Then came those song titles: *Blowin' in the Wind, Girl from the North Country, Down the Highway, Bob Dylan's Blues, A Hard Rain's a-Gonna Fall, Don't Think Twice It's Alright, Bob Dylan's Dream, Oxford Town, Talkin' World War III Blues, Corrina, Corrina, Honey, Just Allow Me One More Chance,* and *I Shall Be Free.* There was no way I could bring this into our home, so I opted to listen in the basement of my car-pooling buddy's mom's house. He preached *Talkin' World War III Blues.* Both of us facing possible induction into the military and college the only shield. The gig at U.S. Steel was sure to end my college career.

Working alongside surly men who longed for me to fail was most unpleasant. Everyone was protecting their jobs. I would collect chunks of sawed-down wood, stack them high on dollies, and steer around the plant. Stuff prefab houses into trucks, twist screws in window frames, sweep sawdust out of the way, and lift T-frames off conveyor belts, stack, and pile them into the backs of trucks. They called me "sheepdog," draft-dodger or whatever insult came to mind. All this grief for a monthly paycheck of $90 before deductions. Summer ending and another semester of college ahead. Inhaling sawdust, and listening to depraved men re-tell anecdotes of past sexual encounters was a bit below my pay grade. Then the letter arrives. "William King, we are sorry to inform you, you've been declined membership of the steelworkers' local …. we understand you are attending college, and wish you well. If you wish to appeal ..." Appeal?

Freewheelin' is ranked as one of the top 50 albums of all time, and rightly so. It is a campus record. It speaks to the "boomer"' generation torn between work, war, and responsibility. Dylan brought us closer to Steinbeck, Guthrie, James Baldwin, the Ole' Miss Riots, rural blues figures, dustbowl balladeers, and asked us to question our leaders and freely breathe in the air willed to us by our ancestors. The beat poets who hung around the "art" fringe of Louisville respected Dylan. It was a time of transition, and that time was influenced by the journeyman nature of Dylan's music.

21

President Lyndon Baines Johnson

President Lyndon Johnson visited Jeffersonville to celebrate the beautification of our post office on July 23, 1966. We did suspect that Johnson was there to sell us on war when he spoke these words: "We believe that we must be strong to protect the things that we have that other people would like to take away from us. And after seeing the headquarters of the 101st Airborne Division this afternoon, we do not doubt our strength. But we do not want to be strong to be able to wage or win wars. We want to be strong so we can prevent war and bring peace. Your government and your administration, is ready at this hour, as it has been every hour since I have been president, to talk instead of fight, to negotiate instead of bomb, to reason instead of trying to force." I'm standing amongst thousands of college students much more progressive and informed than me and upset. A crowd of dissenters start chanting, "No more war, no more war—Johnson is a murderer!" That was my first rally, one that opened eyes and mind to the malpractice behind the war in Vietnam.

22

The Psychiatrist

Dad took one last crack at pinning our troubled history on me. He booked an appointment with a psychiatrist, and insisted that I submit to testing, then counselling. I agreed. The three of us arrived at the doctor's office. I am given a Rorschach test, then asked to answer page after page of personal info and sit for hours of evaluation. The good doctor then asked me to wait outside, and called Dad and Mom in. It seemed an eternity before I was asked to return. The doctor opened with a statement: "We have examined, tested, and spoken with your son. He is highly intelligent, stable, suffers no depression or other maladies, and talked openly about his feelings for the both of you and the conflicts. My recommendation? Bill should move out as soon as possible. We see no problems here. But I would like to keep the two of you for further consultation. Can we schedule a time for both?" Dad looked on mortified. Mom looked at Dad. "Mr. King, it is obvious you are suffering greatly from your experiences of war. Mrs. King, from our discussion and observations, there are signs you battle cycles of depression. I'd like to help both of you." Dad looked over at me. "What about him?" he asked. The doc reiterated, "There's nothing wrong with this young man. He is old enough to be on his own. He should move out." Wham! Since birth, this is the first moment I felt I had an ally who was not a member of the music community.

It's now May, and my college term has ended. While strolling through the house, Dad confronted both Wayne and me, and said, "Every time you boys come in my home, you avoid me. I've had enough of this." He then took a swing at me. I grabbed his arms

and gripped them tight. He struggled. In tears, I said to him,"
Dad, I do not want to hurt you; I don't want this fight. You have
hurt me, called me stupid in front of your friends, demeaned,
threatened, and beaten me. I'm nineteen; it's over." Dad paused,
then exited the room. Moments later, he called a meeting around
the kitchen table: "Boys, I've talked this over with your mom.
We want you to move out; this is my house and my rules. If you
aren't willing, you have to go." He then asked Wayne, "What do
you think?" Wayne said meekly, "If I can live with Billy." Dad
asked, "You, Bill?" I organized my thoughts. "Dad, I've tried my
best to live under your roof, and at this moment, there is nothing
out there I'm more fearful of than you. Even if I must sleep on
the streets, and starve, nothing could be unhappier than living
under these conditions." End of story!

23

Divine Intervention

With grades at Indiana University sub-par, I enrolled in Bellarmine College, a Catholic institution, much less expensive, $250 a semester. First year passed without much resistance or complications, with grades ranging from negligible in Latin to A+ in music composition. Second year, I registered as a student in social sciences.

I had a few good priests, generally conservative concerning religious matters, quite liberal in social regions. One priest supplied us required reading material, James Baldwin's *The Fire Next Time*, the first book by which I acquired a general understanding of race relations as told by a person most affected. The liberal priest told us of his work with the homeless, and marginalized people of colour, encouraged us to do the same, then asked if any of us had visited a whorehouse. It was a strange question in that it was the first semester women could crossover from sister Ursuline College and take classes in an all-boys college. The capper was what he said to the two females: " Please cross your legs and cover the gates to hell. We've got a room full of horny boys." The priest also talked about prostitution and a nearby brothel frequented by college-aged boys who knew the exact locale and telephone number. I rode out the semester carrying mostly average grades courtesy of straight As in music-related programs, Cs in writing courses, a B here and there in social sciences, and nought in French and religion.

Second year and orientation week, I am lounging in the communal cafeteria listening to a replay of English jukebox bands reverberate in the background when, unexpectedly, this extraordinary song comes blasting on: *"I was born in Lil' Rock, had a childhood sweetheart, we always hand in hand. I was in high-top shoes and shirt tails, Suzy was in pigtails, I know I loved her even then. You know my papa disapproved of it, my mama boohooed it, but I told them time and time again. 'Don't you know I was made to love her, Built a world all around her.' Yah! Hey, hey, hey."* Oh, my God! Play it again, Mr. Bill, and again, and again, and again, please!

I played it so many times I pissed off the "buttoned-to-the-neck" Catholic schoolboys who revolted—rose to their feet and waved bologna sandwiches at me as if to say, "Cease, or we're going to stuff these cheap cuts of sandwich meat between your ears."

Two cherub-faced boys marched over and questioned me as to what year I was in. I informed them second year, and warned that they should steer clear. One signalled to me to accompany him to the dean's office—but it wasn't going to happen. I had already made peace with God crossing the bridge between connecting states and survived a fearful moment. Then off he went on a mission. Minutes passed until he returned, accompanied by someone in power who ordered me to follow close behind. I made the sojourn through the sacred hallways adorned in religious artifacts, and took a seat outside the dean's office. A priest invited me in for a chat, my accuser located nearby. A litany of violations was levelled against me, as if I had committed the most heinous crimes. The priest listened to my accuser, and then asked for my rebuttal. I tell him of my love for that Stevie Wonder recording, and that I have no control over the jukebox volume. My accuser interrupted, insisting that I disobeyed an order from a class leader to which I responded, "Who made you warden?" The administrator listened, then suggested that I could avoid expulsion if I abided by whatever punishment was decided by the team leader and his associates. I said nothing, and walked out of the room. Minutes later, a young pimple-faced boy placed a bucket of soapy water near to me. "Mop the floor, freshman!" I stared him down. "Who are you calling freshman? I'm in the second year," I responded. "As far as we can ascertain, you are a freshman here," he said. "You have to scrub the school emblem to clear your name," he said in a mouse-like whimper. I looked over the designated zone and said, "It's not my shoes that scuffed this floor — you clean it up."

I stepped around him and walked back downstairs, unloading a pocketful of nickels, dimes, and quarters to stuff into the jukebox, punched play, and enjoyed more Stevie: "*She's been my inspiration, showed appreciation, for the love I gave her through the years. Like a sweet magnolia tree, my love blossomed tenderly; My life grew sweeter through the years. I know that my baby loves me; my baby needs me; that is why we made it through the years. I was made to love her, worship and adore her. Hey, hey, hey.*" I did not stick around for the 10th play. I timed out!

I Was Made to Love Her, written by Stevie and his mother Lula Mae Hardaway, stalled at the #2 spot behind The Doors' *Light My Fire* on the Billboard Pop Singles chart. I inhaled that beat, those rich melodies, and all that beauty; the love, the song, and inspiration coming from Wonder and concluded the coming days of unwelcome theology and nerd intervention would never again rule my life or interrupt my day or undermine my radical make-over. Jesus loves!

24

The New Rhythm & Blues Quintet

Our first fling with freedom was with the Adams brothers: Terry
and Don. We came through the same society big-band that
still rolls along today in Louisville, Kentucky, the Don Krekel
Orchestra. Don Adams was in the trombone section, a hilarious and brilliant man. Adams was teaching at the University
of Louisville and having one hell of a "free-living" time. Future
member Keith Spring inhabited the sax section and was soon
to be a close pal. We all came together at pianist and educator
Don Murray's Monday jazz workshops at The Arts in Louisville.
Murray and his students were laying jazz charts on us, trying to
bring all the young players along. It was West Coast "cool"—a
bit of vibraphone mixed in with piano, trumpet, trombone, and
easy-walking swing.

A year had passed when Don's younger brother Terry arrived.
Terry, like me, was studying privately with Murray. Adams was
on this Thelonious Monk kick. It was 1964, and the Ohio Valley
Jazz Festival in Cincinnati happened, with a triple bill: Nina Simone, Oscar Peterson, and Thelonious Monk. Adams caught Monk
crossing the lawn heading towards the main stage and offered to
carry his briefcase. Monk obliged. The same night, we stalked
Oscar in the parking lot. "Mr. Peterson, remember me, Louisville, from your school," I asked. "I certainly do, Bill, what brings
you to Cincinnati?" I am shaking in my jeans. "Mr. Peterson, we
live only a hundred miles from here." Dad proudly adds," Bill
practices all day." Peterson smiles and waves goodbye. Dad and
boys watch Nina Simone sing *Cotton-Eyed Joe*. Oh, did that still
the night and silence the audience. Then Monk. Monk hovered

around the piano, occasionally stabbing the keys with his elbow. Dad laughed; the boys looked on, confused.

In Krekel's orchestra, Terry played trumpet. Let us just say there was never a night when the old guard did not want to string one or the other of us up. One player even offered to rope a tin cup around Adam's neck and send him through the crowd for donations, the two of us restless clowns. Throw Don Adams into the mix, playing slide trombone and wafting spittle on the back of unsuspecting necks; the bandstand was never safe. After Krekel, we all strayed into rock bands. Young women were plentiful, and the old "dudes" who wore cheap smoking jackets banished to the sidelines.

Terry began growing a shoulder-length mane—the rest of us something less daring. Here's where things got wild. Louisville was under siege with sit-ins and sluggishly addressing civil rights concerns. The Vietnam war was raging, and Bob Dylan was preaching *The Times They Are a-Changin'*—sex, free love, and rock 'n' roll. If you were not there, you would not recall the daily harassment, the threats, the punch-ups, and beatings. There were no video cameras to catch police brutality or a redneck hell-bent on busting some open-minded thinkers. I was wary of crossing those lines, so kept a distance. Terry Adams played with fire, antagonized, and incited. It was lunacy on a local scale that would keep all in Adams' company on guard.

The Adams family had a passion for roots music. Even the family fireplace had a cut-out poster of Tennessee Ernie Ford, a country and western "good ole boy" and comic, hands locked into prayer position, where logs burn. Drummer Charlie Craig, another member of the youth rhythm section with the Krekel Orchestra, the Adams brothers, Spring, guitarist Steve Ferguson, and brother Wayne and I assembled at Eddie Donaldson's bar, the Shack, on Bardstown Road in Louisville for the inaugural run of NRBQ. We had no idea there was an advertised band named for the jam session. We would soon learn about The New Rhythm & Blues Quintet. We played Muddy Waters, Terry played some wild Monk, and we staggered through a few blues classics, and then off we go. Not long after, I move into a "frat boy" house on

Baxter Avenue in Louisville, Kentucky, and the parties began. I was trying to salvage what grades I had managed at Bellarmine College, and failed miserably. Nights came with beer-swilling contests and pure craziness. Adams and Ferguson would mysteriously surface with objects removed from construction sites and light up the party den. There were girls and students and enough chaos and crudity to get us evicted a few weeks in.

Adams, Wayne, and I triple-date and find ourselves at either Jerry's Family Restaurant or Frisch's Big Boy burger joint in Jeffersonville. It was one of those late-night eateries where rednecks bring dates and feed them cheeseburgers and lots of *Hee Haw* squealing. While sitting with our girls and awaiting menus, the doors swung open, and a half-dozen guys and dolls sporting cowboy apparel — girls in puffy square dance outfits— arrive. I avoid eye contact, but with Adams close by, it was a given something out of the ordinary was about to occur. As the square-dancers get situated, one male decided it was time to impress his date, sidled up to our table, hovered above, and asked, "What are you girls doing with these pussies?" Say what? The clodhopper lingered a good minute or so. Then his puffy-skirted date tugged and pulled him back to the laughing brood. Adams, big hair waving and sporting a goofy grin, strolled over to the table, leaned in, and asked one of the girls: "What are you girls doing with these pussies?" That was it. War! Threats flew, as did swearing and chest-pumping. The room erupted, when a night manager intervened, separated everyone, and shoved them back to their home areas. A fork came flying from above, crashed, and bounced off our table. Adams turned to see the hillbilly table laughing, flung a knife back at them, and then watched as it dive-bombed and struck an adjacent table. That was our cue to get out of Dodge.

Outside, and dates safely back in the car, an older man tapped on the window closest to Adams. Terry rolled it down. The senior tells Adams what he thinks of long hair, and insists he is a girl. Adams then says "fuck off" to the old bastard, sending the man into a rage. The man punched through the glass, as Terry wound up for a punch.

Small wars started when someone called you a Beatle. How many times did someone ask, "Are you a Beatle?" We were young jazz hounds—why not, "Are you Woody Herman"? There was something contemptuous in the tone. Men still saw The Beatles as their mortal enemies, and any length of hair thicker than a crew cut was an insult to the military mindset of the day.

Not long after, I hooked up with Terry at the Kentucky State Fair. We dropped by to see Tim Tyler, an influential WACKY radio jock and a big supporter of local bands, including The Chateaus. Tyler had the power to put local groups on the big shows. Walking across a converted cow pasture, I noticed Adams carrying a foghorn, like something you see on a watercraft, a loud, in-your-face instrument. I asked Terry, why the equipment? "Self-defense," he said. It seemed the closer we got to the grandstand, the more threatening the "horse-headed" rednecks were. As they started to move our way, Adams would point the marine horn in their faces and blast away. It was beyond hilarious — he was scary, and then another sprint to the exit.

By 1966, we all parted ways. Adams and Ferguson moved on with NRBQ, and worked until they became a full-fledged music machine moving from New York to Florida. NRBQ played an average of 250 shows a year, mostly bars, connecting nightly with 200-250 loyal jubilant fans. The band was tight from day one, blending a mix of Sun Ra/Thelonious Monk smarts with good old-fashioned rockabilly. It made for some great over-the-top live shows.

25

Down the Road Apiece

I dreamed of breaking free; those long drives musicians reminisced about through the south, past fields of sprawling kudzu, down fog-shrouded backroads, the perfect way to decompress after a long night playing on the funk side of town. I was ready to climb on the band bus or into the back of a station wagon and begin my journey.

The many one-nighters I had already played were mostly local, no more than a hundred miles in all directions. I knew radio was the best company a carload of musicians could ask for to free the mind of setlists and missed opportunities with local groupies. No time for a sleep-over or three-dollar T-bone steak. I had already ridden in a crippled station wagon, taken on road grime and patches of red clay; the windshield a graveyard of suicidal beetles, palmetto bugs, wasps, and grasshoppers. Above me, the sleeping branches of tall pines; in the distance, weeping willows near where a mockingbird eyeballed and serenaded all-night drivers.

I imagined my next gig would be with one of those southern touring bands, a 225-mile drive and arrival just past noon. I envisioned a stopover at one of those WLAC kinds of stations and a DJ yelping like he was riding an amphetamine high. Then there was the insomniac basement preacher with a 100-watt transmitter selling Jesus and recipes for warding off imagined demons. "Satan will boil you in a pot of blood and snakes." I could hear the radioman bark, "Don't forget tonight at Round Hall, The Mob—big funky rhythm machine from Chicago. $2 off if you bring a date." During the '60s, nothing much happened after 7

p.m. in rural communities, other than those night creatures troll-
ing the landscape for a good meal.

It's three in the morning, Otis Redding on repeat cycle, and a
DJ storytelling long into the dark hours. I fantasize about what
it would be like playing in a soul band and singing much like
Ray Charles and Otis Redding. Curve those white notes into
blue notes and "sweet-sing" the unexpected. The DJ rambles on,
"Did you know young Otis ran barefoot through these woods
surrounded by copperheads, diamondbacks, and coral snakes
and spiders the size of small animals, the son of a preacher man
born of hard Georgia soil? There you have it, one solid hour of
Dawson, Georgia's own Otis Redding, born 1941 right down
here where the smokehouse hams it up, and bird-hounds chase
peasant for sport, this is Captain Ray Williams WXBX signing off.
We'll be back on the air in three hours with the farm report."

Eventually, we pull into the next town, set up, then play four
sets of Wilson Pickett, Willie Mitchell, Ike and Tina, some Little
Richard, Bobby "Blue" Bland, Lowell Fulson, and Otis himself.
After the gig and mostly sleep-deprived, we laugh, eat shitty
food, and reclaim the same seats we came in. With trailer packed
and all accounted and another 111 miles to Tallahassee, we fall
back into a radio trance; drummer mumbling some nonsense
about some sweet honey left behind he would marry if time
permitted. The white noise of roadside cicadas alert us to roll
front and back windows tight. Through the hours I watch the
miles click by like a late-night newsreel. I am the boy in a band
of men, and never sure of what they are laughing about, but I
laugh along. I downed my first beer at sunset, the last after gear
packed. Good Lord, I've got to have a piss. Can I get a witness?

26

California Dreamin'

It is 1966; change is inevitable. Folk-rock, psychedelic, soul, funk, pop music, you can call it whatever — somewhere out there, bands under the influence of everything that paid well, new groups focused on innovation and originality, and compensated next to nothing. I longed for a change of scenery. University and college were killing time for me, grades straddling somewhere between failure and passing, not enough to keep me enrolled or engaged. It was an accidental encounter at an A&W Root Beer stand in New Albany, Indiana, that launched a different path.

I'd occasionally cruise the "night-burger" stands and do what most teenage boys did: scout *pretty women*. One night, I meet two men who not so long ago relocated to Manhattan Beach, California. The thought revived those Beach Boys sea and sun anthems buried in the brain. By night's end, the guys sold me on sunshine, women, hot sand, open seas, and a promising future, then invite me to ride back with them offering accommodation until I got on my feet.

I returned to my newly decorated apartment in Louisville, Kentucky, one I had roller-painted the interior jet black, with kitchen cabinets fire-engine red. The hanging Chinese lanterns gave the impression I was living in a Yakuza gangster hideout.

Wayne flitted in and out, mostly focused on a young woman he had been dating, and unaware of my imminent departure. The time between decision and change was only a matter of hours. I packed my portable Farfisa organ, Bogen amplifier, and Jensen speaker cabinet, clothes, a few records, and set out to meet my travel partners. Along the way, I passed Dad on a side road. He had been tipped off and was scouting for me. He signalled me over. "You're leaving for California, and not telling your mom and me?" Dad wore the look of resignation yet spoke with authority. "What do you think you're going to do out there?" I thought for a moment and said, "Something different. I play music, that's what goes on there." I could read his face. No longer in charge, he climbed back in his car, and sped away. Those were the last words we would share in the coming years.

Early morning, I make my way to a communal house in New Albany, Indiana, meet my travel companions and am introduced to a 1946 hearse parked just beyond the front lawn with four tires strapped on top. I spot a couple of "hippie-like" individuals clutching paint cans, dipping brushes, and scribbling slogans on both sides of the "dead-man" vehicle. I asked myself if this was the right location. "California next stop," a voice from behind shouted. Everything looked unfamiliar; my new travel companions, the cryptic looking hearse, the rooming house in the distance, even the street where the corpse car parked.

Two hours passed before seven of us finally crammed into "black beauty," and began twisting our way out of town, loaded with clothing, luggage, my equipment, and a single mattress, and only a moment to introduce ourselves. There would be no overnight stopovers, just the road ahead. My touring companions, Jim and Rick, already had good jobs at TRW (Thompson, Ramo, Wooldrige Inc., pioneers in electronics and aerospace) in Redondo Beach, California. The women, Janice and Jim's girlfriends, were in limbo, and travelling with us. A gentleman from South America they referred to as "the Latin lover" was just along for the ride.

The first 100 miles or so was high-energy talk; that "getting to know" everyone thing about "you" chat. I had plenty on my mind. I had just walked away from Bellarmine/Ursuline Catholic Colleges, somewhat relieved of the daily grind and the anxiety of going to a religious institution to which I was in complete opposition. I remembered the sub-par grades and dropping out of Indiana University, and felt the pressure. Thirteen-and-a-half years of routine school and work. That brief tenure at U.S. Steel and band gigs gave me a fair taste of what eight-hour day labour and six-hour music gigs were all about. There were not enough hours in a day to play music and attend college. Something had to give.

Crossing America was a balance between wide-open highways, roadside diners and suspicious patrons. Most stops were a challenge: tall hats and guns. Those wary of travellers whiled away the days hating anyone sporting two weeks of hair growth or chin whiskers. Rick and Jim wore close-cropped hair, posing no threat. I had grown a few inches of hair down below the ears, enough to arouse catcalls from truckers and snickers from female companions. The long drive was a "give-and-take" conversation between those situated upfront, and the rest of us sequestered where the dead slept amongst piles of clothes, a mattress, my organ and amp, a few tools, and plenty of laughter. While crossing the Midwest, there were moments the temperature rose just above bearable to near-suffocating, and the drive less than memorable. Through the mountains, I wrapped myself in whatever was available as the temperature dropped. When we hit the desert, those brochures from under my bed came to life — the long vistas and howls of mating coyotes. Driving was Jim's domain. He never asked me to steer the big wagon. The trip, for the most part, was uneventful until we hit Oklahoma.

Just outside of Oklahoma City, we passed a contingent of Hell's Angels, then spotted them again at a roadside diner. Not long after, others arrived on motorcycles, followed by two large semis. Over lunch, a biker approached our table, bent over, and asks me if I had any grass. Mr. "Wiseass" me replied, "There are fields of grass out there; in fact, miles of it." The biker shot me a cold look, then informed the posse there was a "smart-ass" sitting amongst us. Whatever possessed me to pop-off at these guys was quickly neutralized when Jim told them it was my first time out of Indiana, and I didn't know any better. He was right.

Outside the diner, we crossed paths with the bike crew near the hearse. I noticed blood dripping from the backside of one of the bikers, and overheard a conversation between him and another gang member: "You've got to get that taken care of man;

that shit is gonna get worse." The guy looked down on his blood-stained jeans and said, "I got the best of the motherfucker, didn't I?" A third biker spoke: "But he stabbed you in the ass — do something about it. Don't just stand there and bleed to death. Get to a hospital!"

Things did not go as planned with the hearse. Jim flipped the ignition and there was quiet. Again, and again. We then gathered at the backside and pushed, while Jim tried to jump-start. Where gravel met asphalt, it became evident that none of us had enough leg strength to push the massive beast into a full roll, and down the highway. Help arrived in the form of five or six Angels to the rescue. The big push and shove, anything to get the death-beast moving at a reasonable speed. It soon choked, swallowed enough gas and air to please the carburetor, came back to life, and then we waved goodbye.

California was something I had read about in brochures. I imagined it to be the epicentre of west-coast rebellion, where movie stars and rock prophets got together to plan the takeover of America. That story told through the pages of *Time* and *Newsweek* magazines, and where hippies and flower children congregated with musicians along Sunset Strip in Hollywood. I am ready to rumble, but uncertain of my musical abilities. Competent, but far from seasoned or privy to music beyond my local region. Then, arrival! Manhattan Beach, California, adjacent to Redondo and Hermosa beaches. I had heard of Hermosa Beach and the jazz club the Lighthouse from gig postings in *Downbeat* magazine, featuring the Gerald Wilson Big Band and a host of other jazz icons. I also had those Beach Boys surf songs to reference: the easy life ... beach life.

Jim and Rick resided in a sprawling apartment complex not far from the beach. I claimed a small corner of the living room and set up shop; unpacked the organ and amp and started playing, which earned me a quick rebuke from the inhabitants of the adjoining apartments. I brought with me the sum of $90, along with my few possessions. Beyond that, I had no recourse when funds ran out. I learned a lesson in culinary survival: Birdseye TV dinners at 33 cents a pop. Three for a dollar. Mashed potatoes, a chicken thigh, and green beans. The beach complex was spacious, with a swimming pool and a constant flow of female flight attendants. I didn't see this as a long-term stayover, but the visuals were no less appealing.

Night one, and down North Ardmore towards the beach pier, I hear a jazz trio playing at one of the local haunts with more than a few well-schooled players jamming. The quality of playing was way above my grade level. I soon learned these were the top L.A. jazz musicians working a calendar night.

By day I would walk the beach. Swimming was out of the question, as fall season tides were rough, and undertows treacherous. On one such walk, I made it to Hermosa Beach and the famed The Lighthouse. With a handful of dollars, I dropped three, and sat back in the wooden church pews to listen to the Gerald Wilson Big Band. The band was beyond terrific, and a reasonable introduction to the L.A. jazz scene.

A week in, Jim and I started trading barbs, much of it "manplay." Nevertheless, I sensed the invitation to stay to be shorter than expected. Four men, two women, lovemaking, and outsiders. Not the right mix. The following day, I dropped by a local music store, and noticed a bulletin board and phone number advertising for a keyboardist. Supposedly, the band had good-paying gigs and "big" promise. I dialled up. A day later, two members of a local group calling themselves the Royal Teens of Redondo Beach came by the apartment; one with a guitar. We jammed a few songs, and they asked if I knew *A Taste of Honey*, Herb Alpert's version. On this, I soared. A few other Beach Boys covers and '50s teen ditties thrown in. I get the gig, and am told rehearsals are scheduled in the bandleader's parents' home, leading to my first encounter with plastic furniture covers. It seems Mom was big on wrapping couch, chairs and dining room set in zip-up, see-through plastic, and by her standards, not enough protection. When seated, she asked me not to lean back on the couch. I sat near the edge, catching the panic in her eyes.

The players were amateurs, who had decided to enter a band competition at Redondo Union High School, the then-alma mater of comedy duo The Smothers Brothers. The grand prize: a

Fender Twin Reverb amp. Positioned somewhere in the middle of 10 bands, the Teens were slotted to perform one song and one extra opportunity to impress. Our song? *A Taste of Honey*, featuring the mighty organ lead and soloing of Mr. B.K.!

That Saturday, most of the competition was DOA, and left at the starting gate, bogged down tuning instruments. From the downbeat, we had the crowd. *A Taste of Honey* popped along as expected. I threw in a dash of technical wizardry: a few blue notes, uncommon in this arena. We left the stage to cheers and high approval. In attendance, a Catholic priest, a friend of the family who came to me with an outstretched hand; congratulated me, then patted me on the back. The gregarious priest went on to tell me how the Smothers Brothers were still the biggest stars from Redondo Union High School. Maybe we would be next.

A day or so passed, and I heard nothing from the band. While skimming a community newspaper, I read about my bandmates and me, and how we had won a Fender Twin Reverb amp and first place in the competition. I left messages with the family, but no response. I made the short trek from one beach to the next, and visited the parents' house. Dear Mom intercepted and informed me that I was no longer of any use to the band or her son.

"With that win, the boys are on their way to the big time," she said. I had never experienced such callous behaviour. She then went on to say, "Please don't come back here and make trouble, the amp belongs to my son. He organized and entered the competition." Life lesson #1.

On a return visit to the music store where I first connected with the Teens, I jotted down the telephone number for a Roy and Dan — the last names evade me. The business card advertised: "We specialize in Memphis Soul." I'm in. I contacted the brothers, arranged a jam session, and discovered Roy to be a decent soul singer and brother Dan a competent rhythm guitarist. Putting together a set of soul material was easy. We knew the same songs. Roy booked a gig, down the coast in a cavernous room in Gardena. The three of us and a drummer pounded out the soul classics of the day. It was on a break I first heard Aretha Franklin's *I Never Loved a Man (The Way I Love You)*. I played the song over and over and over, much like Stevie Wonder's, back at Bellarmine College. Several days passed when the club manager walked over and asked me to stop dropping nickels in the jukebox.

The next morning, with a few dollars in hand, I live my passion and shop for records at a local retail outlet. It was the start of building a recorded library of jazz, blues, soul, psychedelic, folk, and gospel music. The beauty of browsing and engaging? The cover art and the spell that they cast over you. LPS were much like classic paintings, meant to be framed and hung.

While flipping through the record bins, I uncovered *Fresh Cream*, by the British trio, Cream. Three guys bathed in unfriendly lighting, all wearing aviation gear. Back at the communal apartment complex, I coaxed one of my housemates to let me drop the needle on my new acquisition, reluctant at first and even more so after hearing the power trio grind away on less than adequate speakers. The shock of hearing the first play was overwhelming. I was ready to announce to the world what I heard in those grooves. I called Dan and Roy and asked to drop by and play it for them. The needle dropped and the record spun. A perplexed Dan didn't know what to make of the dense, often distorted guitar chords. "Man, I prefer George Benson," he said. Roy, on the other hand, couldn't get enough. "I can see what you are saying. These guys can sing the blues too; it's something entirely different — and that bass player," said Roy.

Dan borrowed the record overnight, and late the following day, brought it back, and said he bought a copy for himself and confessed he was confused by it all. He didn't know whether to alter his style, or forge ahead in a Wes Montgomery tradition. The rest of the week, the phone goes silent. I then call and it's Dan: "Bill, I need to think this over and practice. I don't know if this new music world is for me. We are taking a break from playing for awhile. Roy's wife laid down the law. Roy has got to find a day job. I'm living with Mom, and she is cool with me practicing. Talk to you soon." Dan. Cold, man — cold!

Weeks after performing in the beach communities along the southern California coastline, with Roy and Dan a distant memory, I magically wandered into the not-so-impressive city of Westminster, California. It was there that I secured work in a Mexican rock band led by the Sabori brothers, Andy and Rusty. Both were flirting with revolution. We had three things in common: a love for rock 'n' roll, a distrust of the police, and long, shoulder-length hair.

Bassist Andy and I rented an apartment nearby, and spent hours where he gazed into a floor-length mirror, grooming every precious follicle at the end of a narrow hallway. By night, we played before beer-swilling crowds of middle-aged men who paid admission to spew obscenities at semi-nude topless dancers. Strip clubs dotted the landscape from San Diego to Seattle; not the life I had envisioned, yet it provided temporary wages. We rambled through the psychedelic hits of the day, then weekend excursions north to Hollywood.

The Sabori family offered me a rare glimpse into the home life of California Hispanics. White America did not socialize in the homes of people of colour. I had seen residences from the outside, but had yet to enter the house of someone who wasn't white. Momma Sabori lived much the same as my aunts Mildred and Ann, religiously watching afternoon soap operas. She also moved about much like my grandmother Nellie, from the kitchen to living room, to back porch, with plates of food in hand. There were no awkward moments, uneasiness, or ill-will directed at me. The brothers harboured plenty of anger for whites and black folks; the bandstand was neutral ground. The Sabori brothers of Westminster were imitators, content with posing, lacking even the basic music skills. Andy faked bass, relying on a broad grin to divert attention from false posturing. I worked double duty playing left-hand bass, chords, and lead lines on the right hand. Rusty smiled a lot while keeping a less than consistent beat. Rusty's voice sounded much like a melancholy coyote, mating in front of a desert moon. We played a mix of Bob Dylan, the Rolling Stones' *Under My Thumb*, the Kinks' *You Really Got Me*, The Standells' *Dirty Water*, Music Machine's *Talk, Talk*, Question Mark & the Mysterians' *96 Tears*. Anything that kept the beer flowing, and the girls amused.

27

Sunset Strip

My first visit to the Sunset Strip—38 miles north — was to the legendary Hullabaloo Club. In Indiana, I watched the weekly TV broadcasts, featuring guest hosts like Petula Clark and Bobby Darin, and assumed that this was the place it originated. To my surprise, the club had no connection to the show other than capitalizing on the big-budget series connection with progressive-rock music. Bands like the Buffalo Springfield, the Doors, Gregg and Duane Allman's Hourglass, The Standells, Spirit, and Leaves often played the venue, and exposed young people to new and alternative sounds. You could be as young as 15 years old, and slip past security. Hollywood offered a glimpse into my future. Home to street hustlers, pimps, and voyeurs, preying on the most vulnerable with promises of easy access to a fantasy world beyond the poverty-stricken boulevards and streets.

Upon entry to the Hullabaloo Club, we noticed the only seats available were down in front of the massive stage. The club was formerly the Hollywood landmark the Moulin Rouge, where Hollywood beauties paraded, and then the Earl Carroll Theatre, home of the stars. As we worked ourselves upfront to two vacant seats and down an aisle, we crossed paths with the master of ceremonies and a one-time teen idol, Paul Petersen. Petersen noticed, then singled us out for one of those infamous '60s calls to combat: "Hi, girls! Excuse me, they're not girls. Whoops, I made a mistake. It's getting where you can't tell the boys from the girls." He then waved arms about as if fishing for big laughs, striking a nerve with Andy, who I sensed wanted to strangle the asshole.

We were there for the debut of Toronto soul act, Mandala: November 26, 1966. I didn't know what to expect from the group until the band started playing a high-energy fusion of soul and blues. When the band cut loose, I found myself consumed by the moment. Lead singer George Olliver spun, twisted, and danced, a white man's impression of James Brown. A strobe light kicked in, and the crowd revelled in the unexpected frenzy. Dressed as costumed gangsters, not exactly the style of the times, unless you were playing lounge gigs in Vegas, the band had something different going for them. Andy and I got with the band's energy and drummer "Whitey" Glan's rapid-fire footwork. We nudged one another as guitarist Domenic Troiano shed a few cutting licks, becoming instant disciples. Mandala was the momentary rage of Hollywood, making a return visit a week later and packing the place, yet there were signs the "white soul man" routine was not in step with the times. Just as fast as they arrived, they faded from sight.

One grand January night in '67 at the Hullabaloo, the featured act for this occasion, The Buffalo Springfield (Stephen Stills, Richie Furay, Neil Young, Ken Koblun and Dewey Martin), The Seeds and organist Stu Gardner's trio. Gardner would go on to become Bill Cosby's music director. On this night, the Buffalo Springfield caught fire with *For What It's Worth*. The Seeds, by comparison, were a weak Hollywood opening act featuring lead singer Sky Saxon, a poor man's Mick Jagger. Saxon struggled to elevate his rambling stage act, playing their radio hit *Pushin' Too Hard* — nothing more than a clichéd bit of stage antics. Riding high with a cameo appearance in Lee Marvin's classic film, *Point Blank*, the Stu Gardner Trio took the stage.

Gardner straddled the line between Vegas schmaltz and Sunset Strip hip. Between soul, and psychedelic. One moment the groove would be percolating James Brown, the next, a slow descent into lounge-act hell. There were long extended jams with solid organ riffs and lots of testifying. Fortunately, for Gardner, the late-night crowd had arrived, and teens vanquished to the Sunset Strip. Gardner played a popular soul-pop style of Hammond B-3 organ, part funky and part middle-ground. The Sabori brothers recalled Peterson's catcalls and took it personally, taking leave of future excursions up the Hollywood freeway. I took it in stride. Besides, I had lived through so many stupid one-liners in Indiana, for me, it was just harmless ridicule.

Andy worshipped his white Chevy Impala, a long-awaited purchase. Each drive, Andy would situate himself behind the leather-wrapped steering wheel, adjust the rear-view mirror and slowly twist the ignition key. He would then give it a bit of gas, wait and wait and wait. On one occasion, I lost patience with the routine, and asked Andy to speed the process up. Fed up, he ordered me out of the car and told me to walk. At the ritual's end, Andy fastened the seat belt, lit a cigarette, and sank five or six inches below window level, eyeballs to the horizon, and then pulled away. Damn funny!

I began to commute between the north and south regions of Los Angeles by thumb and foot. Rides were infrequent, and interrupted periodically by vigilant highway patrol officers scouting for draft-age males. I hiked alongside freeways through drainage ditches and past oil rigs pumping minimum crude, most roadside oil wells dry, casting an eerie pall over the parched landscape. During those long walks, the nails in the heels of my Beatle boots pushed upwards into the binding and through to soft skin, causing my feet to bleed. Mostly tired and numb, I rarely addressed the pain. While hitchhiking, I would walk the side roads, highways, and fend off sex-predators and hostile Mexicans who would pull near. The Mexicans would stop and offer me a lift. Just when I was about to climb in, they would speed away laughing. It must have been a freeway sport or something less compelling. Car rides from men with bad intentions kept me on guard. Some would sweet talk, and inquire about my well-being, while others would uncoil a lecherous hand. One aged white-haired predator tried to assault me, and I fought back. He refused to stop his convertible and let me out. I wrestled the steering wheel from him, and pointed the car towards a concrete barrier, crashed, then abruptly exited, sprinting across the highway and leaving the guy to deal with his own carnage. Then I disappeared into a Compton neighbourhood.

Compton was way off my radar. I found myself lost and walking the side streets, old folks eyeballing me as if dropped from an airplane. A few young blacks passed me on the sidewalks and stared me down, until a sympathetic man directed me back to a safe on-ramp.

28

An American Rock 'n' Road Story

Nightly I would stroll the lanes up and down Hollywood Boulevard and Sunset Strip. I would meet the strangest characters. One night while hanging with another longhair, the guy signals a vw bug over and begs for a ride. The two of us get in, and are immediately offered tabs of acid. I rejected it, but the guy I was with squealed like he had won both the lottery and a chariot ride to heaven. A few blocks down Sunset Strip, the "keeper of the acid" signalled the driver to drop him off. The driver looked back at us and said, "You know, that guy's famous, that's Owsley — the acid king."

On another such occasion, I was walking not far from the Whisky a Go Go, and a guy pulled to the curb in a Rolls-Royce and offered a ride. "How far you going?" he asked? How far? I had no idea. "I'm just out walking," I responded. "You want to come with me to get the Rolls washed?" he asked.

We drove around L.A., scouting for a car wash and shot the shit. "Whose car is this?" I asked. He paused. "It belongs to Brian Wilson of the Beach Boys. Don't ever mention that I picked you up. You look cool. When I'm done at the car wash, I've got to drive over and deliver it to the Whiskey (A Go-Go), so don't say anything, and I'll get you in."

I agreed, and off we went. It just happened that the Sons of Champlin were playing a late afternoon set. The driver talked us past security into the balcony where Hollywood's elite rockers and record producers would hang. One after another, he introduced them. "That's Phil Spector, that's so and so." I soaked in as much as possible, then left.

The (Sunset) Strip was a touring caravan of teenagers, mostly from the suburbs, with the clubs along the way being the draw. In-play were Pandora's Box at 8118 Sunset and Crescent Heights, which started as a jazz club in the 1950s. November 1966, Pandora's became the scene of a riot and fights, as nightcrawlers went about protesting a 10 p.m. party curfew. I made one tour of the property with its purple interior and exterior— Day-Glo paint and The Doors playing as the soundtrack to partygoers' acid-dropping and sucking back reefer hits. Then one day, the building is bulldozed. No evidence of its whereabouts.

During another late-night walk, I turned up at the Omnibus Coffee House situated on North Cahuenga Boulevard, near Franklin Avenue, the exterior covered in wood and concrete, just above a multi-coloured sign displaying the coffee house logo. Inside, a wood-framed interior, giving it a quaint farmhouse look. It was here I would encounter a nightly flow of young people lost in a world of cosmic dreams and psychedelic intentions and where Scratch, Rick, Denny, Carol, Flower, and I would first meet.

I started to hang around Hollywood more. The 56 miles of freeway between Westminster and Hollywood began to wear me down. I would hitchhike days and nights and walk just off the highway and atop walls built to dampen the roar of vehicles, rides few and far between. The occasional dog would give chase as would a vigilant neighbour. Before sundown, the police would patrol the side lanes, stop and request ID and draft card. This happened to me numerous times, and I was warned to stay off the highway or face arrest. One return trip, I kicked open the front door to my apartment, and landed face down on my bed and slept 16 uninterrupted hours in my bloody Beatles boots. I so wanted out of Westminster, and that region of southern California.

On my final journey north, I took up residence in a skid-row hotel. The lobby entertained a bizarre assortment of derelicts, aging Hollywood damsels, and habitual criminals. At times, the foyer erupted in violence when one or two crazies would assault the hotel newspaper and mail box. Little men with no real life ahead — mouths cocked, and loaded with complaints. Paranoia and inevitable homelessness. What few women sheltered there were poorly kept. A good many sported lipstick smears from ear to ear. Whenever possible, I'd attempt to communicate. Jammed between the derelicts were young, hostile drifters who'd violently explode over any miscommunication. Everyone would scatter down the hallways, and hide under beds until the police arrived. I would usually squeeze out a back window.

There were afternoons in the Omnibus I spent sketching the menacing symbol of the Hell's Angels on the back of denim jackets worn by the occasional artless biker who relished the sanctuary of dimly-lit rooms. Drawing was my thing, something I spent many hours engaged in as a kid. This all came about when I was spotted doodling on a drink coaster, and a member of the Angels clan laid his denim jacket in front of me, and asked if I could do a better job. I ink-traced an outline winning their approval. There was a sense of security around the Angels, but I never trusted their intentions. I gave them exactly what they asked for, and let it be. Besides, it was the sight of young "free-spirited" women parading about in tight, see-through material that kept their eyes occupied.

Tucked away in various corners, on the rooftop or in back rooms, the occupants of the Omnibus slept near their possessions. I first met Scratch and his girl, Flower, holed up in a vault-like freezer at the rear of the building, then warned them both of the danger. They ignored the message, content with the security of their surroundings. Resting passively in his hands, a vintage Telecaster. Flower curled next to Scratch, rarely leaving his side. Tall, thin and with pointed features, Scratch allowed a loose strand of blond hair to cover one eye. A yellow tint coloured his anemic body, the consequence of a hamburger-and-hot-dog diet. Flower's short brown hair complimented her sensual mouth and deep-set eyes, her clothes lightweight East Indian fabric, accentuating a lovely figure. The two fought continuously, occasionally withdrawing for a session of therapeutic lovemaking.

Scratch's father was a career diplomat stationed in Panama. When Scratch sensed his finances shrinking, a call to father would bring a few hundred dollars via Western Union, arriving in time for the next Jimi Hendrix side. Scratch played with high energy. A style based on East Indian scales, a tonality that worked itself into the psychedelic vocabulary with a touch of rockabilly. Nothing bluesy or jazz-influenced. Just an odd take on music.

Evenings spawned endless jam sessions, attracting an eccentric variety of transient musicians and clueless beatniks. During one of our late-night sessions, a hip-looking guy wearing John Lennon spectacles emerged from the crowd and asked to sit-in. Already mugged by an endless stream of inept conga players and resilient folkies, we agreed nothing could be worse and worth a jam. All 98 pounds of "small man" pulled three drums, hi-hat and ride cymbal and fixtures to the stage, then we hit with Dino Valente's *Hey Joe*. From the downbeat, Denny kicked in with a solid groove. Next, Dylan's *Like a Rolling Stone* and blues anthem *I'm A Man*, and then *Smokestack Lightnin'*. Denny played with all the energy and freedom of The Who's Keith Moon. We were delighted to ride Denny's good sense of time. I played left handed bass, and locked the unit in place.

Following the set, we discussed the possibility of forming a band, but Denny seemed reluctant. He had options, and this was just another in a growing list. After more jamming and serious discussions, we decided to proceed, yet still lacked a frontman who could sing. Denny mentioned a friend from North Hollywood named Rick he thought might work well in this situation. A call was placed and an invitation extended. Rick accepted.

When Rick first strolled through the hallway of the Omnibus, I had difficulty putting this picture together. Here was a guy with the physique of a baseball player; coal-black waist-length hair, and wearing what looked like a three-foot-tall Stetson positioned high on the skull, the original suburban cowboy. Rick was loud, friendly, and ready to rock Jim Morrison-style. Rick's adopted persona complete with spastic stage moves was more suited to sucking up baseball grounders than rock choreography; a voice no worse than most around Hollywood, short on range and dynamics, yet loud in delivery. Stage footwork by military design, embellished with double-spins and boot camp swagger, most resembling a two-point military about-face. We learned to appreciate his exuberance.

The band began rehearsing, then performing nightly at the Omnibus, attracting a modest following. Eventually, club owner Mike Raven took on the management of the group. Raven was involved in launching a series of concerts in Griffith Park, which he called "be-ins," with his wife, Heather Rooney. Anti-war protesters, longhairs, musicians, and bikers frequented the early gatherings. As the international media coverage picked up, the events would transform from "be-ins" to "love-ins." The rallies in Griffith/Elysian park were a mix of vibrant dress: young teenaged girls resplendent in bright rainbow-coloured madras, wreaths of crowning dandelions and decorative facial paint. The boys wore painted denim, long bushy hair, incense blazing in hand. Everybody was peaceful and friendly except for the numerous Hell's Angels in attendance. The invading gang chilled an otherwise perfect mix, striking fear in the Beverly Hills kids who easily coupled with danger, but scampered when things got out of hand.

We would soon find ourselves performing at a second such gathering at Griffith Park for over 30,000 flower children. NBC News dispatched a camera crew to cover the event. That evening we appeared at 6:00 p.m. on the NBC Huntley-Brinkley Report playing our crowd-pleaser, *Hey Joe*. The news of the happening was mostly favourable, focusing mainly on the free nature of the participants. Mike Raven was ecstatic. He saw this as an opening for the band. The Hell's Angels drew their share of media attention and a few comments about their violent nature. The excitement in and around the Omnibus triggered fantasy and grander schemes.

We floated around Hollywood, playing one free gig after another, hoping to be booked at the Whisky a Go Go, where mostly dance-oriented bands dominated the music policy. Then Scratch suddenly came up with the idea for a lengthy tour of America. We bounced the idea around and agreed every aspect needed careful consideration from planning to finances.

We debated our way through a representative list of possible band names, settling on The Yellow Brick Road, until a few weeks later, we spotted a marquee on Santa Monica Boulevard, advertising the debut recording of a group billed as the Yellow Brick Road. We played one other love-in as the YBR when one of the band members uncovered a brochure promoting a show at an exhibition centre, The Great Western Exhibit. It sounded epic, the kind of name no one could deny. We assumed we could live with it, even though we had no idea what it meant. Consequently, it was kind of a stupid name. What were we? Potted-plant cowboys?

We were naive about approaching a booking agent, with no idea where they even existed. Scratch volunteered to be the point man in these negotiations. He first telephoned his father seeking financial assistance. A few days later, $1,000 arrived via Western Union. We hustled down to Wallach's Music City at Sunset and Vine, purchased a Fender Dual Showman and a few other gadgets for the guitar. Scratch then visited a used-car lot and invested in a duo-tone black and white '57 Pontiac sedan. From there, he rented a U-Haul trailer. Now, the cross-country adventure was looking like a possibility and coming together. With 300 dollars left, we gathered around a tabletop in the Omnibus and charted our destination.

The Omnibus was coming under persistent FBI scrutiny, local authorities on the lookout for biker gangs, draft-dodgers, and other felons. The evening before our departure, the LAPD stormed the building in search of an armed-robbery suspect. Club owner Mike Raven was ill-equipped to scrutinize every freewheeling outlaw who passed through the café doors. That night, the police went about inspecting draft cards for inconsistencies. I had in my possession a student deferment card, status unclear. My name hadn't surfaced on any suspect lists, so I hid in the shadows. The police carried photos and composite descriptions along with the identities of young men suspected of draft evasion. From that day forward, everyone who frequented the Omnibus became fearful of the harassment. I was the only one in the band with a potential problem. The others received medical deferments. March 27, 1967, after receiving numerous noise complaints from the derelicts a few doors down at the "crazy people" hotel, the Omnibus was raided. Raven and ten guitar players were arrested.

Raven had failed to get an entertainment licence.

Two weeks passed until the morning of our planned departure, Rick, nowhere in sight. Rick and Denny, both California boys, never ventured beyond the secure beach communities around Santa Monica. Rick got cold feet, had a girlfriend and responsibilities as a little league coach and other significant duties. We were not giving up. Scratch worked magic on the telephone, luring Rick and his new love, Carol, to the Omnibus. Upon arrival, we discovered Carol to be easy-going and relished the opportunity to travel and possibly a stop-over visit with parents in Minnesota. A deal was struck: drop Carol some 90 miles north of Minneapolis with her parents, and Rick was on board. Carol would prove to be a calming presence: blonde, blue-eyed, friendly, and comfortable. She never let hardship rule, choosing to find something positive in adversity. Rick relented, called family, and received their blessings. With music gear, clothes, and trunks loaded, we journeyed down Highway 10 up through San Bernardino, connecting with Highway 15 through Barstow, eventually turning on 40 East, out and beyond the California border into Arizona.

It was somewhere between Barstow and Kingman, Arizona, when reality struck. We had been laughing and speculating about the future, then suddenly realized that we knew nothing of touring or booking a band. Scratch had this confident air about him, and convinced us he could sell our band anywhere in America. We had no reason to doubt him. He earned the job.

Early the next morning, we arrived in Williams, Arizona, the temperature hovering near freezing, none of us dressed for the sudden drop. It was mid-April, and, in our minds, something was drastically wrong. A service-station attendant reassured us that once we descended through the mountains, the thermometer would rise considerably, and by the time we reached Flagstaff, it would be in the high '70s. We also determined our travel money would not last more than a week, so we were desperately in need of a gig.

It was mid-afternoon when we motored through the heart of Flagstaff, tired, and less confident about our journey.

Roadside, Scratch spotted a country-and-western joint and opted to approach the owner about a booking. The first sight of us shocked the lunchtime crowd, who were all sporting tall hats, dressed much like "Hollywood Rick," crowded around a long bar. More than a few redneck heads whip-snapped, spun around, and belched obscene remarks. The cowboys had seen our type on TV, certainly more curious than threatening.

The owner was quite taken with Scratch's audacious sales pitch, and looked upon us as a low-cost diversion. He asked one patriotic question: "Any of you boys flag-burners?" All-American Rick assured the boss we were different from those radical protesters. We were a true-blue, hard-hat-loving band. Rick had obtained a medical deferment for a gimp knee, injured in a sandlot football game. Otherwise, he said, he would have enlisted for Vietnam, bypassing boot camp. The owner bought our act, offering us $20 for an evening of suspect entertainment.

Western folk piled in ready for a twilight set of Hank Snow classics or a Porter Wagner jamboree. As we cleared the doorway, the tall hats giggled in synch along with their bovine mistresses. Scratch tuned his guitar, then spun into action. Rick executed one of those basic military training pivots, whipped his long black mane about in a swirling frenzy, the voice strained, monophonic, and absent the God-given charm of a George Jones. The dog-faced audience looked on in disbelief. As far as they were concerned, we had arrived from some far-away planet. A few tall hats grilled the owner and asked if this was a set-up for a practical joke. The regulars persevered, and politely requested we pack up and leave before midnight; the jukebox was preferred, and would be less invasive than a travelling pack of peculiar musicians. The owner was a straight-up good guy who thought this was a grand idea. We collected the negotiated fee, $20, and sped away unscathed on to Albuquerque, New Mexico. That $20 stretched a reasonable distance in 1967, enough to feed six nomads and fill a gas tank.

Upon arriving in Albuquerque, we took note of the numerous empty lots and western bars. Scratch noticed a stand-alone bar situated dead centre in a used-car lot that looked safe for a caravan of misfits. He then worked his way past a cluster of roughnecks and heavily made-up women. Somehow, he convinced the owner to rethink his music policy and book a psychedelic band and topple the resident Billy-Bob act. While dragging equipment into the club, I came face to face with the day manager who in no way was as amused as the owner or the man who booked us in his Flagstaff bar, and far more demanding with terse instructions: "If we like you, we'll pay you. If not, you'll be gone."

Before showtime, we endured a set of weepy bumpkin tragedies, sad-faced cowgirls, and a lonely hombre. With the rock-and-roll zeal of a high-speed tank engine, we crashed the stage, Rick pumping fists, whirling and twirling, the rest of us loud and foreign. I quickly sensed the mood shift amongst the lizard-skinned patrons lining the pine bar. It was if they were making plans to stuff us in a wood-chipper rather than tolerate any more of this nonsense; everything repulsed this conservative ass-kicking brood. Near set's end, it seemed apparent we were not going to collect payment. I signalled Scratch to cut the set short. As if on cue, the big boss man walked over and reminded us the opportunity was there, and we had blown it, as witnessed by the crowd's reaction, asking why he should pay us a dime. Scratch shouted back, drawing an ugly response. I had seen enough, didn't care, and was plenty tired of dragging band equipment back and forth after a long drive. The manager gave us two alternatives, get the fuck out of his face or endure an ass-whipping. With a few dollars stashed, we cut our losses and penetrated the Texas border.

As with any mention of Texas and longhairs, the possibility of being interred in a Texas jail was a given. Although we were free of drugs, we knew Texas authorities had ways of manufacturing criminal offences. These guys were masters. Every male with hair drifting below the ear was considered a "commie draft-dodger" in need of "fixin'." We knew the key to our survival was not attracting attention, which we planned to do.

We drove around Amarillo, looking for any evidence of shoulder-length hair. Down a side street, we caught a glimpse of a paranoid-looking guy dodging pedestrians. My first thought? Here's our guy. We waved him to the curb, then inquired about the local music scene: clubs, parks, dances, or whatever. He lowered his head, and gestured us to drive down a side street away from the throughway, and park across from a low-rise building where blinds were pulled. Inside, a half dozen freaks near-invisible and seriously paranoid. Scratch retells our story, and asks about any possible engagements around the city. The fellow politely picks up the telephone, dials and secures a Saturday night dance, and $200 pay for the band. We could not believe our good fortune, knowing that the amount could take us to Minnesota. The guy then directed us to a military base on the far side of Amarillo. The word *military* rocked the nervous system.

"What's the catch?" I asked. "None," he said. "Other than playing a Saturday night dance for couples in a mess hall." We were then given a contact name and directions. The offer set the mind spinning. I envisioned armed guards with guns ready to abduct and escort me to a military stockade, and some "hup, two, three, four" down a hellhole — Scratch was unfazed.

Getting past the military police was a sight to behold, when two beefnecks signalled us over for inspection, offered up a few goofy hippie jokes, then telephoned ahead. Bingo! Safe passage past heavy armaments and a cadre of dreary, marched-out troops. The designated concert hall, a giant feeding area dressed up for prom night, with several mess-style tables removed, and a room frantically redecorated for the social affair; instruments to be arranged in a central locale near where we imagined adoring fans would gather. I thought, this isn't so bad: good pay, a decent room, and a fair sound system.

Before we hit the stage, we are ushered into a space the size of a footlocker and far from military personnel. There were rumblings we might be draft-dodgers or drug merchants, there to inject liberal poison into the veins of our nation's finest. I tried avoiding eye contact. What do you say to a three-bird colonel with two pounds of polished brass dangling from the chest and an angry disposition? "I hope you like the tunes"?

The evening arrived without much aggravation, the room pulsating with corsage-garnished damsels clinging to their stiff-necked dates. Before the night began to roll, the occasional officer-in-training would sidle up and say, "Hey buddy, I used to have long hair like yours. Have a look at me now. They'll get you one day, too." We were facing men and women, mostly our age. Then this punk-ass junior officer arrived. Let the games begin. "Hey, hippie, do you squat when you piss? Are you girls? Do you have wet pussies?"

Rick's demeanour turned volcanic. He screamed back, "Shut the fuck up, peckerhead, or I'll beat the snot out of both you and your ugly date. I come from a military family, too." No, no, no, I say to myself, this is not good. "Come down here, turd-boy, and I'll yank that funny wig off," yelled another. "What wig? This is real California hair you grapefruit-headed Mississippi asshole," yelled Rick. Please, slow down, Rick, please. In real life, Rick was one of those beer-drinking, anti-hippie flower child types. His "get up" more costume than commitment. The band kept a distance even though a table of date-deficient troopers kept ramming a hard metal table at us, trying to bust our kneecaps.

Then showtime! And what a show it was. The GWE plowed into The Seeds' *Pushin Too Hard*, one of our endless jams, followed by a working set comprised of 10 songs of not much variety, and an epic 25-minute "acid burn" jam. I could sense the debutantes growing impatient, and watched as they yanked the neckties of their dates and eyes rolling into the backs of their heads. No one danced. It was if we were playing to an audience of Formica tables. "Play something we can dance to like *Woolly Bully*," someone yelled. "How 'bout something slow by Gene Pitney?— I know, *Town Without Pity*," a disgruntled voice pleaded. "She wants to jump my bones. Let's get it going over there, or no one gets fucked tonight." What a mess. "We're from California, and we don't play that shit," Scratch responds. A voice shouted, "Why don't you guys take the night off, and we'll get someone to spin records, some real music?" "Deal," an authoritative voice from the crowd confirms.

I am banking on the $200. Scratch said, "No, that's fine; we'll keep playing. Here is one I know you all know, *Light My Fire* by The Doors. We soar into the body of the tune without mishap, then the screeching of chairs. Before the 20-minute guitar solo, I make out the silhouettes of the remaining couples slither out of

sight and parade into a side room. Necks bend and whisper in
the dark. Then a military representative nears, "Could you guys
just stop playing — just leave, this is all wrong. For your safety,
we'll help you pack up and find the highway." Scratch looks the
guy straight on and says, "We still have two more sets to play
and need to be paid. We're just warming up." The guy pulls us
aside, "Look, you'll get your money. Just get out of this room, it's
a security matter now." Then the insults.

"Hey, 'big-beak' come over here and suck on this," says a pork-
face guy. What? Rick and I shift into a whip-ass mode. "Did you
hear what he said?" asks Rick? "Let's get the one with the mouth
full of shit and pound him into 'ass' pudding. I've been watching him undress Carol all night with that goofy grin," screams
Rick. "He's got insane fucking eyes." Bingo! DJ and songs of
yesteryear. The house music begins, and the couples pair up. We
quickly become yesterday's nightmare.

While loading, a broken-down soldier waltzes near, "I love you
guys. I love acid, too. I'm so high right now; I'm feeling electric,
I may never come down. You want some?" While carting instruments away, an invisible hand from behind slaps the back of my
head. I do a quick turn-around and see three guys staring in the
opposite direction and one giggling. I call up a few rebuttals, yet
leave well enough alone. Then the catcalls and shoving start. The
military police then intervene and move the "square-headed"
boys a safe distance away, and escort us to where an officer in
charge apologizes, then confides his love for "anti-social" music,
especially Tommy James & The Shondells. He then proceeds to
write us a check. A check? What the hell? We argue back and
forth in favour of cash, yet he insists on "military" procedure. He
then suggests we return Monday morning, and he would arrange
to cash the check, the only hitch is it's late Saturday night, and
what the hell does a longhair do in Amarillo besides hide out on
a Sunday.

We took up residence in a roadside park. Soon after, our
downtown zombie friends invited us over to *party*. We dropped
in for an hour or so, but couldn't handle the relentless paranoia.
Everyone was on a watch list—guys and girls. I understood it

was way too easy getting tossed into the back seat of a Texas police cruiser, and even more challenging fixing broken bones and concealing facial injures. We spent Sunday walking circles around the rest area. Monday could not come soon enough. Early morning, we arrived at the front gates of the military base, met by security, and escorted to the moneyman. The officer lived up to his word, and paid us $200 in cash — cordial and respectful. Next stop? Des Moines, Iowa.

It was a wet and miserable eight-hour drive from Amarillo to Des Moines. We arrived late at an all-night diner inhabited by farm boys and preening small-town girls. The boys looked well-fed, much like the livestock they tended by day, and as vocal. "Look at those long-hair pussies — why they are as pretty as Mandy the heifer, the one Hubert screws," says one clod-hopping rowdy. The six of us dine on burgers and fries as "jacked-up" farm boys begin to close in and play us for laughs. The louder the girls hooted, the more excitable the boys became.

We paid the tab, walked towards the Pontiac, and climbed inside. Ten miles or so down the road towards Minnesota, blinding high-beams hit the back of our heads. We couldn't detect if it was a provocative gesture, or just someone looking to pass. Scratch signals the vehicle to drive around. As the car blows by, you could hear obscenities reverberate across the sleeping cornfields, and the roar of howling farm boys diminish as the car lights blended then faded into the distant horizon. Miles down the road, we observed a sliver of light edge towards us then a sudden surge into our lane at high speed. As the high-beam widens, we realize the farm boys are playing a game of "chicken"; we hold ground, expecting they'd reconsider, unaware they were in this to win. A split-second before impact, Scratch flips the steering wheel, and points the Pontiac into a cornfield — a terrifying moment. The farm boys stop, back up, jump on the hood of the car, and "monkey-shout" obscenities. We talked amongst ourselves, hoping this wasn't an opening salvo into a night of violent rage.

As quickly as the theatre of war erupted, the "Billy Bob" show scurried back down the highway towards Des Moines, leaving behind the "fearful six." It was several miles and a good 30 minutes before the tremors subsided. Middle America rarely changes. There's always a demon to chase, and in '67, if it wasn't black, it was someone sporting long hair.

We faced a six-hour drive returning Carol safely to her parents. Rick's "love interest" was losing interest in him. Carol was one of the fortunate young adventurers who did not attract harm or flirt with poverty. Her parents trusted and knew she was in control, and the brief interlude in California was more exploration than rebellion. The two of us spent hours in the back of the U-Haul, riding high up on blankets and falling between suitcases just talking. Those periods caused a bit of friction between Rick and me, but nothing more than two people comfortable in conversation. Carol was of old country Swedish stock, hearty and good-natured, and in control. I appreciated the female company.

The drop-off outside Minneapolis went smoothly. None of the over-the-top dysfunctional stuff when a child returns after extending their wings. It was now time to concentrate on finding more work. Scratch was on the move, which meant tracking down more longhairs and engaging artsy types in and around Minneapolis.

The road leading into the downtown called for a drive past a headshop. Like most cities, every young person paused at one-time or another, especially musicians, and would stop for rolling papers and hash pipes. The odd thing about us? No one did drugs. It was a no-no. We certainly looked the part, but with similar backgrounds, there was a greater emphasis on work and Christian-like play. Unlike other promising music scenes, we had encountered, Minneapolis was a business hub. When people went to work, the main street stood barren. As for music, there was still a connection with the '50s and oldies bands from that area.

Danceland was the top teen club. Not a venue for longhairs but bouffant hairstyles and close-cropped boys. The room was in transition, a considerable distance from those Rolling Stone types or anything comparable. When we asked about playing, we were told to start by working down the gig chain and build an audience.

The GWE landed a job in a pizza parlour called Magoo's, playing our brand of psychotic jams for three weeks. Local freaks and geeks all dropped in. We pocketed $600, enough for food and possible lodgings. It was there we made our second appearance on national television, a segment performing at a love-in and protest concert against the Vietnam War. Once again, NBC was on hand. Just after 6 p.m., Scratch, Denny, Rick, and I appeared on the Huntley-Brinkley Report. Word spread around Minneapolis about this edgy band from California, and we packed Magoo's. Then the bombshell. Without informing us, a party was organized for a local hero.

We arrived to see Magoo's decorated in party balloons, and staff secretive. In the middle of the second set, the guest of honour arrived, greeted by the enthusiastic cheers of admiring fans. Bob Dylan! We are asked to cut the band break short, and play a few more numbers; that's when "Hey Joe" came in handy. We never spoke to or got near the folk icon, other than watching him walk about smiling and socializing, shaking a few hands and nodding. I thought: wouldn't it be cool if I could get close to him, and tell him about my pal and our morning drives to U.S. Steel and the cultural awakening the both of us underwent listening to *Freewheelin.'*

After searching for a short-term rental with zero success, we are taken to a doomed building, condemned for the wrecking ball in the centre of a highway expansion. Thankfully, the structure still had running water, but no electricity. It was a crash pad of sorts, taken over by a group of young party dwellers; some intent on saving it from the encroaching highway, others in for a good time. It was a hard slog.

This Minnesota spring came with damp, bone-chilling nights. Days? Long and indifferent. We still had that band passion, but there was something absent at the core. We could pick up one-off gigs: park concerts and freebies, but the pressure of relentless hustling strained our relations. Rick was uncomfortable with the lack of amenities; Scratch and Flower couldn't care less. Denny and I just floated about as if we had few options. In the background, I could hear the "drums of war." Vietnam was never far from my mind; neither was the fear of being drafted.

We eventually met Minnesota's number one band, The Castaways, known for the hit record, *Liar, Liar*. These were college-looking boys, committed to no cause nor fashionable, just decent, friendly folks. We talked and befriended the gracious folks, who then lined up a show at Danceland for us without complication. As we took the stage, a full house looked back at us as if we were circus freaks. Something was not right with this picture, a total time-warp. We played a set of hard-core psychedelic acid-rock before a confused room. I thought to myself, there's Betsy, Mindy, and Shirley—over there, Bobby, Stewie, and Brett; all right out of the glossy pages of *Teen Beat Magazine*. The heartland of America was not the best place to abandon Dick Clark's Bandstand playlist. I don't think a soul spoke to us. It was all about the spectacle, something the clean-cut kids could whisper about before church.

We were hanging around a local head shop and listening to *Sgt. Pepper's Lonely Hearts Club Band*, Jimi Hendrix, *Are You Experienced*, and John Mayall's Blues Breakers, believing there was more to this scene than presented. Then the night of reckless debauchery. We throw a party. The few friends we attract invite their buddies; the mob arrives, frat-boys clutching cases of beer along with a few long-haired stragglers. An hour or so in, the party swings out of control. When the banging starts, we disappear upstairs. Down below, I can hear hammers and boards creaking, one gigantic drunken orgy of nail pulling, wall bashing and paint slinging. I had never witnessed such teen carnage in my short life. On our way out I stop in front of drunken kids, most covered in paint, the floors watered down in spilled beers and busted plaster and think to myself, what kind of fucking idiot gets a kick from such nonsense. We quickly exit.

The following day, we are driven out into the country and shown another abandoned property where freaks crash. We spend the night in unforgivable conditions, no heat, no food, no blankets, just body tremours — then decide to put Minnesota behind us. Scratch had an aunt living in Ironwood, Michigan, who owned a lodge, so he made a telephone call. She agreed to hire the band and help us secure more work in the Upper Peninsula. As we worked our way up the highway, we found ourselves in for the night from hell.

After nearly a month on the road, the temperature rose to seasonal. It was muggy, and night closing in. We'd been driving for hours, counting deer, dodging roadkill and patching tires. Down to our last replacement, the left-back tire blows. Far from civilization, the only light a still moon gazing through the blackened silhouettes of towering pines. It was an eerie feeling as if all wildlife were watching and calculating our miscues. Scratch pops open the trunk to discover no jack, which I assume was left roadside some two-hundred miles back when tire number three blew like a birthday balloon. We were screwed. Circling above, a billion-strong flying army, as if Satan summoned his bug militia in for a sumptuous buffet. Parasites fly in from all directions, wings whistling, blood on their lips, highway to the cloud deck, the blackest of black in both directions.

It is well past midnight, and Scratch quickly gathers reams of firewood and builds a campfire middle of the road. We remove all blankets from the back of the U-Haul and huddle next to each other. The attacks escalate. Denny and I agree to jog to the next town and ask for help, fill a plastic container with water, soak a couple of towels, wrap around heads, and assure everyone of a quick return.

It was a slow jog/walk at first, but an aggressive army of insect assailants made striding near impossible. As the night humidity and sweat intensified, so did the assaults. We bump up the pace. An hour or two passes with no sign of a porch light or humanity, not even the framework of a working farm in the distance. We eventually spot a house set back off the highway, lit by a small beam and knock on the door. No response! This was cottage country; apparently, most inhabitants not around. Heart-pounding, legs tired, and with few options, we began to slow walk; the mosquitoes returned in a fury. Itching from head to toe, face and neck an open wound, Denny and I curse, laugh nervously, trade stories and shout back at the surrounding forest, sweat dripping at an alarming rate, the canister of water running low. Over the next hours, we shuffle forward like zombies in a B-grade flick, wounded, exhausted, but not yet defeated. Then the first light of morning. The darkened forest begins to give way to broad fields covered in long-stem sunflowers, lit by a rising sun. It's Sunday morning!

Coming up the highway, a station wagon, and inside, a woman wearing a bonnet nestled high on her head. She stops and asks, "Boys, what are you two doing out here this early?" I thought to myself, glory hallelujah, a church lady. "Why don't I take you to the police station," she says. The fearless soul invites us in, drives back five miles, and drops us in front of the cop shop. Two officers greet two somewhat bug-eaten long-haired drifters. Denny and I recall our claustrophobic adventure as like that Wes Craven horror movie featuring zombie mosquitoes. The on-duty enforcement officers listen intently to our freak story, then question us about the details. "You sure about this? Never heard of anything like that happening around here," says officer one. A second officer walks outside, packs a tire iron and jack, and points us to the backseat of the cruiser and suggests we retrace the mishap. "You two say you ran all night and left your friends huddling around a fire," he asks? "Yes, sir, and we're hurting," I say. "You know, if you had walked from the other direction, it would have been five miles to town. You just travelled forty. Are you boys lying to me? You must have got a ride; you cannot be in that kind of shape. Hell, you're long hairs." Denny and I had covered an astonishing forty miles in eight hours. To this day, I question why we didn't collapse face-down in the middle of the road and die. There is something to be said about will, perseverance, endurance, fear, and survival.

Bathed in a low-lying fog, and still draped in blankets, we arrive to find Scratch and crew huddled in the centre of the road. Overnight, the team locked themselves in the car and sealed every possible entry point and massacred the intruders. Stacks of burnt wood and smouldering ash lay near the Pontiac. A police officer popped the trunk, extracted a jack, walked over, spun the tire iron, then retreated to his cruiser. "Fuck that," he yelled. The entire return trip, he accused Denny and me of bullshitting.

Faced with the same enemy, he panicked, swatted and scratched his face, dodged when possible, then retreated to the cruiser, partially rolling down the window and saying: "If you boys know how to fix a tire, do it!" We thanked him, and had a good laugh. He then yelled, "You know, I thought you boys were a bunch of draft-dodging freaks, but anyone who can survive out here at night ain't so bad." Denny and I settle in, crack a side window, and invite the fragrant mix of air, moisture and tall-pines to massage us to sleep.

Scratch's aunt provided a lovely interlude. The family had long roots in the Ironwood, Michigan, community. We even found refuge in a rental cottage: rainbow-trout fishing and boating. Two days in, and several rainbow trout in Scratch's sports pack, the good times come to a sudden end when the owner discovers Scratch holed up with Flower, and unmarried. "I understand there's that free-love stuff going around, but in our community, we are Christians, and I can't change that. You folks have to leave in the morning," he says meekly. Damn, this place was so lovely and far nicer than the shitholes we inhabited. There was even a foot-long stuffed trout posted over the master bed.

Night time offered us one last epic outdoor Michigan adventure. We played an off-road game, where one of us would ride the hood of the car, Scratch dimmed the lights, and the rest of us would scream like 3-year-olds: a "dare to be scared" contest. Each of us took turns and it was fucking scary. Last up, Denny. Speeding down a country back road, Denny clinging to the hood ornament, Scratch cuts the lights. Denny yells "faster." Scratch accelerates, then pops the headlights. The high-beams catch a terrified black bear and cubs crossing the road. Scratch quickly brakes. The bear turns as if ready to charge, rises, and without thinking Scratch cuts the lights. Denny leaps from the hood and sprints to the far side of the Pontiac and climbs through an open window. Holy shit! Scratch then floors the car before popping the high-beams back on. Terrifying. Fortunately, he was able to fumble and open the lights just before a bend in the road. Later that evening, we sat around the cottage joking about that fat trout mounted above the bed, and the look of fear in Denny's eyes, which by now had turned to relief.

The drive north to Ironwood, Michigan — located near the Montreal River adjacent to Hurley, Wisconsin — follows. We meet Scratch's aunt. Mid-afternoon, we catch her sweeping leaves from the entrance of her small boutique hotel. She had promised a gig playing for teens and vacationers and she came through. We spent the evening performing for sweet faces and even caught a gig leaving town. There was an innocence about these kids and the most delightful temperament.

Just off the main highway, surrounded by a blackened forest, a college pub. It just happened to be a place where all kinds of alternative bands played. Word got out we were coming, and the bar quickly filled. A group from California carried weight around here, and curiosity. Throughout the night, we thundered through our repertoire of psychedelic jams and the place roared with excitement. It was if we brought with us the imagined vestiges of Sunset Strip and Haight-Ashbury. While basking in our new-found fame, a young man approached the bandstand and asked, "Are you Bill King?" I read his face and thought to myself, it has been a year or so since I left Indiana, and hidden in the north woods. Who would know me here? "Bill, it's Frank—Frank Mimms from church." Sure enough, my good pal from Meigs Avenue Church of Christ in Jeffersonville. "Damn, Frank, how the hell did you end up in this giant forest," I ask? It seems Frank got a summer job logging and in forest-management work, all part of an accredited college program. "Bill, this is unreal, how's it going with the draft? I hear things aren't well." No, they were not going well, nor would they! Frank was the smartest and kindest college student in our congregation and never one to walk the same path as me. Between sets, we talked and shared words about war, home, and road stories. Who would go, and how would the good folks in church accept our decisions?

After the gig and goodbyes, the band found its way to an all-night diner connected to a strip bar. Students would cross state lines from alcohol-dry Wisconsin to Michigan to drink after hours. We take a booth near a small window facing into an adjacent room where dancers strutted about on a stage. You could see and hear "horse-headed" Billy Bobs bend and squeal with each suggestive spin, the moronic catcalls and arms raised high in beer salutes. As we're about to order food, asshole number one approaches. "Do you boys squat when you piss?" How many times have we heard that? Is there not an original line to be had?

I spot two police officers sitting far end of the counter, approach, and ask them to intervene. Reluctantly, a junior officer plays the good-ole boy card. "Come on, Melvin, leave the pussies alone, you've got better things to do." Melvin then demands we present our draft cards. "Those queers are all draft-dodgers—why aren't they in Vietnam, he says?" I counter, "Why aren't you in Vietnam, shithead." Melvin runs at me with a cop in pursuit, "Listen, fuckhead; it's you and me outside." A smiley face comes poking through the mini window leading to the strip bar and says, "Hey kids, he's a big-ass idiot. Pay him, no mind." Stripper to the rescue. "Melvin, leave these kids alone. Why do you bother every hippie who comes here for a meal and leaves? Damn you," she says. "They're pussy draft-dodgers; that's why," says Melvin. "How do you know that?" she inquires. "Just look at them, they look like women with all that hair, they got to be pussies," he says. Melvin insists we take this outdoors. We ignore, pay up, and make our way back to the Pontiac — Melvin, and friends in pursuit. We climb in and drive up the road to a service station.

While filling up, Melvin and posse arrive. Without talking, Scratch moves back of the Pontiac, pops the trunk then distributes the stems of four microphone stands between Rick, me, and Denny and himself, then waits behind the driver's wheel. As we gas up, Melvin and his band of restless assholes taunt, threaten, then charge. Like Zulu warriors, the three of us rush forward and swing wildly in defense. Melvin retreats a safe distance with his gang of all-night losers and waits. One by one we climb back inside the car, Melvin looking foolish and defeated. On the road again!

We had been talking about Canada for weeks, me recalling my summer session with Oscar Peterson in 1963, and how liberating it was wandering Yorkville Avenue. I had heard about Canada's embrace of draft resisters and resistance to the war in Vietnam, and talk of alternative sanctuaries like Sweden and Australia, and how Canada was openly accepting. I knew of the music scene and Toronto being a sizeable city — much more diverse than any of these back-lane towns and racially-divided cities where we had begged for gigs. A vote was taken and it was decided: Toronto, here we come.

Upper Michigan was like driving across Ohio, miles and miles of emptiness and roadkill. The second night of the drive, we pulled into the late-night diner. I'm the first to enter and told, "We don't serve longhairs or draft dodgers." I ignored it, and summoned the crew. We lined up along the counter, and I ordered a slice of lemon pie. An ageing waitress ignored us. As time passed, I politely asked, "Can we place our orders?" She responded: "We don't serve dogs in here. Dogs stay outside." That was it. I asked insistently, "Who's the mayor of this town?" A lone voice from the room yelled out Mayor So-and-So. I walked to the diner entrance, scanned a telephone book, searched for the mayor's name, and dialled. "Hello, who is this?" a voice on the other end demanded. "It's Bill. I'm from out of town, and here with my band, and trying to order food, but the waitress won't serve us." "Don't you know it's 3 a.m.?" he asked. "Yes, sir, we are trying to get served and drive on and have every right to be here." Pause. "Who said they wouldn't serve you?" I shout out: "Ma'am, what's your name?" She answered, "I don't give a rat's ass who you are talking too, I don't serve longhairs." The mayor overheard, and said, "Put her on the phone now." The conversation went something like this: "Mr. Mayor, the Rolling Stones are here, and they look all shaggy and stuff. I don't have to serve them." Then we hear, "It's fucking 3 a.m., serve the kids, and stop the bullshit. Bye." Served!

Early Sunday morning, we arrived in the Canadian border city of Sault Saint-Marie. A customs agent informs us we cannot bring the car into Canada without specific insurance, and tells us of a cousin who would pay cash. Sold! Before doing so, we drop the U-Haul in a U-haul parking lot with a note saying, "Rented in Los Angeles, it's Sunday, and no servicemen on the site." We then move all the luggage and equipment store them at the train terminal, and await boarding. There was something genuinely liberating ditching the car and opting for a train ride: no more fill-ups, flat tires, or oil changes, just a clear view out theatre-size windows of the horizon and weatherbeaten landscape. The trip was nothing special, other than the feeling of being deflated and not defeated. A grey pall shadowed the long stretch of the countryside to Union Station in Toronto.

Upon arrival, we stored most everything in lockers and headed towards Yorkville. It was the week leading up to the July 23, 1967 performance of the Jefferson Airplane at Nathan Phillips Square. The five of us land in Yorkville, fan out and search for a week's lodging. Denny and I located a flat on Huron Street, the others close by. We then gathered in Yorkville and canvassed for work. First stop, Boris's, and club manager Bernie Fiedler. Scratch conjured his best lines: "We're a band from California, and we've played the first love-ins in Griffith Park and across America, and this would be a perfect situation for us." Fiedler was not buying. Outside we meet musicians Luke Gibson and not long after, Keith McKie. Both suggested other options along Yorkville that hired bands. We made additional inquiries, but established venues showed little to no interest until we came across Jacques's Place. We booked three evenings, and were instructed to walk about Yorkville promoting ourselves. We did just that. Doing so I meet a young woman who introduces me to several musicians playing various clubs. She escorts me past doorkeepers, in for shows and down the front. Most of what I saw were remnants of the British Invasion, bands in dated mod attire, or lounge acts. It was Luke and the Apostles who were of the most interest to me.

The GWE mark time and, after a week, lose all interest in Toronto, until invited to City Hall for a concert featuring the Jefferson Airplane, and we made the downtown run. I am guessing some 20,000 packed the square. From our vantage, the band sounded as if it was playing through a megaphone. New York City seemed a better fit. On the rails again! The trip from Toronto down through New York State: a quiet passage and exhilarating. None of us had ever played or visited the grandest city in North America, and as exciting as that seemed, it also scared the shit out of us.

29

Greenwich Village '67 / The Street Is Not a Home

If there was one place in America where homelessness could either be a monumental disaster or a liberating experience, New York City in the '60s was that place to be. That connecting zone between optimism and reality helped me sort through the difficult days ahead. I had never envisioned living broke out in the open. Most days, I had a few dollars tucked away, and a place to sleep and friends close by.

We arrived late at night in Penn Station, unloaded, and searched for a taxi to cart luggage and band equipment to Greenwich Village. A first driver asked for $50 and said he could round up another four. All we had between us was $250. We tried negotiating and offered $200. No go. A flatbed truck then approached, and two bearded freaks pulled over. "Where are you going?" "Greenwich Village," I say. "If you've got $50 between you, load her up and get in back." Wow! We arranged all the items, climbed aboard, and talked amongst ourselves. "This can't be happening!" Once in the Village, we asked to be dropped off in front of the Night Owl Café, an iconic venue we had read about in magazines. A night drizzle dampened our outer clothing, yet we wore big broad smiles.

We then huddled under an awning, away from the rain with no plans, no friends, no place to live, and no idea what we were doing. A young man and his companion ducked under and join us. He introduced himself as Roy Michaels and said he led a band called Cat Mother & the All-Night Newsboys. We asked

Michaels for places to play, and he suggested we give the Café Wha? a visit: a venue welcoming to new and visiting bands.

Midday, Scratch takes charge, left us with Flower and headed for the club. An hour passed before he returned. He then informed us he had arranged a gig; in fact, the house manager, named Tex, offered him and Flower accommodations for the night. Scratch also met a street hustler named André, who asked to join us for the gig and share frontman duties with Rick. Much depended on the afternoon audition.

The band arrived, set up, and in walked the flamboyant Puerto Rican. André came dressed in tight satin pants, shirt open at the waist, and scarf whipping about his neck. He then climbed on stage, and called out an assortment of counter-culture anthems of which we knew maybe two. Rick didn't buy-in, already thinking ahead and seeing no future in this room. When it came to who was the better singer, it was a draw. Amongst the street people, André assumed the role of a hustler and wannabe rock star. He talked as if we were the next Beatles or possibly the Rolling Stones, and it all hinged on his leadership. André went on to brag about sleeping with Linda Keith, Keith Richards' girlfriend; in fact, he made plans to take us by a friend's place at 11 Horatio Street. He said he was friends of both, who would invite us to crash until we found lodgings.

We carted our possessions over to said friends' flat, unpacked everything we owned and waited around. An hour passed when this so-called friend arrived. This does not go well. André introduced us as his new band, and said that we needed to crash until we could rent a space. The guy looked on mortified, eventually relented, and allowed Rick, Scratch, and Flower to stay; Denny and I are assigned the streets. André told me not to worry, he had something in mind, then he disappeared.

Night One on the NYC streets came after a long day pacing up and down MacDougal Street, then down Bleecker to its conclusion. Early morning, sanitation crews picked up debris left behind by tourists who mostly ignored the overflowing garbage bins. To me it was invigorating, an epic high. Nothing could derail my optimistic inner soul. Life in Indiana was two steps to the right side of hell. I am now on the street of dreams!

Manhattan streets came as a much-needed release and passage to unchained freedom. When hungry, the mind screws with the stomach. I noticed that many of the transient kids panhandled. I had never imagined such a scenario for myself: stick a hand out, tourist types and business people drop a quarter in your palm, and just as quickly push you off their radar. I met a couple of teens adept at kindly begging and took a few cues. Twenty-five cents bought a slice of Sicilian pizza, or a double-decker Neapolitan ice cream cone, enough to coat the stomach's inner lining until late in the day. At first, I was way off my game; then, after a half-hour or so of novice soliciting, I stockpiled 75 cents. I felt a sense of pride walking into a pizza parlour and slapping down a quarter for a slice. New York pizza, with a layer of home-made tomato sauce and pepperoni on top of a deep thick crust, never tasted so good in life as at that rescue moment.

The street brought me in close contact with persons flirting with varying degrees of insanity, addiction and saddled with debilitating loneliness. I met a vagrant named Jesse from Louisville, Kentucky. Jesse was black as the night sky with hands as thick as a welder's mitt, who addressed me from the side of his face, rarely eyeball to eyeball. We shared a stoop where the Blue Note Jazz Club now resides on West Third Street, then called the Four Winds Café, and watched tourists mill about and converse for long hours.

Jesse's back story was one of severe alcoholism and long stretches away from wife and family. He loved people-watching and did not mind sleeping in doorways on a humid summer night. No one approached him. Jesse had a fearsome bark that could make wolves tremble. I loved talking about music with him. We agreed on organist Jimmy Smith and hummed a few bars in unison of *Walk on the Wild Side*. We discussed the gladiator-type horn sections and Smith's soul-fetching organ. Jesse would hoist a brown bag masking a liquor bottle, take a long swig, then sing a melody associated with one of those itinerant bluesmen he had come across during his travels. Yet not all was peaceful within Jesse. Jesse had this contemptible habit, practiced over the years, of what he called "ass swiping." A young woman would walk by, and he would reach out to give her a slap on the butt. It was like a grenade going off. Wham! He would jump to his feet, big mitts extended, slap, then scream drunken prose at a female backside. Then step back in place. Men rarely got involved, and few would ever confront him. Jesse understood, and taunted. I never asked why. For Jesse, I assumed it was summer sport.

As my day came to an end with still no place to sleep, I slipped backside of the Four Winds, and located a gardening shed complete with tools and workbench. To me, it seemed odd, since there was not much space out back for a patch of dirt, let alone a tomato vine or mischievous weeds. Stacked high on a side shelf was a pile of old newspapers that I could use to cover the surface of the bench. I then spread my long legs both sides, centred my back, and fell to sleep. Suddenly, the door popped open, and a menacing voice bellowed, "Hey, you fucking tramp, get the hell out of my shed. See this hammer; I'll bust your skull if you come back here?" I slithered past the guy and to safety.

The following evening, I ran into Denny, wandering the streets with no place to crash. I told him about this shed out back of the Four Winds, and how maybe we should give it another try. We squeezed between buildings to find a padlock on the door. Outside, a stack of cardboard was tied together, most likely refuse from kitchen supplies. I noticed a crawlspace beneath the building, and suggested we slide under it for the night. The two of us pulled reams of the cardboard beneath us and created a mattress separating dirt from the body. We then fell asleep. Well after midnight, an intense beam of light shattered my face. "Come out from under there, you fucking bums. I've got my hammer, and I'm busting your legs, in fact smashing every bone in your bodies." Holy shit, he's back. Denny and I slid out and faced the wrath of the building manager. "If I ever see your faces around here again, consider yourselves dead. Hear me?" Off we go!

Shaken and our morale reduced to nothingness, we separated, and I roamed in search of sanctuary, resting no more than minutes at a time. I tried sleeping in doorways, blocking people from coming and going. That did not sit well with tenants. Then I spotted a telephone booth on LaGuardia Place lit up as if the sun had pointed a magnifying glass directly at it. I placed my back to the door, and stretched my legs to the far side — able to wedge myself in such a way as to prevent unwanted intruders. Minutes passed, when a burly fellow frantically pounded. "Open up — I've got to make a call." I accommodated, and waited for a good 20 minutes as he argued and screamed obscenities at an ex-girlfriend. Once gone, I reclaimed my position. Cops arrived. "Come here, kid!" The interrogation began. "Why are you sleeping in this area? Are you homeless? We should run you in." They talked among themselves, then one responded, "Don't be around when we come back. Be gone, asshole!"

After a brisk walk around the block, I returned to the booth. It was now four in the morning, and just as I was about to doze — bam! "Hey, hippie boy. Let me in." I looked up to see a large black man clothed in a long overcoat carrying a knapsack. "I won't be long, and then you can do whatever you're doing again," he said. I noticed a hammer dangling from his right hand, and was reluctant to vacate. He banged again. "I ain't gonna fuck with you," he said. I insisted he step back a good 20 feet. "Kid, I'm not going to bust your face, I've got small business in there." I weighed my options and exited. He then rushed in, and in one vicious swing, slammed the hammer down on the telephone's shell and beat it until gobs of coins came pouring forth. He then withdrew a pair of wire cutters and snapped the umbilical cord of the phone, stuffing the prize receiver in a cloth bag. He looked back at me and said, "Sleep well, longhair."

The night ran longer than envisioned. Morning could not come soon enough, with two days out, one hour of sleep and far removed from friendly surroundings. I entertained numerous aches, plenty of stress and fatigue, and then met Wandering Bridget. By day, it seemed Bridget walked the side streets and, at times, in a rush, others, meanwhile conversing with the moon. Visually, she was lovely, with creamy white skin, thinning blond hair, blue eyes, and a slim frame. Bridget roamed about in a purple crushed velvet cape, much like an exemplary good witch. I had to get acquainted. With one remaining quarter, I talked my way into her presence and offered to buy a slice of early-morning pizza. No go! Bridget, I would learn, was on the 11th day of *acid-tripping*. The fairy princess had been dropping daily for nearly two weeks. Bridget noticed things crawl up trees, jump buildings and sprint down the back alleyways. She would "acid pause," as if slapped with unshakable fear, then laugh out loud. I played along, anticipating a moment of companionship but no such chemistry. Bridget was crazy. She was going for a world record: the most "acid-baked" brain on planet Earth, and was not stopping until authorities locked her safely away from herself. In the coming days, I'd see her flitter to and fro, up and down Bleecker Street as if adorned with wings poached from butterflies.

The following night came without much fanfare after a day of panhandling quarters, pizza slices, and colas. Sleep disagreed with my body, placing me on the losing end. Then I met young Laura, also quite beautiful. We chatted for an hour or so until she invited me back to her place, which happened to be only doors away from that demolished telephone booth on LaGuardia Place. Laura's flat was decorated in brocade fabric — deep reds, blacks, and tassel-covered lamps looked as if fashioned by a New Orleans madam. I noticed a queen-size bed and imagined what comfort lay ahead. Minutes passed when Laura said, "I've got to get my rest; I have a day job. You can sleep over there." "Over there" came as a surprise. It was a patch of barren floor near a choking radiator. I grabbed two chair cushions, and assembled a not-so-orthopaedic bed, curled up, and contemplated the lovely creature covered in all her brocade goodness, debating if I should make a play, or just be a gracious spectator. Moments passed when I heard, "You should leave now; I can't sleep with you here." The words pierced my brain as if knifed by an intruder. "Seriously, I don't want you here in case my boyfriend shows up. Bye!" A boyfriend? I hadn't thought such things existed in Greenwich Village, other than a roommate or love interest. Boyfriend sounded so much like a burger night outing in Indiana. The more Laura spoke, the greater the hostility in her voice, "I want you out of here now: I need to get some sleep. I work, you know?" She works; I lurk!

It was now late morning, and I dragged myself to Washington Square Park. I recalled the surrounding neighbourhood from the movie *Barefoot in the Park* from screening a year or so ago at one of those triple bill cinemas, when I developed a boy-crush on Jane Fonda. The adjacent buildings looked familiar, and I speculated Jane still lived in the apartment across the street and left a key under a doormat for me. To my left, a field of winos, vagabonds, bikers, conga hackers, and drug addicts, not quite as I had imagined. In the distance, a public fountain near where I claim a small patch of grass, and I would rest my long frame on neutral ground. Every moment or so, a stranger would drift by and advise me to tuck my possessions under my stomach. I had few. Most everything I owned was still in the backroom of that Horatio Street flat, the rest in my side pockets. Until I found permanent residence, I prayed the guy did not shove my possessions to the curb.

Under a brilliant night sky, I counted stars and observed distant constellations as I drifted in and out of sleep, eyes fixated on the neighbouring porch lights. I thought about home, the dark times and recalled my last conversation with Dad before leaving and saying to him, "nothing out there could be worse than living here," and how at this moment, no matter how difficult or how problematic, this was still paradise in comparison. Streaking comets rocketed across the horizon and then suddenly dimmed. I smiled and watched with a child's enthusiasm never fully understanding why I was gifted with a "faith gene" made of cast-iron optimism. As rough as the days were, I never felt as relieved, confident, and positive about the future, New York seemed all-embracing.

Early morning, I was back at my post observing tourists and watching dump-trucks parade a last haul of night-refuse out of view. I was sitting on the steps of Miteras, a diner at the corner of MacDougal and West 3rd street, when suddenly a convertible slowed to a complete stop, and a young woman yelled, "Bill, is that you? Is that you? It's me, Toni. Toni Ballard from church!" Christ's sake, it's my great friend Toni from Meigs Avenue Church of Christ, cruising the village with what looked to be a

'60s style urban cowboy behind the steering wheel. "What are you doing here and up so early?" she asked. I invented some story about loving early mornings and a peaceful start to the day. She then introduced her partner Bob Slawson from Vevay, Indiana, up in Switzerland County, the lead singer in the band The Chicago Loop. Slawson reached over, shook my hand and then looked away. Slawson looked much like a cross between Roger Daltrey of The Who and country singer Porter Waggoner, and would later patent the moniker Drugstore Cowboy. I sensed Toni was on the upswing, and far from kissing this pavement. The two of us exchanged good wishes and promised to meet again. Toni was the only female in the church who seemed destined to leave the community. We would roll our eyes back at each other during church services as the older women would drag the spirituals to a shrieking halt. There was no true rejoicing, even if the words were written that way. The voices were long on suffering and void of optimism. Toni lived freely, and in a few short years sadly died from cancer.

At 6 a.m., the rain ceased, the streets steaming up to near 90 degrees, a gift from the day before. I strolled down MacDougal and noticed the path leading to the nightspot, Café Wha? blocked; two cops with ill-fitting uniforms standing close-by, adjusting garments. A voice screamed from behind, "Move back; you're in the way." I retreated and took a position on the top step of a nearby head shop, and watched a surreal moment blanket the neighbourhood. A man came sprinting at top speed past me with a camera crew in hot pursuit, behind—two cops in the chase —one screaming, "Halt, halt, put your hands on your head." A second cop tackled and restrained. Then all hell broke loose. "We're shooting a goddamned movie, you fucking assholes. This shit is not real. That is fucking James Coburn," screamed the director. I watched in disbelief. A mistake had been made. The cops apologized, and reminded the director they oversaw the apprehension of crooks. Coburn deflected, and strolled back around the corner, repeating the action, and ran directly to the Café Wha? then disappeared downstairs. The director yelled "cut," and closed in. A Volkswagen bus coloured in decorative psychedelic symbols stood by as the crew huddled outside the club. I questioned one of the gaffers, "What's up?" He responded, "We're shooting *The President's Analyst* — it should be out by Christmas." I asked, "Was that James Coburn you were chasing?" All I could think of was the movie *Point Blank,* one of my favourites. I don't collect autographs, yet at that moment I would have entertained the thought.

An hour or so passed as the residents from the Village slowly rose. Long Island soul band the Vanilla Fudge, reportedly managed by a member of the Lucchese crime family, could be heard blasting *You Keep Me Hangin' On,* from a neighbourhood bodega. The Young Rascals' *Groovin',* and Lovin' Spoonful's *Summer in the City,* played endlessly from pizza parlours to headshops. The honking of taxis, big-throated laughter and duelling record shops blasted hippie anthems along with Latin rhythms, the soundtrack to my new day.

Just as I was starting to get comfortable with my surroundings, André returned, "Your band boys are gone, and the guy wants your gear and stuff out of his flat today, or he's tossing it to the curb." Catastrophic. "Don't worry, let's get dressed up," said André. Let's get dressed up? "Man, I've got no place to stay, and you want me to get dressed up?" André paused, then offered a simple truth. "You're from Indiana, right? I am from the Bronx. You are walking on my ground, and I'm trying to help you. I got some suits — Carnaby Street style. If we put these on, everyone will notice and pay us respect." Hesitantly, I buy in.

André walked me across Lower Manhattan, up the steps of a handsome brownstone, pressed the buzzer, and a voice yelled from above, "Where the hell have you been, you Puerto Rican fag? Come on up but leave your boy-toy behind." André invited me into the building, up two flights, and then knocked. "I told you to leave your boy-child outside. I don't need another thief coming around here," the muse said. "He's not my boy; he's my keyboard player, and where are the suits?" he asks. The woman brings out two attractively packaged boxes, opens and places them in front of André. "This one's mine, and you put that one on, Bill." This is crazy. The young woman says, "Don't put them on; deliver them to the person who bought them." Andre slips into the suit, preening like one of those young English rock moguls. Even at 165 pounds, I had difficulty getting into my assigned get-up. "Look in that mirror, Bill, look at the both of us, we look magnificent; we look like money." The young woman is not amused, "Take those suits off before you get them all filthy," she says. "Can't do, got to deliver to Linda." André pulled me out the door, and down the street we go. It is now hotter than purgatory.

A few blocks on, André says, "That's it. You wait right here, and I'll be back." André disappeared into a nearby building, leaving me seated in a parkette, dressed much like Michael Caine, or a reasonable facsimile, when the catcalls start. "Hey, pretty boy, why don't you come up here and suck my pussy?" I imagine I am hearing a recording of the Mothers of Invention, or maybe the Fugs. "I'm talking to you, white boy, don't you like pussy? There is a whole bunch of it up here. You are so skinny, when was your last meal? Pussy will fatten you up." Then a blast of laughter. I look up and recognize I am only yards from a women's prison. Damn funny. I absorb the weird humour and earn my quota of humiliation.

An hour wasted, I work my way up the stairs of the tenement building, pause in the stairwell, and ask if anyone had seen a strange looking guy in a funny suit, "You mean André? He's in there fucking." I pound the door, André answers, and invites me in. Before me, a naked woman. I mean, not any ordinary naked woman, but one extraordinarily stunning looking woman. "Take off the suit. We've got to leave it here; this is for her clients," André demands. "But I have no clothes," I say. "Here, wear this." This? An ill-fitting T-shirt and short pants.

We make our way back to Horatio Street, enter, and André rummages through a dresser drawer and hands me a pair of jeans and a T-shirt. "Put these on; they look like they fit." I do just that, thinking the two of us must have similar builds. "I've got shit to do, meet me back here in three hours. You can't be here now, we'll find a place for your stuff later," he says. Three hours pass when I arrive back as scheduled, knock, and await a response. The tenant opens the door, looks me over, and asks, "What do you want?" "Remember me, I'm Bill, we met a week ago, and I'm back to collect my belongings. André says he's found a place for me to stash my gear." The guy looks me over then says, "Where did you get the T-shirt and jeans?" I hesitate, then answer: "André. We came by here earlier, and André handed me these items and told me to wear them." The guy explodes, "You stole my clothes, didn't you?" I felt a sickness strike my limbs, and weakness in my joints and say, "Never! I have never stolen anything in my life." The guy pauses, "I don't believe you. Get your shit out of here now. I'm calling the cops, and you're fucked." I move my gear to the curb, change clothes and wait for André. André returns, sees me sitting outside on my keyboard and amp, lets himself in, and overwhelms the guy. I learned André was bi-sexual and screwed his way around the village, any and all comers. "Bring your shit back in here. It can stay here until you find a place, but you can't stay here," the man says.

Back on MacDougal, I encounter Carol, a sweet, heavyset woman who sold ice-cream bars, cigarettes, and trinkets, in a small cubicle. She confided in me of her long-running affair with Jimi Hendrix, then proceeded to open an envelope and carefully withdrew the many postcards Hendrix addressed to her from various locales around the world. There were others like Donna, who snuck up and grabbed me from behind in a neighbourhood newspaper/variety store, and then brought me to her apartment for a private dinner. Over a plate of half-cooked spaghetti, I notice hanging on the kitchen wall side by side, naked photos of Hendrix and ballet star Rudolph Nureyev. "Looks good, don't you think? You want to be up there?" she asked. I passed, and returned to the streets. Most days, I would catch her coming and going from one small Village business to another, one storefront bedroom to another. The women carried with them the roots stories, those first-hand encounters with the cultural icons of that generation.

Meet Louie Pigeon, leader of biker gang the Vagabonds on West 3rd. During my long hangs with Jesse from Louisville and near the Four Winds Café, I would observe Louie's bike club go

about business. There was a turf war taking place in the neighbourhood, and the Vagabonds were suspected of murder. Two
young teenage addicts had been burned to death inside their 11th
street apartment, the method of punishment rumoured to have
been borrowed from the Vagabonds' "get even" playbook. All
exit doors wired shut, the two rolled up in a rug, bound together
with wire and lit on fire. It was the same building folksingers and
Vanguard recording artists Roger and Wendy lived, who I would
meet a few weeks down the line.

Then there's streetwise Eddie. Eddie was a junkie hooked on
amphetamines and burdened by an uncontrollable twitch that
danced to a tortured rhythm. Eddie took a liking to me and soon
declared "us" a team, and set out to find a room for us at night.
An hour later, he returned, handed me a door key, and said, "You
take the room tonight and get a good sleep. I paid for it at the
Hotel Greenwich. I'm too fucked up — I'll sleep tomorrow." I
had no idea the room was in the Hotel Greenwich, a prison-like
flophouse on Bleecker Street.

I worked my way past a front-desk clerk who resembled an
outpatient from a 19th-century insane asylum. "Three flights
up, if you care to walk," he says. I took his advice. The third
floor reeked of urine, vomit and booze, the shower area a mix
of bathwater, piss, derelicts, and madmen, a few men shaving
— most in a toxic stupor. My assigned room — scary. In one
corner, a bunk protected by a mutilated sheet punctuated with
an assortment of cigarette burns, situated near a brick-lined window overlooking a back alley one could imagine sketched from
a horror flick. A single bulb lit the room, and when unscrewed,
trapped everything in darkness. Atop the doorway, wire fencing,
there to keep everyone segregated. Looking around the room, I
speculate about the person who slept on the sullied mattress the
night before — the night before that, and weeks past.

That night, it seemed every conceivable parasite feasted on
my skin until I fall unwillingly, into a deep sleep. After a brief
interlude, I'm awakened by a fist-pounding at my door, "Let me
in you fucker, let me in now," a voice insists. I ignore. "I know
you're in there, and I'm going to kill you if you don't unlock the

door," a determined predator demands. Beyond tired and fearful, I yell back, "Go fuck yourself." The voice continues, "Give me the light bulb, if you ain't using it." The episode lingers a good fifteen minutes until the prowler wears down, and I drift back to sleep, his last words, "I'll get your ass in the morning motherfucker. You can bet on that." I wondered about the interlude, and the possibility the man feared darkness and that light his only salvation.

As surreal as the night's sleep was, it was the first in four days since the band abandoned me. All I could think of was a warm shower, but the area in question was highly suspicious. Early morning the shower stalls stood empty. I quickly soap up: wash and dry. On return, I discover my belongings ransacked. Before sleep, I hid my wallet high above on a ledge and between the wire mesh and window sill. A voice again threatens, then a face appears, "I'll kill you, you prick. I'll kill you." It is the same scrawny-ass fucker with a big mouth and plenty bold. In passing, I look down at him, laugh and say, "Eat shit, asshole!" He quickly scatters like a wounded rat.

Eddie was able to score a week's stay eight flights up in the cockroach-infested Hotel Earle. The upside, he never slept. The downside, he rarely stopped mumbling crazy thoughts. Eddie offers me the bed, which for sleeping was much like lounging on patio stones. Eddie would look out the floor-length open window, smoke and converse with himself. Middle week, Eddie returns and offers me a hit of acid. I refuse, he pops. Somewhere between three and four in the morning, Eddie announces, "I can fly, I can spread my wings and fly." I awaken to see Eddie's backside, feet and legs dangling outside the window arms flapping as if readied to take flight. "Bill, Bill — I'm leaving — I'm going to fly away from this shithole," he yells in a celebratory voice. Tonight's the night." I freak out, rush forward and grab Eddie's upper body and pull him back safely inside. Eddie continues to hallucinate and talk nonsense. I then walk him over to the bed and lay him dead-centre and cover him. Moments later, he drifts off.

I was hanging on the streets talking with other vagrants when someone suggests I meet Georgy, a guitar player who had a nightly gig at The Underground, a local tourist trap. It seems Georgy had a falling out with his regular keyboard player and was auditioning for a replacement. We hook up, jam and I'm hired. The pay? $15 cash a night! Georgy also had a place for me to crash.

I revisit the flat on Horatio and gather my possessions, collect the Farfisa organ, bass amp and trunk of clothes. The proprietor demands I pay storage and for the laundering of a borrowed T-shirt and jeans. I remind him he refused to let me sleep a single night in his apartment, and that I'd endured a week on the streets holed up in the cockroach-infested Hotel Greenwich and Hotel Earle, and the fact that he made that all possible. I was in no mood for this idiocy.

Painted in dayglo and walls smothered in a surreal beam of fluorescent light, The Underground was similar to an outsized comic book, entirely appropriate for seducing tourists at hyper-inflated drink costs. On stage, Georgy and I were much like semi-caged zoo animals, there to give the visiting hoards something to remember. Rarely did we agree on songs, but mostly jammed for 30 minutes at a time, change keys, and occasionally alter the tempo. There was no doubt the two of us hit a few peaks, and had plenty of technique to delight onlookers.

Georgy hooks me with an ex-girlfriend on Jones Street who offers to let me spend the night. The apartment smelled of Tigress perfume and day-old sex. Even her clothing: the feather boas and frilly pinks looked as if they were stolen from an inattentive chorus girl at Paris's Moulin Rouge club a half-century before. One night of sleepless madness was more than I bargained for, much like serving nine months of hard labour on a work farm. Night two, I decide an additional stay at Hotel Greenwich preferable; the penthouse suite $5.00, with a proper bed, a floor or two above the derelicts. Next morning, I pass my favourite "kill-boy" still spitting profanities at some helpless rummy in the shower area and tell him to eat an extra bowl of shit on me.

Night three, Georgy and I fall into a groove. The music rolls as does the applause. After food and boarding, I have now saved $30, back on the streets and feeling good about myself until I encounter André on the hustle. "Man, where have you been? I've got so much action happening out here, and having a tough time getting the band back together." I ask myself, what band? André asks," Do you play drums?" I am thinking, what the hell is the guy up to? "I have a guitar player, there's me, and I'm the showman; and if you can play drums, we've got a gig at the Café Wha? It pays $15." I reluctantly agree. It's the early afternoon set just before N.D. Smart and Kangaroo. Two songs in and my ankle weakens. I continue to slap about the drums with little control over my right foot. "Let's pick up the tempo," André begs. I last eight bars, and return to the same tempo. $15, and we part ways.

A night or so later, I run into André, hustling a pair of teenage girls, the two wearing the look of absolute innocence. That rescue side of me kicks in as a drunken middle-aged man walks near. André sizes him up. "You're looking for pussy," he inquires? The guy wobbles about then responds, "With those pretty things? Hell, yes. How much?" André says, "These two, twenty each." The guy opens his wallet. "I only have forty dollars, and I've got to get back to my room. How about just one?" André reaches down and takes the man's wallet, empties, and returns, "You just bought both bitches, now fuck off." The guy grins, "Let's go, girls. Papa's waiting." The two scream "Go fuck yourself" and walk away laughing. The guy then goes after André, "Hey, you bastard, you fucking thief, I want my money back." André doesn't budge. "Who are you going to tell, that cop over there? You going to tell them you like them young?" The guy threatens, André pushes back, "I own these streets motherfucker; never fuck with me." The guy backs off. André was privy to everything going on up and down Bleecker and MacDougal. He knew the bands, shared the women, accompanied the hangers-on, and fleeced the willing. André continually led me down back allies into the strangest circumstances.

Early morning, as the two of us meet on Bleecker Street, André suddenly pauses, catches a glimpse of this shadowy figure moving slowly up the street, attached to two women. "Do you who know who that is?" he asks. I watch in silence. "That's Jimi James — I mean Jimi Hendrix. Bill, he's the next big thing in rock 'n' roll. He's just finished his first album in London, and it's going to be a monster." I knew nothing of the man other than that he sported an elegant looking woman on each arm. Hendrix arrives dressed in what appeared to be a stylish crushed-velvet military jacket, a knotted scarf loosely tied around the neck, and sporting a wind-blown Afro. The girls looked as if they had survived a vigorous shopping spree; every item seemingly purchased at some upscale Manhattan boutique. André glances back, and signals me to hang close while he approaches Hendrix. A few words pass, then he summons me. "Bill, this is the man, the next great rock superstar, Jimi Hendrix." I shake "the man's" hand and quickly direct my eyes towards the two attractive vixens, and slow march up Bleecker. André asks Hendrix where he is headed, and he invites the both of us along. Moments later, we are situated behind a large round oak table in an upstairs café called the Tin Angel next door and above the Bitter End nightclub. André banters on about the recording and release date, his aspirations to perform and record, all the while sweet-talking one of Hendrix's entourage, until a waitress arrives with a scratch pad to book orders. My cue to exit. Let's face it, I could not even afford a cube of butter, let alone a cut of bread, so I politely excuse myself.

The Village introduced me to folksingers Roger and Wendy Penney and their friend George, who worked as a barker outside a Bleecker Street night club by nights, and by day, took acting classes at The Actor's Studio. Roger and Wendy were gigging at the Four Winds Café and invite me in. I had seen the place from around back, below and now indoors, where I should have been from the start. I caught a clear view of the owner—my prospective executioner — and steered clear. As the folk duo made their way through a set of charming songs, I noticed a lovely young woman staring out a front window, inhaling a cigarette. Close by, a cast of folk believers. The woman with the short-cropped blond hair, smooth, flawless skin, and classic Mediterranean features intrigued me, not at all like the white-bread, middle-American faces camped along the village streets and parks. Greek by origin. As the disciples of the new folk wave swayed to the counter-rhythms and political implications of the moment, I focused on her.

"You're a fan of folk music," I ask? She ignores me, and continues to blow a steady stream of smoke out on to the street. I wait. "Not really, it's the view." I counter: "It's my first time seeing the room in daylight; I didn't even know they had an upright piano in here." "I guess so," she says. "You're a musician, I assume?" she asked with the coolness of a '40s dramatic actress. "I think so. But you wouldn't know it from the past week or so; it hasn't been going exactly as planned." I ask if she lives close by. "No. Queens!" "Queens!—how far is that?" "A subway ride — I come in every weekend and hang with some of the guys in the Mothers of Invention." "Frank Zappa?" I ask. "No, Jim Black." I pause, then say, "I saw Zappa biking around the village the other day with his baby girl." She responds, "I don't know him that well—I like the band, though. I'm Patti, and you are?" The conversation rolls on a good two or three hours. "So, where do you live?" she asks. "Nowhere—I'm alone and looking for a place." "I stay with a friend on 8th Avenue. I'm sure she wouldn't mind if you spent the night." Roger and Wendy smile back at me as I depart for worlds unknown.

Patti was white heat and smouldering hot. That is how fantasy played in my imagination. I stood a foot taller, but certainly appreciated her compact physique, reserved disposition, strange haircut, which at times irritated her eyes, and B-movie grip on that ever-present cigarette. I scribble the girlfriend's address on a napkin, and arrive just past 6 p.m. Everything was grand. Patti leads me into an adjacent room, insists I rest, and orders sleep. Somewhere past midnight, I am awakened by what sounds like a choir of mischievous "jazz bikers." Patti pops the door and says, "Bill, I want you to meet my friend, Jim Black. There are others in the living room from the Mothers of Invention." I unwillingly dress and enter the action. It is party time, and this does not work for me. I am far too tired and optimistic in thinking Patti was in play. I didn't give a thought to the fact she had many connected friends and a club traveller's music history.

The following afternoon I catch up with a motoring Patti. We talk and make plans to meet later. Patti invites me to accompany her to a new celebrity haunt, Salvation, at 1 Sheridan Square, where Jimi Hendrix is said to be opening the club with his band the Experience. That night, we hook up and cut past a thick forest of disco timber; mostly gay teens, well outside anything this Indiana-bred boy has ever encountered and nose to eyebrow snobbery. I distance myself in the upper gallery, far away from the fashionable "Flushing Express" wolverines. Inside the chrome disco arena and as promised, Hendrix takes centre stage. The trio, bathed in soft blue lighting, runs through what would soon become a stellar catalogue of hits, which this crowd found an annoyance. The dance zombies whined about the lack of a beat. Me? I considered walking below and informing the trio that they had at least one friend in the house. Maybe possibly request *Hey Joe*. I then notify Patti that I had to meet someone. For Patti, there was a sprawling night ahead, and more shallow dipshits to entertain; for me, the streets. Years later, I would learn that the brash club manager who scowled at me like I was a homeless panhandler was none other than Tony Sirico, "Paulie Walnuts" Gualteri of *Sopranos* fame. In those days he was known as Gennaro Sirrico. Salvation survived for less than six months after my visit, long enough for the Mafia to suck the rich kids dry.

In the weeks that followed, I would occasionally cross paths with Patti and try to resume our conversation, but Patti was always on the move. I certainly didn't share her clubbing spirit or keys to her revolving disco planet. It wasn't as if she had suddenly dropped me. We were not together long enough to develop a relationship other than being good travel companions. I soon learned she was 17, and a perfect fit for the neighbourhood. Young girls abandoned the suburbs on weekends and concealed their ages; boys, much the same. At 15, Barbra Streisand would catch a train in from Queens and sing her way through the Village. It seemed every weekend the streets would fill up with teenagers—a good many from Queens, Brooklyn, or New Jersey, mostly Jewish. I soon learned a flat was more than a personal sanctuary; it was a desirable crib.

I had earned enough coin to book a second week at the Hotel Earle at Washington Square; $40 did the job. I secured a bed, a battalion of loyal cockroaches, an unobstructed view of most things outdoor green, and, most of all, shelter. Georgy and I were holding our own at The Underground when I start picking up work here and there, and landed a gig at Louis Jordan's piano bar, a block away, and just below street-level next door to the Bitter End. Situated in the front window and facing the street, a small baby-grand piano stood atop a sawdust-coated floor. Big Russian "Maxie" greeted everyone upon entry, with hands thicker than bear paws, and bald head the width of an oversized bowling ball. It was a jazz gig, my first in the big city, and it came through pianist Jeff Labes of Van Morrison's iconic recording *Moondance*. Jeff would hire me as the occasional Thursday replacement, sometimes on weekends, subbing for jazz pianists Jane Getz or Burton Greene, who would duo along with bassist Abdul Malik.

My final days at The Underground represented high drama. A young woman named Chrissie approaches the bandstand, and asks me to go for a walk, me a bit reticent but willing. I had recently concluded only Natalie Wood could rightfully seduce me. Wood had toyed with me with such vigour on the big screen; I pleaded to her to drop those pretty Hollywood boys and pay close attention to this street jester. Chrissie would morph into Natalie Wood — same height. popping brown eyes, hair parted much like my dream girl; sly and blessed with a convincing smile. While on a break, we slide down a side hallway of The Underground when suddenly Chrissie shoves me against a wall and starts massaging me, leaving me at a loss for words. She then insists we go somewhere. I sarcastically say, "I'm guessing you like sex?" She looks up at me as if she had just landed Barney Fife of Mayberry, USA. On to the Hotel Earle.

The next five days were bedroom warfare — a real game of endurance, with me on the losing end. Every few hours or so, I would excuse myself, run downstairs, and inhale a chocolate Yoo-hoo drink and down a Ring Ding cupcake: high nutrition, then back to action. Day four, I begged off and hit the streets, and my favourite record store on 8th Avenue. It was my first hearing of the Fania All-Stars. Rotating on the turntable, I asked to buy it, but told it had been sold, so I settled on the latest Willie Colón.

It was then I observe a telephone number on the side of the cash register that would soon disrupt my dependable gigging in the West Village. "Band in need of Hammond B-3 organist. Organ supplied. Plenty of work." I make the call, and hook up with a group from Brooklyn with engagements galore. We meet, and jam and I take the gig. I returned to tell Chrissie of my good fortune, but found her nowhere in sight. I search the hotel, the hallways then back to the streets. No Chrissie. I return and am packing things when a knock comes at my door, "Where's my sister?" a voice demands? I answer and Christ's sake, it`s an ordained nun, beads, headdress, and all. "What have you done with my sister?" she inquires. As I attempt to explain my absence and upcoming gig out of town with a band, Chrissie coolly slips into the room, stuffs her clothes in a small make-up suitcase and says nothing. The nun-sister goes off on me about living in sin, and taking advantage of a young woman with a compulsive sex addiction. I was not about to take the hit, and fired back, grabbed my belongings and then instructed the two to close the door behind them. Goodbye Hotel Earle and cockroach posse!

While waiting for an elevator, a weird guy approaches. "Hey, are you the boy Chrissie is living with?" he asks. "No, she was staying with me," I say. Really? "She spent the weekend with me. Damn, she wore me out. Oh man, that tie!" Fuck off!

A couple of weeks pass, and I'm hanging on MacDougal, when I meet two of my street pals, and we talk. "Bill, that girl Chrissie was way more than I could handle. Then pal #2 interjects—me too. Did she pull that Colonel Sanders string-tie routine and beg for a whipping?" Holy shit!

The streets of the Village came with the unexpected. It was mid-September 1968, and I am hanging with my usual contingent of street people, musicians, and hangers-on when I hear this choir of men half-cheering and half-hollering. As I turn, I come face to face with this diminutive big-busted brunette wearing a tight yellow sweater and miniskirt out for a stroll, so it seemed. I watch as the crowd behind her multiplies, and marches in step with her through the streets of the Village. I walked to the edge of the neighbourhood, and watched as she disappeared with a marauding band of spineless men. Five-thousand men tagged behind as Francine Gottfried worked her way up and through to Wall Street. Gottfried was an employee of the Chemical Bank New York Trust, and the escapade was a stunt. This is why hanging out had its moments.

I am out front of the Bitter End on a set break from Louis Jordan's, where there's always someone of note on stage, run into club owner Paul Colby, and chat him up. Those short talks paid dividends. Colby would occasionally pop out and take a break from the club pressures. That night I heard a voice so angelic one would have assumed from heaven. The sound drifted from the smoky interior out onto the streets. I stood there, soaking up every phrase, even the lovely down-home patter between songs then noticed the room overflowing. Colby slides out and offers me a seat back of the room with a warning: if a tourist asks for a stool, you will have to leave. I lasted three songs. But those songs cut deep into my soul. I watched newcomer Joni Mitchell's every gesture; from the tuning of the guitar to the drama in every scripted verse and marvelled at her features, so delicate and not of this planet. Then I'm told she is from Canada. The following week I catch a full night of her at the Anderson Theatre.

On another occasion, I'd hear wild applause and was denied entry. Colby asked me to be patient. I listened, listened, and listened but did not buy in. Colby says to me, "This guy is going to be huge; you wait and see." Neil Diamond owned The Bitter End that night. I did not get it!

Hanging around the Bitter End, I would soon meet keyboardist Moogy Klingman. Klingman was tight with guitarist/producer Todd Rundgren, and always on the move. We shared keyboard stress, talked amplifiers and gigs, then one afternoon he invites me in for a hang inside the Bitter End. On the left side of the stage, a Hammond B-3 organ, right side, an acoustic spinet piano. "Why don't we jam?" Moogy suggests. Moments in, I look up to see this big Afro move towards the organ. Moogy relents. The jam rolls on. Then I notice it is Sylvester Stone. Not far behind, David Clayton-Thomas. Clayton-Thomas was living in the Village and playing with The Shays.

The act that most excited me was The Electric Flag with Mike Bloomfield and Buddy Miles, and one of the rare shows for which I laid down money and paid a cover charge at The Bitter End on November 24, 1967. The band was on fire, and played everything I longed to hear in a crossover blues/soul unit. I sat directly in front of drummer Buddy Miles, and absorbed the brute strength and muscle behind the kit. The band, from my vantage point, was America's greatest.

30

533 E. 6th Street

The real game-changer for me came when I met Hunter College student Richard Quattrocchi. Richard was hanging in front of the Fillmore East, and I just happened by and was introduced. Someone mentioned Richard was searching for a roommate. Rich had secured a flat at 533 E.6th Street, just around the corner from Tompkins Square Park. The rent, $52 a month. Split both ways, $26 each; in today's terms, $3,000. All I had to do was wrap up a few loose ends at the Hotel Earle and move in. The two-room flat was perfectly located, newly renovated with a fresh coat of blue paint and a tub in the kitchen area which doubled as my bedroom. This was to be my first sense of well-being.

Richard was handsome, serious, and fully dedicated to his studies at Hunter College. He would commute mornings, study at night as I slept by day, and prowled the city's hot spots. We'd share a few laughs and small talk in passing, but mostly "strangers by day and night."

Ground floor housed a budding actor and student in theatre at New York University: Vincent Schiavelli. Schiavelli was the oddest-looking man I had ever come upon. Double-jointed in every limb, seriously funny, and a big fan of jazz and life in general. Each time we crossed paths, Vincent would offer me a carafe of fine wine, a few good theatre stories, and a joint of marijuana. Victor would one day catch the attention of Czech director Milos Forman, and carve a modest yet memorable acting career in movies like *Taking Off*, *One Flew Over the Cuckoo's Nest*, and *Amadeus*. A floor above, cartoonists Roger and Michele (Wrightson) Brand of *Underground Comics*. I would pass the two going and coming.

Most days, the door to their flat wide open. Both were incredibly friendly and up on music and always curious about my next gig. I was just as curious of the images drying in ink, so would interrogate both. Roger was known for the horror and eroticism in his work, especially *Tales of Sex and Death.*

Richard and I lived on the third-floor landing, wedged between the most eclectic gathering of young talent. Just above, Canadian Susan Oppenheim. Susan was close to folk singer Richie Havens and his family. We would cross paths when I was leaving for a gig or checking in late at night. She also gave refuge to a somewhat troubled Kenny Rankin. To this day, Susan and I are neighbours and remain friends.

I only visited the top floor once, the invitation courtesy of the building's hostess vixen. One evening, the young woman knocked on my door and invited me up for a chat, then confessed she was short on a rent payment and about to make a deal. "I don't know you that well, but you look clean. How about I fuck you for $40? Any diseases?" Gone boy, gone!

Having a drink and hanging around Louis Jordan's, was a band called The Third Eye, working on music for an off-Broadway production called *Conquest of the Universe.* They asked if I would like to contribute to the music score. I was curious, but unsure where this would lead. With little warning, I enter a world far beyond the unique island I'd been circling: that of director John Vaccaro's *Play-House of the Ridiculous.* When introduced, Vaccaro quizzes me about my music past and passion for jazz. He was a big fan of Herbie Hancock's Blue Note sides and avant-garde jazz. I had one foot in the free-thing, two in psychedelic rock, and rock and soul, yet willing to stretch.

During the interview, a naked man parades past Vaccaro. Vaccaro slaps his backside, and unleashes a few sarcastic comments. I take it all in stride, and stay focused. Vaccaro asks, "What do you think?" I had not a clue how to respond. "Think about what?" I reply. "Not bad, huh?" I quickly usher the conversation back to music. Vaccaro continues with the insults as the muscular man walks about towelling off, oblivious to the remarks. I pause and wait out the debasing banter. Vaccaro, slumped in a white wicker chair, draped in a white robe, hair sprinkled in glitter, looked secure in his spacious and artfully provided loft. He then looked up at me. "Let's make a date, young man. I think we can do something together. Here's the address; think about what you can compose."

I follow his advice, and show up at the given address. The room came supplied with a small stage and workplace, with a giant fake log positioned down the middle. All around, men flittered about in semi-drag accompanied by a few hardcore-looking women. Talk about being out of my element; I thought I'd just entered a galaxy even NASA telescopes had failed to report. I look around for the band, and am told they would arrive a night or so after a cast and director run-through.

The acting troupe mingled, smoked, and chirped when suddenly the writer shows: Charles Ludlam. I had not a clue who this antsy guy was. Everything quickly turned high drama! Ludlam did not like this actor or that, did not like the amateur cast, and did not approve of where Vaccaro was taking his coveted play. I had never heard grown men shriek at each other, then be reduced to tears over a few clumsy paragraphs. Vaccaro walked about, waving his hands. "Charles, Charles, you are brilliant, brilliant, but I'm in charge." Ludlam: "If that's the case, then why do you show me so little respect, John? I'm leaving." "But Charles, it's pouring rain out there. Please stay, you haven't seen my staging yet; just see it through," Vaccaro insists in a comforting tone. Ludlam pops an umbrella, and starts for the exit with a handful of dedicated supporters not far behind. Vaccaro chases, then embraces; both disappear in an adjacent room.

Then a voice from the wilderness commands, "All right, back at it, we need six fire boys on the log. Hey, you with the long hair, take the back seat." I find myself trapped and strapped to a fake theatrical log. "Wait! I want boy, girl, boy, girl, boy, girl." Now I'm buzzing, the last link on this log and a female ahead. "Start the music." The music begins, and Vacarro yells, "Start humping — heavy humping." The log wobbles as bodies writhe in ecstasy. "Moan!" Moaning begins. "All right, switch! I want men on men, women on women." The switch happens, the motion starts in earnest. "You in the back. Throw your body into this, you're not emotionally involved. I can't hear you moan. Much closer, please." I felt this guy from behind apply maximum thrust. That was the moment I determined acting was not for me, and excused myself.

It would be years later when retelling this moment; a friend would inform me the play was a ground-breaking production called *When Queens Collide* and a first for the queer avant-garde theatre, and still popular today. Ludlam would become a prime figure in the movement until his death from AIDS in 1987. Vacarro died at 86 in 2016.

It is a cool March day when I get wind the Jefferson Airplane is in for a week's stay at the Café au Go-Go, and work my way past security. It just so happens the room is packed with music industry scouts and bigwigs, and opening for the Airplane, Canadian unknowns The Paupers. Verve Records' Rick Shorter walks by and introduces himself. I had no prior knowledge or association with the label or Shorter, just a friendly hello. The band takes the stage, lead singer Adam Mitchell decked out in the shortest Nehru shirt imaginable. I'm by then no way a style merchant, but the unusual dress caught my attention. The band kicks off with *Think I Care*, and it was if the floor of the building lifts and relocates two blocks away. Drummer Skip Prokop reached the same level of rhythmic intensity and skill of my hero, drummer Buddy Miles, even throwing in a lesson in classic military-snare drumming. Bassist Denny Gerrard was all over the fretboard, slinging fistfuls of nearly unplayable patterns around the beat. It was a set of sure-fire magnificence, one I believed would catapult the band to national prominence. Not long after, I catch the group for a second look, which proved disastrous. The chemistry and goodwill of showcase night was derailed by what I saw: Gerrard was going off the rails. Lead singer Adam Mitchell inhabited the good ground, but something raging underneath was about to undo this promising band.

Richard and I got on big-time. Two strait-laced guys, one a student, the other a musician. I'm now rolling in pocket change; coin earned on weekends and enough to buy a black and white television and fold-out portable stereo. Richard had seized the back bedroom and converted to a study/sleeping quarters; I bunked near a small dining table. A tight bathroom, much like a telephone booth, faced on to the back fire escape. It was our *West Side Story* even though we lived on the east side, absent Jets and Sharks, yet in a neighbourhood of Marias and jealous lovers. Down below, there were fights, agonizing screams, and arguments that harmonized seamlessly with the cacophonous roar of the street. The buildings would act as sound reflectors, each channelling the braking of cars and honking of taxis, much like a classic "tone row" written for symphony. The rumble below rocketed upward in a reverse avalanche of jangle sifting through the gated windows. Most nights, I would hunch on the iron-cut fire escape and let imagination ride. Evenings inside were often lengthy and steamy with little ventilation. Outside, the occasional tenor saxophonist would rummage through a batch of jazzy pentatonic scales. After midnight, and while Richard slept, I would tune in a classic black-and-white movie and entertain myself until dawn.

One late Saturday afternoon, just as I'm waking up, I hear the screams of a woman under duress. I scramble three flights below to the street and view a man, much like Stanley Kowalski in *Streetcar Named Desire*, slap and punch. During the ruckus, I watch her grab the windowsill, pull herself half-way out and cry for help while both swear and strike each other in front of a growing audience. The plea for help rocked me to the bottom of my stomach. I yell upward, "I'm calling the police; let her go." It was her response and the looks on the faces of the passers-by that pretty much summed up how my intervention was about to play out. "Mind your own business and go fuck yourself, asshole." Not spoken by the attacker, but by the woman bruised and battered and on the losing end of a lengthy fight.

Every neighbourhood came with a level of violence and a malevolent guy hanging in front of a tenement building. I had my personal heckler. Whether walking for a cola or coming home from a gig, the same guy sat on top of the same garbage can and yelled at me: "Eat shit." Early on, I was terrified. Not so much from his physical presence, but from the tone of his rants. "I'm going to kill you tonight, you wait and see. Die, die, die. Never turn your back; eat shit." I tolerated the nonsense for weeks. I'd spot him a block or so away, cross to the far side of the street, dodge, then turn a corner onto what I perceived to be safer lanes. One day I cross the street and enter a local tavern just doors away to make a phone call. As I'm talking, I see all eyes focused on me and chuckling. After hanging up I take a closer look at the room; the shoddily dressed me in the middle of flat greys, soot-covered walls, and half-empty beers. "You're that hippie across the street, aren't you? I see you're scared of the idiot." I listen. "You know he doesn't have a proper mind," says another barman. "What do you mean?" I ask. In a serious tone, one responds. "He won't hurt you. He's been sitting on that garbage can since he was a little boy. He's like a fat parrot, just mouths what he hears others say." I thanked the men, had a good laugh, and was much relieved.

There were nights after returning from a gig when I would stroll into a crime scene. The whole street tied up in one giant police ribbon — the chase, rooftop to rooftop. I asked one officer, "What's the deal?" He turned to me. "The Puerto Rican Olympics. Robbery and foot chase. Roof to roof. No one crosses the finish line."

31

Movieola

The Indiana Kings mostly caught movies at a nearby drive-in theatre. Films like *The Robe* with Charlton Heston, or Disney's *Lady and the Tramp*. If Jesus had a part, we were parked and loaded. It was during the Beatles' film era I began crossing the bridge connecting Indiana and Kentucky. Eventually, Wayne and I take in a Doris Day/Rock Hudson flick. I can't say we were privy to thrillers and dramas with a small, small viewing world. Back home it was either war stories or westerns: Bette Davis or Humphrey Bogart nowhere to be seen. New York City was a far different scene for this culturally deficient Hoosier boy.

Early afternoons, I began catching movies, something I did mostly late nights on TV in the flat; something that felt alien, almost unnatural. I still had this obligation gene — like I'd be pre-empting the classroom for pleasure. I wandered innocently into St. Mark's Theater at St. Mark's Place, originally named the Astor, St. Marks — undergoing a name change in 1926. Through the '60s, St. Marks became known as The Itch, much to do with a local chapter of the Hell's Angels living in a tenement building at 5th Street and 1st Avenue who retained the front row of seats. By day, a triple bill of world-class movies played; most I had never been privy too. There were stars from the far side of the world, mostly subtitled films in rotation: French director Jean-Luc Godard, Jane Fonda, Deneuve, Belmondo, and Simone Simon. *Ship of Fools, Alphaville, Belle de Jour, Repulsion, Days of Wine and Roses*. Lee Remick, *The Odd Couple, The Fortune Cookie*, Walter Matthau, Jack Lemon, *The Apartment*, Shirley MacLaine, *8 ½, La Dolce Vita*, Fellini, Warren Beatty, Natalie Wood, Michael Caine,

The Balcony. A brave new world. A world so foreign it was as if I had discovered an alternate universe never to be abandoned. Five afternoons a week I would absorb a triple bill, gig at night, rise at noon, then off to another movie venue. Gig at 10 p.m., and over by 2:00 a.m., then on to a café and light hang with the street people. Then back to the flat and watch another movie until dawn — all I needed in life. Complete European indulgence. Big-screen salvation!

Two films spoke to me. *Splendor in the Grass* and *Days of Wine and Roses*. Up until then, I'd never endured such big-screen heartache and feelings of loss and sadness. Two women, Natalie Wood and Lee Remick, brought the pain. I so wanted to intervene in the Woods psychodrama, and save her for Beatty in *Splendor*, or hide those unopened liquor bottles that stole the heart and soul of Remick in *Days*. I cried those nights.

Catching movies along 42nd street was another story that could cripple the mind. The big hassle? Pimps, 3-card monte card hustlers, hookers, and pickpockets. What coin I had I buried deep in my pants, along with my selective service card and expired Indiana driver's licence. One afternoon, I catch sight of a marquee featuring the image of a squinting cowboy draped in a poncho, puffing the remains of a stogey, all too intriguing and genuinely worth a one-dollar buy-in. It's a double-bill afternoon and playing is *A Fistful of Dollars* with Clint Eastwood, alongside another film of no merit. I recognized Eastwood as sidekick Rowdy Yates from the TV series *Rawhide*. It was the vibe of the film that worked me over. Slow-moving, brutal killings, and one man's command of the big screen. From start to finish, I couldn't wait to get out and spread the word. The badass western was back. Not long after, *For a Few Dollars More* arrives, a second big thrill! Same reaction, and then *The Good, The Bad and The Ugly*. Most movies on my watch list came packaged as films you should never miss, but probably had. This one was a premiere.

I had this thing about sitting dead centre in all of the cinemas: middle seat, middle row. On this occasion, I find the perfect seat, and drop my jacket across my lap, look around, and see that the venue is mostly empty. Then the crowds arrive. From both sides of the aisle, I watch as they close in on me; not two seats away, but situated right and left of me. I then asked one guy to move down a seat — no reason to cramp me. He smiles, but stays put. The movie rolls with opening credits, and I'm now engaged. Thirty minutes pass, and I am following Clint Eastwood through the desert, in cinema heaven and time travelling, when I feel pressure on my right leg. I look down to see this hand snaking about, and so I whack the guy. I then turn and put a hard stare on the guy to the left of me. Both take off running down the aisle. A voice from behind creeps over my seat. "Shut the hell up, hippie, we're trying to watch a movie. Wear your coat next time."

32

Jack Dina and
The Boys From Brooklyn

I began to gig with The Boys From Brooklyn, and took a week's work in upstate New York. While steering bumper to bumper on Manhattan's East River Drive in the late summer of 1968, a slight chill in the air, one could hear the urban rant of horns, and taxi drivers screaming obscenities. Bassist Stu Wasserman and I return from one of those week-long gigs playing mostly Sam & Dave, Wilson Pickett, and Eddie Palmieri in upstate New York, and socializing. One twist of the radio dial, the sound of tribal tom-toms beating a warlike pattern, then singer Marvin Gaye cuts in: "*Ooh, I bet you're wondering how I knew, 'bout your plans to make me blue. With some other guy that you knew before. Between the two of us guys you know I love you more. It took me by surprise — I must say when I found out yesterday. Don't you know that I heard it through the grapevine ...*" That was it! We nearly lose it. Stu slaps the steering wheel as if mistaking it for a snare drum. I thump the dashboard and stamp my right foot as if pounding a bass drum. It was one of the most blissful drives of my life, and at song's end, we had found common ground and kinship. Stu and I were not satisfied with the one-play option, and did a cross-dial search for a second miracle play. Moments pass, and there it is again, but this time it is a different cast with a female voice: Gladys Knight, killing it good!

Greenwich Village was all about the moment, the time of day, no radio, unless I ran down 10 flights of stairs for provisions at a local bodega. The music was Latin-based: Willie Colón, Fania

All-Stars, Eddie Palmieri, and sometimes the rhythm and soul of the Vanilla Fudge. It was all about sound systems and LPs. The road gigs were about catching up. Who did *not* love Marvin Gaye? Women especially did! Marvin was a second husband to many a housewife. While your man was at work, Marvin was in your bedroom; having a shower, a meal, hanging in your front yard, depending on the capabilities of that transistor radio. Women would say, "I like the Beatles; that's okay if you like boys. Sammy Davis? Too old! Sinatra is like being around a bossy father." Marvin had an open invite into most any female's bedroom. In my world, the greatest voice of all.

The Boys From Brooklyn — Vic Bonadonna, Stu Wasserman, Jack Dina, Jon Prano and, on occasion, Joey Ardigo — would soon become my East Coast family; that big Italian connection, and the craziest fucker in the bunch was guitarist Jack Dina. How could one ever forget that protruding chin, the bluntness, that loudmouthed mob-driving ginger? A *Mustang Sally*-Steve Cropper kind of guitar player with more soul than all those bogus, blue-eyed imitators playing the downtown Manhattan clubs who rarely connected. Dina earned his soul stripes hanging near the street corners of doo-wop Brooklyn. He smoked heaps of weed and needled heroin into his muscle-light forearms. Enough to redefine the words "express junkie," and a hapless free-floating thug with no principles. A guy who'd steal from his bandmates and pawn his ancestors for the next fix. He was also terribly funny, and spoke out of the roof of his head. It was if all those devious thoughts camped under those flaming red curls were comedic props. You needed a hallucinogen to decipher the insane rants and provocative outbursts, and a sturdy laugh rib. "Hey, Billy, you fuck!" That was the tender side of Jackie.

Dina would cruise through the old neighbourhood for hours in his dark-green Lincoln Imperial rental, gossip and retell mob-related fables from late afternoon until gig time. I would be waiting two to three hours on a Greenwich Village street corner before Jackie would show with Victor and John. There was always an emergency stop, a connection for "the boo": hashish, heroin, or pot. Fridays were bag day. Mob work. Numbers collection. Jackie would pocket $200 harvesting paper bags of "loss" money. Then it was off to Columbia Street to cop some "get-high" before the gig, the connection often iffy.

"Hey, Billy, you fuck!" Honestly, I was born laughing. God whispered a joke in my ear. Something about, "In the not-so-distant future, every gig you take will pay less than the guy who sticks his hand down a toilet bowl to remove a flushed clown wig, but you'll laugh your ass off."

The Boys From Brooklyn caught a 9-week posting at the Pines Hotel and Resort in the Catskills, a no-frills Jewish entertainment centre in South Fallsburg, New York, in the Borscht Belt. Down the road, the more exclusive Grossinger's and Concord Resort with marquee stars Buddy Hackett, Tony Bennett, Milton Berle, Judy Garland, Barbra Streisand, and, during my stay, Jerry Lewis. "When I was a kid, I was breastfed by my father," Rodney Dangerfield. That pretty much summed up the shows in the main ballroom; the region was a comic's paradise.

The Pines featured guys with names like Shecky Greene, Myron Stanley Handelman, Charlie Callas doing his best imitation of a flapping seagull, Buddy Hackett, and Marty Brill. The Pines, built in 1933 as a ski resort, in what was called the Jewish Alps in Lake Placid, New York, closed in 1998, as the large casinos of New Jersey and elsewhere altered the entertainment landscape. A mad Austrian ski instructor ruled the premises by reputation. I might be playing a game of 9-ball, and he would walk over to the table, grab the cue ball, and insist I step away. The only TV was a black-and-white floor model in the hotel lobby. The band might be watching an old Jimmy Stewart classic like *Destry Rides Again*, and the big snot would cruise by, change the channel, demand it stay where he set it, then step away. I remember saying to him one day, "I'm seriously thinking of crushing your skull." He quickly put me on *Hans the Austrian* notice. "I am friends with the owners, and here forever. You fuck with me, and you will be hauled away in a vegetable cart." I got the message.

Maestro Sid Wayne led the house orchestra, and had a hit recording in 1959, a song he scripted with staying power: *See You in September*. Sid hated me. "You look like a dog, a hideous dog, a very tall ugly dog — why don't you get a haircut?" he would say. I cut Sid some slack until he developed Pines dementia, and repeated the same tired lines. One day Sid heard me play and said, "You are excellent, and can have the piano gig in my orchestra if you get a haircut, and show me your draft card." That's when I looked Sid in the eye and said, "Sid, you only hire the dead, and they don't even like you." We rarely conversed yet the goofy draft card rant played on: "That hippie dog burned his draft card — I should call Mr. Hoover," he'd repeat within earshot of anyone who would laugh.

The Boys From Brooklyn changed names. Formerly The Compliments, now The New Image. We played poolside, the lobby, on the patio — wherever we were commanded. Nobody cared or paid much attention. We considered "turn the volume down" a compliment.

Bassist Stu "Woods" Wasserman and I roomed in a small servant's cubicle, and slept on cots near a pissing radiator. Each time I would walk down the hallway to the bathroom, this 3-foot-tall Puerto Rican busboy would spring from "busboy hell" and whip out his flopping foot-long ventriloquist dick and insist it talk to me, "Hey, look at this dick, sucker!" Most nights he would roam the hallways in his underwear, juggle his balls, and swat flies with his member. He remained a mystery.

Attaining a good meal took an outside act of God. Runny eggs for breakfast, no bacon, and late evening the big meal, possibly steak with veggies, or the ground bones of gefilte fish washed down with a glass of scrumptious Manischewitz wine. The menu never varied, with that steak rarely in play. The only route to getting a platter of meat I was told was tipping the head waiter $5 a week in advance, which most side musicians did not have. One of Sid Wayne's sidemen hipped me to the routine. "Make nice and tip twice." I once followed his advice, and a steak arrived early week. Day two, the head waiter ignores me and places a rancid fish on my plate. A few passes later I ask him why. "Sid insists you're a draft-dodging dog!" I stopped tipping the fuck.

By day, drummer Jon Prano played knock rummy with the resident comics, and once remarked, "These are some of the

most depressed and unfunny men I've ever met. No one laughs."
Then Jackie brings a date. First up, there is no way you can picture any woman from planet earth, or any adjacent planet, dating Jackie. The language alone was a turn-off. Jackie would say
something like, "Tender is the night," and it would sound like,
"How 'bout I rear-end tonight?" The young woman sat between
us as Jackie drank and horse-played. Spread across the table, six
bit-sized View-Masters, each with a photo inside — dropped off
by a passing waiter. Individual photos taken earlier in the day
of the band. You had to aim towards a light source to catch a
cheesy Kodachrome likeness of yourself, courtesy of the staff
photographer. Mine taken early afternoon after I attempted to
cut my hair. I grabbed a pair of scissors and experimented with
the front and backside — clipped myself pageboy bangs. It was
the unfortunate look of a '30s black-market baby.

Jackie passes the mini View-Masters around, studies each
image, then says, "I'm looking at the ugliest woman on the
planet," hands it to his date. Both laugh, then he passes it on. I
can't wait to see who it is. I squeeze it between my fingers and
point towards a mock chandelier. Holy hell, it's me! Shocked
and embarrassed, I grudgingly smile. Jackie goes into overdrive,
"Let's take a vote. Is this not the ugliest woman on the planet?
Even I wouldn't fuck her; wouldn't you agree?" I held cool in
check before things turn toxic, laugh it off and off and off, as
Jackie nudges conversation back to the photo, at which point his
date exits. I ask Jackie to end the slam, and he says to me, "I'm
concerned for you, Billy. This new look will put you back in the
nursery." I had to laugh. The guy was so damn funny.

On stage, Jackie moved about, fully informed with the music.
He would hand-slash downward across the strings, bend until
the instrument wept. Recently, Dina bought a Telecaster, hung
it from a shoulder and swung it about with military precision.
He idolized Wilson Pickett, and could vocally replicate the blue
notes stationed between the white ones. That crop of wiry red
hair bobbed up and around shadowing his godfather-like chin.
Jackie had this peculiar on-stage movement, a sort of manic side-
to-side sway; feet stuck in place as if nailed to the carpet, not a
come-dance-with-me attraction.

Early afternoon, I locate a grand piano in an adjacent lobby of the Pines where the high rollers hung, sat down, and amused myself before a desk clerk insists that I circle back to economy class. As I'm about to leave, comedian Marty Brill corners me. "You play beautifully; we should write a song together." I thought about the invite, and asked when. He pauses, then says, "How about tomorrow after lunch; let's say 1:30." The time arrives, and I'm sitting and noodling behind the piano with pen and manuscript paper. Brill shows and says, "Play me some chords." I draw from a collection of half-memorized, unfinished material and play a middle-of-the-road chord pattern. "Is there a melody to that?" he asks. I tap out a single melody line, much like the standards played on any bandstand. "I love that," he says. Brill asks the front desk for a pencil and pad and begins writing. Within twenty minutes, a song is born. I play, he sings. The song in question was so dated it could have come from piles of rejected Tin Pan Alley submissions. None of that mattered. I had just met a bona-fide star comic, and was treated with immense respect.

The final weekend at the Pines, Dina surfaces, "junkie" crazy. Stationed poolside, Jackie wore a ferocious look. "King, I'm tired of you and those Jesus eyes. Stop looking at me." Those Jesus eyes? As straight as I may have seemed about drinking and drugs, I was by no means on a Jesus crusade. I'm sure Jesus and the Apostles would have frowned upon my lobby antic. Poolside, Vic counts the tempo in, Dina enters strumming a mismanaged guitar lick, looks over at me behind the Hammond B-3, raises the Telecaster, spins, and swings. Holy shit! A chop at the head, and a sudden memory of those drunken nights with The Don Krekel Orchestra and bassist Joe Goff, this time courtesy of heroin. Dina runs to the right side of the organ, says something about our Lord and Saviour. I grab him and slowly drag him to the pool, then shove him in. Out pops security, rescues him, then escorts Jackie, kicking and screaming, to the front office, out the front door, and hurls him into a snowbank. A semblance of calm returns. Near poolside a side door pops open, raging Jackie stumbles through, then climbs a giant potted plant while screaming obscenities and in attack mode. Once again, security drags him from the building and he is forever banished.

Days later, Jackie stops by my flat in make-up mood, and asks if I wanted to meet his dad at a Lower East Side bar where he was lightly employed. I thought, why not, let's make the drive. How insane could the day get?

East Side drinking holes looked much the same. Noontime, bar stools inhabited by the regulars. No one dressed in weekend duds, just the clothes slept in the day before — sort of like worn-down electrician fashions; serviceable drinking wear. If a pal arrived in red or orange threads, folks assumed he had spent the weekend at a community beach.

Dina, wearing a full-length camel-hair coat, drives us to Brooklyn, parks the big Lincoln out front and exits. "Fucking pops says he has another job for me, I hope the bastard doesn't start a fight and pays me right." We walk past an old "s.o.b." mopping the floor, and scout the room. At first view I see three or four warped pool cues placed atop a two pool tables in need of levelling. Near the cash register where drinks were bought, a disfigured countertop charred from a lit cigarette. Down back, a San Francisco-like fog lingered, compliments of a wood-burning stove and flaming Camels. The men, for the most part, spoke the language of alcohol: boyhood conquests, mob killings, and remembered miscues of former Yankee baseball greats. Even a made-up story about the day Yankee Joe DiMaggio walked into a bar with Marilyn Monroe under his arm circulated as fact. All around, lime-green walls covered with watercolour prints of New York from the early 1900s adorned the room. Middle of the hall, that pot-belly wood-burning stove huffing and puffing.

"Jackie, what the fuck are you doing here? Your grandmother needs you. Did you feed her?" asks Dina's dad. "Fuck her. She sits in that window all day, gaping at the streets and scaring off the kids," says Jackie. "I asked you, did you look after Ma—did you feed her?" "The old witch doesn't know anything. She'll still be sitting there when I get back," says Jackie. "You're an asshole. A fucking loser, Jackie. If you let your grandma die, she'll make sure to shit in your shoes in da afterlife." I'm genuinely warming to this family.

"Hey, there's Izzy. Izzy, did you walk here from Brooklyn, or catch a ride with Godzilla?" Jackie hollers in an amused tone, looks back at me, and laughs again. Izzy was an Orthodox Jew from the old neighbourhood. I'd been with Jackie on other occasions, and witness Izzy walk the bridges — down long boulevards, with Jackie waving him off, then saying to me, "They don't ride in cars. It's against their religion. Crazy fuckers. Besides, I'm not picking him up; it's outta my way."

Ten minutes in, Jackie and Dad are into each other's face screaming obscenities. Dina looks back at me and says, "Let's get the fuck out of here before I cream him. He says I've got to sweep the damn floor. Fuck that, floors are for parking shoes. What's he going to pay me, $2.00 and can of Ajax? Fuck him."

The New Image were the remnants of Brooklyn's doo-wop past. Vic Bonadonna had a couple of regional hits on the Parakeet label, and spoke with a sweet, mid-toned voice, stocked with compliments and good humour. Stu Wasserman, my brother from another universe, laughed often, and was as boisterous as me. Stu was my roomy on the road and ever-present disciple of jazz and soul. Drummer Jon Prano was all class, a neighbourhood legend, and purveyor of that "funky Broadway" beat. How could you not love these guys? We gigged up and down the East Coast, from Newburg, to next-door Poughkeepsie, NY. Up to Waterville, Maine, and down the East Coast to Atlantic City. Wait, let us pause at Waterville, Maine — virgin territory for me. I'm thinking travel brochures, magic booklets stolen from underneath my childhood bed, those beautiful photos of wildlife and sumptuous landscapes.

Waterville, as expected, came with plenty of roadside deer and foxes, yet was the gig that offered the most surprises. A young man in a wheelchair greeted us just outside the venue, and immediately took a liking to the band. He was also horny as hell, and racked up considerable verbal mileage reminding us. The conversation centred on his desire to knock off some "snapping pussy." I had never witnessed such a unique animal. There seemed to be more of it in Maine than the imagination of most college males. "You have to see the girls in this place; they'll go crazy for you. They like hippies," he says. I'm there, and buying in, yet quite content with the young women I hooked up with at the Pines — able and willing. I did keep in mind an episode in

Poughkeepsie that could have put me in the emergency ward.

It was last call, and few options. I approach what I think is an attractive lady. She buys into whatever I was selling, and Prano throws me the keys to the van and winks. We drive to a friend's place, and lie on a cot made for one. I begin the ceremonial disrobing; she loosens her belt and coughs. Not a passing, breezy cough, but a giant wheeze, launched from a subterranean region of her lungs. A bitter, nasty, dead-of-winter rumble. I refuse to give up. She then slips off that sexy wig, and I discover she's not a blonde, but an office type. I am alright with that, until she says, "Can we pause for a moment while I take my meds?" Okay. I am down with that. On return, another couple arrives, climbs into the cot next to us and hammers skin. The guy hits at full force as his date yelps. I look back at my outpatient, who then chokes up another lung-buster. "I'm so sorry; I have pneumonia," she says in a sickly voice. Back to the van, and down that lonesome highway.

Back in Waterville, I am approached by a guy I assume is the town pimp, who dressed and spoke as such — a slick, jive-talking hunk of nothing. Along with him, a young, slightly chunky blonde, maybe a girlfriend, or that's how he portrayed the relationship. Somehow, she ends up in my room and offers herself up for a nominal fee, $10. I decline, which gets the attention of pimp boy. "Not to your taste? Price too high?" The point of this recollection: Pimp boy and I would cross paths in Greenwich Village weeks later, where he offers me girls and a drink. Months later, I am walking the streets of North Beach in San Francisco, and passing a neighbourhood strip bar, and there, situated in the front window, dressed in sharkskin threads, the Pimp of Waterville. The guy recognizes me, comes busting out the front door, onto the streets and gives me a big hug, "Billy, Billy — you've got to love it here. Free fucking love. The girls are beautiful and cost nothing. Fuck that backwoods shit. You can't even get moose pussy up there," he says with all of the gusto of a child finding a shiny red Schwinn bike parked under a Christmas tree.

Back in the motel, the band gathers and votes to pay a visit to a Waterville "sex den" to watch porn. The viewing to be held in a basement — an invitation from a local politician and his wife. At this juncture, I had never seen porn, only heard rumours. After being greeted in the driveway, we're escorted downstairs to the den. Before us, a good 40 folding chairs. Folks in J.C. Penney suits, and mostly a bad dress-up affair. I'm the only person with shoulder-length hair, or in any way connected to the "flower people." A woman approaches and says, "Don't you get tired of having all that messy hair. Bob doesn't have to worry. He's hairless — all over his body." She giggles. Oh my God, *swingers' night!*

The films commence: Super 8, black-and-white, short reels. First up, two naked women, I'm guessing from the Roaring '20s. Not exactly in tune with the times. Next, the blow job. A woman, clinging to her sunglasses, engaged in the awkward act. Meanwhile, deafening silence, all eyes fixated on the fold-out screen. Reel #3. I am assuming an act of fellatio — a "who is doing what to who?" thing. From the bleachers, a stone-silent Victor watches as a head falls between an opponent's legs, then says, "Hey, that looks like an old man chewing bread." Chairs spin, necks twist, one lone patron yells back at us, "You can leave now." I'm telling you, a hundred pissed-off eyeballs, laser-beamed the five of us. We laughed our way out the suburban driveway and back to the street, one crude and unusual encounter later, a small-town misadventure.

We then scored a gig on Long Island at one of those memorable '50s nightclubs where bands did dances; players with slicked-back hair and girls wore fancy pants. It was post-Elvis action and on the outskirts of change. We arrive early afternoon for set-up, haul the Hammond B-3 and P.A. in place, then a meet-and-greet with the club owner who immediately takes offence with my look. "You're not wearing that hippie crap in here tonight are you?" At first, I ignore. "Are you listening, hippie? Men dress like men in here, not like something from a grocer." I ignore.

That night, I arrive through a side door and slip behind the organ. Most of the evening, I dodge — stay out of sight, then the shit hits the band. "I thought I told you to dress properly. People are complaining. Follow me." I do just that. Big Mafia reaches into the cash register, extracts a $20 bill, and places it on the counter. "Take this and buy new clothes, and get rid of those fucking sneakers and goofy tie." Next day I shop, and buy a tie resplendent with fruity oranges, bundled bananas and grapefruits. I then paint the sides of my sneakers in dayglo, slip into my most elegant bright-red Nehru shirt, and return to the gig. First set, I hide from sight. Break time, I see big man fast approaching, "I should knock the holy fuck out of you. Get the hell out of my club now." Fired! Band and all.

Off to Atlantic City. Tony Martz's—Levon Helm and Robbie Robertson of The Band. A gig that made them a virtual East Coast household name. Jon, Victor and I clear the front door. It's a cold, cold late October evening, ocean blowing wild, whipping up heavy seas, air wet, room humid, and we're unprepared and, um, wearing the minimum travel wear. While hauling the band equipment in, Tony Martz pulls Victor and me aside. "You see that sweet young face over there? That's my daughter. Keep your distance and hands off." I look over, and notice she was a younger version of Tony—thick, short, and of good stock. I swore to Tony I wouldn't even look at her. I don't know what Dina was thinking, but he also stayed away.

The place was enormous, with three rooms running bands at the same time and thousands of kids. As time passed, it became obvious: the house bands were the big draw. In a side room, we attracted a hundred or so loopy college kids who'd stop and mingle, then wander into adjacent rooms. At night's end, Tony walks over. "I don't know if you were any good or just bad, I'll let them decide. Maybe I'll call you back, maybe not."

Drugs scared the shit out of me. 533 E. 6th street came loaded with talent and soft drugs. Ground floor, I would occasionally engage with a young woman who worked as a waitress at the Impromptu Club. She gave me a joint of weed and suggested I smoke. I kept it in a jar, and thought about it for weeks. She then gives me a tab of acid; I stash it in the wallet. Early next morning, and nothing on the itinerary until late afternoon and a Brooklyn Boys gig pick-up. Alone in the flat and at peace with myself, I swallow the tab and wait. A soft drizzle blankets the neighbourhood. An hour or so passes, and I begin hallucinating with no one there to talk me down, so I take to the streets. Wearing a broad smile, I occasionally make eye contact, then catch myself laughing, place both hands over my mouth and smother. It was when I locked eyes with a hot-dog vendor — a face transported through history seemingly born in some remote region of Italy circa the 1900s — that I understood my mind was now orbiting an uncovered planet. Laughing hysterically, the guy insists I get help. Help? Maybe a walk through Tompkins Square Park: derelicts, cyclists, love children, and who knows what the fuck?

Not long after, I climb atop a park bench, sit, and wait. The hallucinogenic suddenly kicks into high gear. Wino #1 approaches, looks me in the eye and says, "I get you," then walks away. He gets me? Daytripper #1 wanders over, fixates on my eyes and says," Trippin'?" Oh man, seriously? "Yes, it's my first trip," I reply. "How's it going? Seen anything," he responds. "I heard I'm supposed to see unusual things?" "I think so,' he says. "What should I be on the lookout for?" I ask. "The man!" Fuck me, the man? "Who's the man?" I ask. "You'll know," he turns, then walks away. Next up, a posse of vagrants panhandling for quarters, cigarettes, some recalling hardship, sordid life stories, with "I understand where you are coming from" being the most common reaction. The best moment came from a down-and-out man draped in a long coat that was scraping pavement, a decade of dirt smeared about his face, who says to me, "You, me?" I look directly into his eyes. "You, me?" He closes in, "You, me!" Off he goes, the me reminiscent of my brief encounter with Moondog on 42nd Street. Walking past, I flash the peace symbol and say "peace." Moondog looks up from under his Viking helmet, spreads three fingers, and says "war"!

Just hours before pick-up, I crash a local diner and order a breakfast of bacon and eggs. It just so happens one of my parkmates invites himself along. I ask, "What are you having?" He says, "Zygotes and ham." I had not a clue what a zygote was, but order. "Give my pal an order of zygotes and ham, please!" The waiter looks at me and shakes his head. Minutes pass, and two plates of eggs and pork arrive. The mind is spinning as if it just broke in orbit. I stab at egg #1 and then the unexpected—both yokes rise, quick look right to left, leap from the table and run to the back of the diner. I peek under the table, over at the cook and back at my park pal and say, "Did you see where my eggs went?" A waiter looks directly at me and says, "Your zygotes went thatta way." The remark hit me so hard; I laughed until my stomach nearly burst all its gifted parts.

Jackie and Vic were late as usual. I'm now in "acid hour" number five and walking in and out of a local newsstand, waiting for that promised ride to the next gig, at our designated hook-up joint. I call Vic's wife, Patty, who tells me Vic left three hours ago. Then episode umpteenth! I can't get loose of the phone booth. I'm still hallucinating and over-thinking, trapped in an 18th-century time machine. It was not until a young woman comes by, taps on the door, and guides me to freedom. "Take my hand, all is well," she says.

Vic and Jackie and I eventually connect, and I retell my adventures. "You got fucked up on acid, and you won't smoke a joint with us?" says Jackie. "I'd smoke a truckload of primo weed before I'd ever touch that crazy screw-your-mind shit," says Jackie. So be it! The two had driven all over Brooklyn, missing one contact after another — all for a small bag of gigging weed and late as usual.

I honestly thought I could tame the tarnished chunk of betrayed humanity and help Dina locate the best in himself by inviting him to join me for Eric Clapton and the Cream's first appearance at the Café Au Go-Go. Dina arrives late, fully loaded on drink and drugs: loud, funny, and in for the kill. Minutes before showtime, I scam two seats second row, "Why the fuck are there so many Marshall amps on stage?" Dina begins. "I thought you said this motherfucker could play; all he needs is a short Fender amp. It looks like a Sam Goody's display up there. Is that shit for sale?" Dina laughs, before going deep into himself. How many esses in embarrassed? Dina trash-talks the drum set, the amps, and the in-coming crowd as they gather in seats. "I bet they don't play any Sam and Dave," Dina said, reciting one of those dim-witted rants I'd heard so many times before. That's when I slide out of the church pew and off to the men's room, hide in a poorly lit back cubicle, and watch Jackie twist and itch from afar.

Clapton and crew centre themselves on stage. Dina tosses less than artful barbs at each, which they ignore, until a fed-up Jack Bruce lobs a few choice profanities. Wearing a satisfied smirk, Dina uncoils, twists his neck, and looks back at the audience, chin bouncing, anticipating something in return. Then the band kicks in at maximum force. The volume and intensity knocks Dina to the floor. Big Red rises, tilts head, dips, and nods approval, points at drummer Baker, who gestures as he throws in a of couple improvised drum rolls. Then, without warning, Dina screams, "Clapton, you suck!" What the fuck? You just insulted God? Dina rises, lips quivering, body shaking, and *blam*, a seismic puke stream rains down on two unsuspecting individuals in the row ahead. Holy shit! I could not believe what I had just witnessed yet I stay put. Dina twists, wobbles, looks back, waves, and flips the bird to the band. "You suck, Clapton. This is my gift to you, you fuck!" Hands raised, and covering both ears, Dina stumbles out onto Bleecker Street.

Curbside and speechless, I watch Dina pull himself together. "Billy, I know you meant well bringing me down here to hear this shit, but that band doesn't have any soul. Where's the fucking beat?" His last words before stumbling off into the shadows mumbling junkie jargon.

As the months pass, Jackie would arrive at gigs dressed in a black cape and wearing a ridiculous World War II German-Prussian Pickelhaube helmet; pointy spike on the top, push the guitar volume to the same level as Clapton's, and play with the same unrelenting intensity, yet a key element was missing in his playing. Soul! Dina and "cool" were opposites, and rarely in synch. Clapton wore buckskin and fur; Dina wore hand-me-down mob-style clothing and shapes borrowed from comic books. Clapton spoke few words and attracted a worldwide following. Dina yelled obscenities, pushing even the most curious and devoted fan to the exits.

The New Image hit the road and land in Newport, Rhode Island, at a sailor's on-leave bar, Leo's Last Stop. The building resided only feet from the Atlantic Ocean. Vic, Jon, and I load in, inspect the surroundings where we are met by a handful of hostile barmaids. "Do you guys play anything we can dance to?"

Vic runs down a list of the band's soul classics. "Never heard of them," one says.

Whatever possessed my sidemen to drop acid that night is still a mystery to me. Throughout the evening, I look over at Jackie, then Jon and Vic and ask myself what is causing the weirdness on stage. Jackie sounded as if he was sawing the tops off road signage, and Vic looked as if he had something to say but at a loss for words. Truly bizarre. Near evening's end, we meet Canadian Zeke Sheppard of The Good Sheppards, another blue-eyed soul revue booked in the following week. Zeke and band earned the royal treatment, a group with a solid following and reputation. Zeke compliments the band. I thought about his kind words while trying to decipher the weird abstraction on the bandstand. The room of beer-swilling sailors and down-and-out mistresses seemed all but immune to what was occurring. Out front, a bidding war took place between the desperate soldiers and the women who held the goods. Packing up, I catch a last view of my crew before hitting the road to Massena, New York. Each wore big broad smiles, half shit-faced. Hours would pass before sanity returned.

This is what memory says about Massena, New York, the next gig, and truly fucked up! Just this side of the border from Cornwall in Ontario, Massena was a wide-open border town where underage Canadians could drink and party and say stupid things. My favourite line was "kiss my foot." It was as if the '50s had come back to haunt everyone. The coming days were mind-numbing cold and dreadful. We were hired to play behind exotic dancers in a small downtown hotel, which came with a tiny bandstand next to a stairway leading up to where band and strippers shared quarters. Two local dancers (the main event), our group, and background music. The players thought they could hustle the women while knowing college-age women were no easy mark.

Vic and I book a room at a bed and breakfast, replacement drummer Joey Ardigo and Jackie check into a local motel. None of us socialized until the gig, which devolved into another fearful acid trip. It was decided the gig sucked beyond redemption, and a portion of the band should go full-on weird. Jackie strummed like Pete Townshend—big arm slashes. Joey crashed and banged, me, more spectator than a participant. Nights end, both dancers pleaded with the band play something with a beat. Before the final show, Vic and I are summoned to the local police station where Jackie and Joey are behind bars. The motel manager accused them of running out on their bill, even though it was early evening before the gig, and dress clothes and other essentials remained in the room. Vic and I visit the cop shop, argue, and then bargain with the night sergeant who kept saying to me, "You look like my sister." A deal struck — ransom — at $100. Vic returned to the hotel and got an advance on the night's band pay and both freed. That evening the band held it together until I caught the eye of a couple of stunted Canadians with close-cropped hair. "I want to fight a longhair," says one clod. "Geez, you look like my sister," says another. I pushed my way past and out the front door, and look across the horizon and survey the barren wasteland and asked myself, "Why the fuck Massena, New York? Why am I here? New York, New York, please!"

Back in the city, the band then cops a weekend: Thursday, Friday, and Saturday night at a prime dance club in Manhattan, Trudy Heller's at 6th Avenue and W. 9th. Heller's was the "in" spot for dance-crazed socialites and a tough gig to arrange. Salvador Dali, George Hamilton, and Lynda Bird Johnson were frequent guests. Two house bands dominated, Barry & the Remains and Benny Gordon & the Soul Brothers. Heller handed us a setlist and expected every group to abide. The main attractions: Ben E. King, Otis Redding, Sam the Sham & the Pharaohs.

The Boys From Brooklyn were on the mark. 10 — 4 in the morning, an hour on, one hour off, the off hour spent in a tight back area inhaling deadly cigarette smoke and fighting off raging heat and humidity. Of all the many gigs we played, this was us at our best. The band played with a relentless groove. Jackie and I sparred; me popping out 10-fisted gospel organ blasts, and Dina churning out his best Memphis-style rhythms. Heller complimented the band, and offered a return visit if ever an opening appeared.

Jackie would soon pay Richard and me a visit at our flat and brought along two young women — one Puerto Rican, the other a blonde and thin as a rail. Dina's mission: sex, smoke the "boo," and watch old black-and-white movies. Dina begged me to let him stay over, saying his creepy grandmother never gave him a moment of peace or privacy — and I could help him get laid. The two women in question were late pick-ups from a gig at The Electric Circus. Jackie promised great weed and a party. Jackie lights a thin joint, sucks in, smiles and hands to the girls, and the girls buy in. He then says to me, "Why don't you and she go for a walk, this won't take long." Correct! Blondie and I barely clear the front door when I hear, "Hey, where you fucks going; there's a party up here?" We quickly return. "Damn, I was good, wasn't I," Jackie asks of the stunned woman? "Let's smoke more reefer; fuck me, it's John Agar night. You girls in?" Jackie says with a devious grin.

I never feared Jackie. He was weak and affected. We eventually learn he was behind the theft of the band Hammond B-3, Leslie cabinet, and Kustom sound system. He didn't give a shit about anybody's personal property other than his own, just the next fix! During the '90s it was said that Dina, then wheelchair-bound and living off social services, with no family or friends, would die and be buried in a pauper's field. All sorts of characters inhabit the bandstands of our lives. Sometimes the residue of those stop-overs linger. Dina wrote his epitaph early on and abided with it to death. I'm glad I knew the guy and witnessed his passion for music. We were both drawn to that "fat-back" groove and those huge gospel voices. What we did not share was an allegiance to the numbing consequences of hard drugs and addiction — that long descent into musician's purgatory. We have all known Jack Dinas in our music lives, and remember them as they were. That may be more than enough.

33

A-1 Sound

I had little knowledge of Herb Abramson when Vic Bonadonna and the The Boys From Brooklyn walked me up the stairs to A-1 Sound Studios in Manhattan, clueless; this was ground zero for those early Atlantic Record hits. I was young and fixated on the psychedelic movement — that long-winded organ, extravagant guitar solos and sidewalks crammed with young "free-love" beauties wagging limbs to an obtuse rhythm. Vic knew Herb from the doo-wop days. Herb discovered Bobby Darin and tried unsuccessfully to squeeze a hit record from him. That would come later when Herb's Atlantic Records partner Ahmet Ertegun scored the big hit *Splish Splash*.

The vibe around A-1 was one of utter chaos, with reams of cable streamed from the central control room to the main room down hallways to places unknown. Herb would step around, pause, and disappear into the men's room and return shrouded in a haze of smouldering weed. I was now 21 years old, and Herb past 50. Abramson had a bride half his age keeping the books. I don't know if she and I ever communicated in the same language, but it was not for lack of me trying. She would recite Herb's legacy and remind me I was fortunate to be in Herb's presence. I never disputed that. It was the comings and goings that captured my attention at rhythm & blues central.

Herb was always looking for the next Ray Charles, Clyde McPhatter, or Aretha Franklin. Abramson produced several recordings for National Records of McPhatter, The Ravens, Billy Eckstine, and Joe Turner. Abramson and first wife Miriam were friends with Ahmet Ertegun. Ertegun recognized Herb's abilities, and came with a proposal for a start-up, Atlantic Records, in 1947. They pooled their money, founded, and sliced the venture into shares, and then off they went. 1953, Herb is drafted into the army and vanishes. Enter producer Jerry Wexler. Herb serves out his time, and returns with a pregnant girlfriend. Marriage ruined. Over the two years I would do the occasional session, share a dinner date, or sell Herb a song for publishing money.

A-1, the original Atlantic Records located at 234 West 54th Street in Manhattan, eventually relocated uptown to 76th Street, the main floor of a hotel off-Broadway. I worked in both, and many a music icon recorded there: Jim Reeves, J.J. Jackson, Pigmeat Markham, Johnny Nash, Lloyd Price, Muddy Waters, Hank Crawford, James Moody. Later, demo time with Bette Midler, Barry Manilow and Patti Smith. During a brief period, I was on-call for singer/songwriter Don Covay. Covay wrote song classics *Chain of Fools, Mercy, Mercy, See-Saw* — from doo-wop to funk. Herb would tell me where and when to be hoping Covay would surface. Abramson understood money was made in publishing, and built a catalogue recording one unknown songwriter or singer after another. A certified-gold plaque hung from the wall of the main studio: Medal Music, *High Heel Sneakers*. Every time the song was covered, Herb upgraded the premises with new equipment.

A-1 Sound, for all its history, sounded shabby; technology had long surpassed Abramson's grasp of popular recording techniques. I could hear what was happening outside Herb's world, but could not translate it with the limited equipment. Another problem: every time Herb bought a reputable vocal microphone, some hanger-on would steal it during or after a recording session. It seemed the only ones that survived were the all-purpose Shures.

When Covay and I first hook up, we immediately hit it off. Don would pack a half-empty bottle of Thunderbird wine wrapped in a paper bag and sip as he talked back at me, "I need you to sing some harmony here?" "Seriously?" I can't sing. I could cat-yodel and play the piano. Covay didn't care. Don just wanted to hear specific notes. *Don't Let There Be Any Blue Lights at the Party*: old-time rhythm & blues, deep south, rural Carolinas.

I remember a session when Covay took a swig, then looked over at me and smiled. "Can we do this again? Maybe I won't mess up this time; I can barely read the words on the back of this paper bag." Wow! That was killing funny. Over and over, we run the song. I saw that big grin claim his face. Covay wore those Roger McGuinn, Byrds-style glasses, twisted and bent around the nose. "Bill, sing those harmonies, what do you say?" The two of us gather around a floor microphone and sing as Herb records take after take. Covay's vocal is spot on; me, six or seven yards off-centre. "You are doing it, white boy, you doing it," he would say, and laugh. Doing what, I wondered? Next take, I howl like a lonesome underfed beagle tied to a backyard shed. Don recorded; Herb paid up.

I figured I could get an advance on publishing money if I could get Herb interested in one of my piecemeal ideas. Herb, tangled in cables and chaos, let me roam about. I took advantage of the baby grand piano and wrote a complete song, *Hurtin' World*, a 6/8 soul/gospel, bluesy ballad. I played for Herb, and five minutes later, he whipped out a publishing contract and handed me a $100 bill. Damn! Big time! I'm now a professional songwriter! During the next few weeks, Herb went about auditioning young black female singers for the big session and came across a high school graduate in New Jersey named Charlotte Stokes. Herb never said much to me about it until session day. "The guys are coming in this evening to record your song; you may want to be here." I did just that.

On arrival, I witness the players working through the melody of *Hurtin' World,* and sounding light years beyond my demo. "That's J.J. Jackson on piano, Bernard Purdie drums, Tommy Tucker on the organ," says Herb. I look around, and the place is full of musicians, and in the control room, a beautiful young woman accompanied by her parents. Other than J.J. Jackson, Purdie, and Tucker, I had no idea who the other players were or the history they represented. I could talk about Cream, the Beatles, or the Rolling Stones, but none of the icons in the room. *Hurtin' World* earned its moment when Charlotte sang, and I'm awarded an acetate which I played until the needle scraped the lacquer from the plate. It was so perfect, then lost forever.

With publishing money in hand, I purchase an Eric Clapton look-alike brown leather fringe jacket for $25 at the Mercury Gift Shop in the Lower East Village and now walking the dream, stop by the Café A-Go-Go, the Bitter End, the Café Wha, and show off the exquisitely crafted garment. The street crew compliment, then inquire about my new-found wealth. I tell them of my adventures at A-1 and history. Their response: "How can I get a publishing deal like that, and that jacket?"

Herb would soon block-book the studio and farm out to ESP Records known for those early recordings of the Fugs, Sun Ra, Paul Bley, Sunny Murray, and Pearls Before Swine. It was a much needed, steady roll of money. I would occasionally drop in for a visit, the place sounding as if multiple accidents were taking place. Nothing resembling the refined music of Herb's rhythm & blues parade.

That Upper-East Side apartment Herb called home, with high ceilings and spacious rooms, I assumed cost a fortune by today's standards — each room the size of a small church. Who would have guessed in the coming months and years that *High Heel Sneakers* would once again fatten Herb's bank account? With over 1,000 covers, ranging from Rod Stewart, Jose Feliciano, John Lennon and Sting, to the Grateful Dead, Herb lived large! The years that followed, I would telephone and speak with Herb; that's if Wife #2 would allow, and we would talk of the past. Herb eventually sold off everything and moved west to Henderson, Nevada. He died in 1999 at age 83.

34

Go West

That weekend solo piano gig at Louis Jordan's proved to be something of a showcase for me. British musicians Donovan and Stevie Winwood, jazz trumpeter Randy Brecker and others would stop by from time to time for a beer, catching a bit of jazz. Atop the piano sat a pie plate with brushes, arranged for anyone who wished to play along. Occasionally, a percussionist with excellent skills would sit in and turn the tin plate into a booming kit. Those were the nights jam sessions took on a far different temperament. Enter Frank Zappa's manager Herb Cohen and friend.

I played through my usual set of jazz and pop standards, improvised, and coasted through a bit of blues and country stylings. I took note when the two applauded. Break time, Cohen invites me over for a beer. He quizzes, asking me about everything from drug use, drinking habits to my background in the music industry, who I played with, and knowledge of various idioms. He complimented my playing, billed himself as Linda Ronstadt's manager, then offered me the music director/piano gig. He said Ronstadt was moving away from the Stone Poneys, going solo, and needed someone there to assist her in forming a new band. I did not second-guess the offer, and jumped on board. Cohen left a phone number and address. The following day I call the office and begin negotiations. The money thing was ridiculous. Cohen offered a retainer of $50 a week, and when rehearsals kicked in, $150 a week. A pauper's sum.

Even though I was heading west, I was not giving up my stake in Richard and my East Village flat, but an incident during the final days made me reconsider. Richard's friend Ronald would drop in on occasion and fill us in on the comings and goings of anyone of note in the Village. After a week playing upstate with Vic and gang, I return to find most of my possessions stolen, and my dog Spirit chained to the radiator. Richard had given Ronald a key to the premises, and spent the week with his parents. Ronald pawned my Farfisa organ, amp, and television. Only a trunk of LPs, Nehru shirts and pants remain. Late-night, I surprise Ronald running a street hustle on some unsuspecting tourist and confront him. He starts with the denial, then shifts the blame onto the others he invited to sleepover. Two days later, Ronald drops in on Richard and me, and hands me a ride cymbal from a drum kit and says, "Cash this in; it should be worth some money." WTF?

With the FBI closing in, a trip west was the best chance to relocate and dodge. I would hear rumours of young men being questioned and harassed by agents up and down MacDougal and Bleecker. I'd call home each month and speak to my sister Karen — the only way to get a straight-up report on family matters and those pursuing me. I would occasionally talk with Mom, whose conversations were brief. "Are you working? When are you coming home? Your dad is upset." Dad and I were not on speaking terms. The only news of merit: Wayne enlisted in the army for a 3-year stint. A deal worked out where after basic training, Wayne attends the Navy School of Music in Virginia, then on to the army band in South Korea.

Cohen informed me he was pairing me with guitarist Lee Underwood, and the two of us would drive west and hook up with the rest of Ronstadt's newly formed band. I found travelling with another musician comforting. Underwood served as singer-songwriter Tim Buckley's guitarist from the downbeat, and was a proponent of free jazz and an excellent guitarist. In the 1970s and '80s, Lee would become a brilliant music journalist and a contributor to *Downbeat* magazine, *Rolling Stone*, and the *Los Angeles Times*. Underwood and I and Lee's girlfriend hit it off big time, both easy-going and storytellers with much to share. On the road again!

During conversation and a drive across New York State, I suggest a late-night stop in Pennsylvania at Nellie's farm. I promised

Lee the best Italian food on the planet. Lee and partner buy in, but we arrive too late for the main course. It was well past 11, with most folks sleeping, yet that didn't hinder Uncle Ronnie from climbing out of bed and fixing us a late-night breakfast. Memories of early Williamsburg mornings, those 3-egg breakfasts and piles of smoked ham danced about the brain from Manhattan to Williamsburg. Ron did not disappoint. "How many eggs you want?' he asks. None of us spoke. We let Ron have his way. Then the capper. Direct from the smokehouse, freshly cured ham. Lordy, Lordy. Salt pork, burnt to a crisp and tastier than imagined.

Lee's woman friend slept a good part of the journey as we crossed from Midwest to west. "Do you realize the two of you have talked non-stop from New York to Colorado, rarely taking a breath?" she asks, easing out of a long nap. That summed up the kinship Lee and I found as the two of us trade stories of mishaps, happenings both big and small, and events on and off stage. Otherwise, the trip was mostly uneventful except for a stop at the Grand Canyon, one magnificent view of the expansive west forever logged to memory, and my first encounter with Native Americans, the Navajo.

We arrive In Los Angeles with limited dollars between us. Cohen paid for gas, but that was it. He also promised, on arrival, there would be another $50 waiting. Let's just say the difficulty in collecting was more than I bargained for. A first western visit with Cohen saw him do a 180-personality reversal, knowing he was now in charge. Lee helped me find temporary lodgings with Buckley's co-writing collaborator, Larry Beckett. Beckett let me crash until I found accommodations. He also had a younger sister who became a constant companion. The two of us hung out, and walked the streets of Santa Monica. Big joy, big laughs. Then two episodes that would turn my world upside down.

Walking along Santa Monica Boulevard, a fast-moving sports car hits the median and shreds in front of us. The shattered remnants of the car fly in all directions. Broken chunks of the sports car lie strewn on both sides of the median. Near us, a headlight comes crashing to earth. Frightening! A second episode only days later. The sound of sirens whistling up and down the boulevard, and then a motorcade. As the open-air car approaches, we see the figure of a man waving as if leading a victory parade of sorts. From the backstreets people cross the median bearing flags, and frantically wave. Bobby Kennedy! Not as eventful as when Harry Truman drove down Main Street in Jeffersonville and his hat was blown off by a brisk wind, or LBJ during my college years, but Kennedy had momentum and charisma.

A first get-together with my future bandmates is arranged at bassist John Keski's apartment. Keski split his fidelity between the Stone Poneys and organist Lee Michaels. The two of us got along much like brothers. Keski allowed me to stay below in the basement cellar until I could find an apartment. Let's just say spiders and centipedes are not the most appealing bedmates.

The rehearsal. We gather and await Ronstadt. When she does arrive, it was if a goddess from some imaginary planet appears. *Different Drum*, the Stone Poneys' hit followed me across America, penned by the Monkees' sideman Mike Nesmith. Ronstadt was going solo, and up for change, and I was hoping the song was tagged and archived. Then a list of potential songs is presented of which Keski was privy. We worked our way through the bones of the material. Canadian songwriter Adam Mitchell penned a couple, along with outside submissions. Situations like those can be unnerving, as we were still in meet-and-greet form.

Ronstadt arrives, pauses, chats, then shares the piano bench and asks me about my past and if I had written any songs. I tell her of the song *Hurtin' World* and my experience with producer Herb Abramson, and then play. She gives a nod of approval. As the conversation transpires, I'm nerve-wracked thinking about the woman next to me — so damn beautiful and gifted with the voice of an angel. Three days in, rehearsals planned, then cancelled. Players would congregate, run through the material, and await Ronstadt. After the third rehearsal and walking out the door, Ronstadt invites me for a run around Hollywood and a drive to a beach community. We drop in at RCA, and catch up with her friend Lester Chambers of the Chambers Brothers, then off to visit experimental-rock band The United States of America at a beach-style cottage. While all of this is transpiring, I phone home and get the unwanted news the FBI is closing in on me. I then telephone my old apartment in Greenwich Village, and learn the FBI had come knocking and issued a warrant for my arrest. I decide I should at least report for a physical and see where that leads. I get word from Herb Cohen that the FBI stopped by Capitol Records, and threatened Ronstadt with a subpoena if she was caught in my presence. I didn't know where to turn — gig done!

Over a breakfast at the International House of Pancakes, I meet a young woman and tell her of my journey — the good stuff, not the military hassles. She invites me to spend the night up the coast in Tiburon. Everything was going well until I mentioned I was a possible draft evader. That was it. The room turned as cold as winter in North Dakota. She came from a military family, and had a brother in the service, and I'm the enemy. Not a single word spoken during the drive back to L.A.

I tried stalling the military. During my previous cross-country journeys, I would randomly stop in cities and re-register for the draft, ensuring six months of leeway. Feeling pressure from home, I decide to report for a physical. I call the Santa Ana branch of the Selective Service System and set a date, then make the long bus ride and discover I arrived a day early. For me, this was more than an epic journey; it was one I did not wish to repeat anytime soon. The Ronstadt adventure ending, I had to find work and new lodgings. How the next episode occurred is still a mystery.

I find myself sleeping on the bedroom floor where the L.A. band The Merry-Go-Round congregated. The place doubled as a drive-in marijuana dealership, and before me were giant bowls of weed. Whoever ran the house allowed me a corner in a side room to sleep. I could watch people coming and going, and then a first encounter with bassist Rick Dey.

Rick was the bass man for Paul Revere & the Raiders and pot courier. I watched as he stuffed bales of marijuana into the back of a Fender Dual Showman from an adjacent room. Dey was prepping for a drive from California to New York City to meet a buyer. Months later, I would discover that buyer to be a future bandmate of mine. Before I leave, a knock at the door and in walks Jimmy Page and manager Peter Grant of Led Zeppelin.

Grant rolls a joint, complains about the taste, lays down some cash and departs. Last words spoken by the house manager: "What a fucking asshole."

Before departing Ronstadt, I convinced manager Herb Cohen to pay me for time served. Reluctantly, he coughed up $100 and told me to take care of the draft problem. With money in the pocket, I went about Hollywood searching for lodgings. I soon discovered a decent rental just off Hollywood and Vine. Out of work, and a month's rent paid, I started hanging around Local 47 of the Los Angeles musicians' union in Hollywood and scouting for gigs.

The basement of Local 47 came with a recreation area, pool and ping-pong tables. By day I would hang about and shoot Nine Ball, a game I would learn on the fly, and gab it up with the most in-demand Hollywood studio musicians of the era. A good many would congregate between session calls, and profess to be in the middle of the cultural shift, though many were already in their 40s and 50s. Then I meet a guy named "Scooby." Scooby was an old-school L.A. musician who knew every player of note. He immediately takes a liking to me, and divulges that rock icon Chuck Berry was looking for a backing band. Berry needed to book a rhythm section for a concert at the Los Angeles Convention Center. I dialled up the members of Linda Ronstadt's band and pulled it together.

Scooby was older than most of the hippies in the neighbourhood, and a guy who could not get a handle on the love generation. But he liked the perks, played saxophone and did a few pit-band gigs, the most memorable when he was hired to play behind The Temptations. Scooby was the only horn man in for the show. Given a score written for six horns and told "Just play the parts, all of the parts, muthah.....," Scooby professed it to be the scariest night of his life.

35

Chuck Berry Scares Me

Ronstadt's band commits and arrives willing to roar with Chuck. The opening act, the original edition of Fleetwood Mac with Peter Green, second billing The Chambers Brothers. Forty minutes into their set, I was ready to rip that throbbing cowbell out of the frontman's hand and scream "time's up"! Then, here's Chuck Berry! Give it up. We are on!

Keep in mind, Chuck Berry does not rehearse, or lay a setlist on you, or speak to you. I stood back and watched the roadies haul a colourful psychedelic-trimmed Fender Dual Showman onto the stage in front of 10,000 reefer-sucking teenagers, followed by an old upright piano, wheeled into place. I thought to myself, "This must be for me." Berry appears sidestage wearing an electric-blue polyester Nehru shirt. I wanted to inform him I once owned a dozen custom-made Nehrus, cut to fit from the Mercury Gift Shop in the East Village, yet thought it better to keep a distance. Chuck's shirt looked like a Uniroyal tires prototype. More tread than thread.

As we take the stage, well-known pianist Barry Goldberg and drummer Eddie Hoh show up. Goldberg cuts me off, and insists he's replacing me on orders from Chuck. I think about the interruption, then ask Goldberg to bring Chuck over and work things out. Goldberg fires back. "Look, man, Eddie and I played with Chuck last night in Chicago, and we flew out here to play with him, so back off." I pause, then ask, "How much is Berry paying you?" Goldberg shoots back, "We're here because we want to be." I respond, "We're here because we're the band, so get lost." Case closed! Who says rock 'n' roll is mellow? Goldberg sniffs around, corners Chuck, and tries to draw him into the line of fire. Berry coolly looks back and says, "I don't care who's on the stage, just as long as they can play." Goldberg loses it. Starts telling me how he would make sure I would never work again in L.A. Hell, who the fuck even knows of my whereabouts? Who's Goldberg going tell? My landlord? The folks at the Spot Dog Diner, home of the 10-cent corndog and my favourite hangout?

Chuck kicks in, roaring louder than a road-hungry diesel. The Dual Showman cracks with distortion, making it difficult to differentiate between single notes and chords. I was sure the amp had arrived with a busted speaker. Sound issue aside, the next 50 minutes were rock 'n' roll nirvana, every song came with a piano solo and an approving nod from The Man. Between tunes, zero conversation, no word of key signatures, or next song, just keep an eye on Chuck. At times scary, at others, exhilarating.

The crowd stomped, hooted, rocked, and rolled. Chuck duckwalks, leans forward, smiles at the throng, then walks back my way and says, "Play some more." Berry then ends the dynamic set with *My Ding-a-Ling*. When Chuck got to the words *my ding-a-ling*, 10,000 rockers wave arms as they sing along, with extra emphasis on the hook. The crowd went wild. At set's end, I leave the stage feeling as though I had conquered not only the west coast but a good portion of the universe. How many times back in Indiana playing with The Chateaus had I played *Johnny B. Goode*, and tonight I understood the original intent and passion behind the song. The same for *Memphis*. That plodding rhythm and overpowering guitar. You couldn't escape the pocket. Maybe next up for me, second keyboardist for The Doors? Hey, why not?

With adrenaline pumping, the four of us congregate sidestage and await a promised crisp hundred-dollar bill, settle-up time with Berry and promoters. Anticipating, I determine it appropriate to exchange cordial words between the iconic headliner and me — possibly a "Thanks for the opportunity!" and "What's up?" goodwill opportunity. That said, the conversation was brief. Mostly me talking to myself! I cooled it while Chuck busied himself counting money. Berry then rattles off, "Four-thousand nine-hundred and seventy, four-thousand nine-hundred and eighty, four-thousand nine hundred and ninety — wait a minute, you shorted me 10 dollars." The ordeal repeats itself. Promoter A recounts every dollar. Chuck argues, and comes up 10 bucks short. The scenario repeats again and again. Promoter A, $5,000; Chuck $4,990. After what seemed an hour of haggling, Promoter B steps in and says, "Who gives a shit? Give the cheapskate another 10." Without looking up, Chuck Berry lays aside four 100-dollar bills, scoops up his stash, rises and begins to walk away. Fool that I am, I assume it's time for another shot at "get acquainted time" and lightheartedly say, "So, I guess you're taking the band out for steaks?" Oh, man, not good. Berry throws me this hissing viper look I will never forget. Let me translate into words: "Get lost loser, before I snap your head off with wire cutters, shrink-wrap it in one of my discarded Nehru shirts and feed it to starving gulls. Excuse me, I have a plane to catch." Chuck never called. Then again, he never knew who I was, yet he did say "take another chorus" throughout the night. Good enough.

Not only did Scooby get me the Chuck Berry gig, but also a 6-month trial union apprenticeship. Union rules allowed applicants to play casuals — no six-night "steadies" around the area. To make a bit of cash, Scooby offered me a gig picketing on behalf of Local 47. It was there I made many friends, one being a singer, "Mama Lion" Lynn Carey, daughter of actor Macdonald Carey. The voluptuous Carey attracted far more attention waving placards picketing Gazzarri's on The Strip, home of The Doors, than my partner or me. You could hear The Doors blasting away as teenagers came and went. I remember commenting to Carey, "Will we ever get away from that song? It's everywhere, Break on Through (To the Other Side). We never did, yet we made $32 each for the weekend.

36

Last Walking Bear/Kent & The Candidates

My newly acquired apartment came with an abundance of young working and underemployed women and a spectacular drummer named Pete "Last Walking Bear" DePoe. Pete was playing the "chitlin'" circuit in and around Crenshaw Boulevard with organist Ron Johnson, a buddy from his home area, Neah Bay (Seattle), Washington. I would hear Pete practise by day, and marvel at his technique, amazing footwork, and perfect time. I'd followed the two to a jazz bar and sat in. Early one afternoon, I catch Pete with his young kids and wife, and beg him to start a band with me knowing Pete was tied to those bread-winning gigs. Then one day, a letter arrives from the Department of Interior, a notice of settlement between the Native Americans of his tribe and the U.S. government. A series of cheques worth hundreds of thousands of dollars to be sent at six-month intervals, all part of a land-claims settlement for DePoe's tribal ancestors — Southern Cheyenne, Turtle Mountain Band of Chippewa Indians, and Rogue River/Siletz.

Then a hard knock at my door. "Hey man, let's go, it's here." It's Pete with a first installment, ready to open a bank account asking me to tag along. DePoe approaches a teller, hands in the cheque, and informs them of his intent. The teller signals the bank manager. The bank manager's face lights up, then cools after reading the amount. Pete fills out the necessary papers. All was going as planned until Pete asks for $10,000 in cash. The manager refuses, lectures Pete on fiscal responsibility of which DePoe was having none. Pete lets loose, and shouts the man down. "It's my fucking money; give me the 10-grand. I want to buy my kids' things on my terms. If not, give me the cheque back." Pete got the $10,000 and bought his kids plenty.

I tried on other occasions to interest Pete in starting a band, but without a schedule of paying gigs, it was out of the question. Not to say things did not work out in the long run. DePoe joined the group Redbone, played on three albums, and the real capper, drums on Bobby Womack's classic, *Across 110th Street*, one of my favourite recordings of all time.

A lost soul wandering the streets of Hollywood Boulevard, I hook up with jazz pianist Corky Lang in a restaurant and learn he played solo late afternoons at the jazz haunt Shelly's Manne-Hole at 1608 N. Cahuenga Boulevard. I'd walk past the Manne-hole numerous occasions and read the listing of jazz giants who played the joint: John Coltrane, Miles Davis, Bill Evans, Abbey Lincoln and others and dreamed of catching one of my heroes, but never had enough coin to pay the cover charge. Lang said he'd work something out for me. Lang then invites me by his apartment to play his 9-foot Steinway, a rental coming at a steep $90 a month, Lang barely able to keep up payments with the occasional paying jazz gig and days working as a parking-lot attendant. Corky and I hung together long enough to collect that gesture of goodwill between players: The Horace Silver Quintet in person at the Manne-Hole. Unlike the spacious Arts in Louisville, the Manne-Hole came with a tight stage. It seemed the players played shoulder to shoulder. I got a clear view of drummer Louis Hayes and snare-drum face tilted towards me, sticks bouncing at a modest tempo. Silver slamming fistfuls of block chords. It was all about the groove, deep and steady.

I'm criss-crossing a parking lot on Santa Monica Boulevard when I cross paths with this smooth looking guy in a suit who calls me over. "You look like a musician," he says. "I own that recording studio over there — Paramount. Why don't you come by and play us some of your music? I might have some work for you. Be there at 9 a.m." Skeptical, I agree. I've had these kinds of encounters dating back to my first recording session. Most never pay, yet with nothing promising ahead, I dash back to the apartment and prepare for the following morning.

The Brolin family-built Paramount Recording Studios during the early '60s: Actor James Brolin encouraged brother Brian to open a studio on Santa Monica Boulevard; in fact, a young carpenter named Harrison Ford found employment there. 9 a.m., and to the minute I arrive, packing song sheets. Even *Hurtin' World*. I connect with the mystery man from the parking lot who says, "Great, we'll check them out a bit later. But for the moment, would you and so-and-so mind measuring the floors throughout the building?" WTF? Naive and anxious for a paying gig, I get down on my knees with tape measure, and then enter digits on drafting paper. The guy alongside views me as competition and goes about shredding. Late day and fed up, I ask, "Can I play the songs now?" The main man pauses, "Why don't you come back tomorrow? I have a few more chores in mind." I ask how much it pays. He says, "You're working your way up like everyone else who starts from the bottom. Soon." I buy in.

The following morning, I return. The same gentleman then ushers me to a back area cluttered with broken flooring, and orders me to lift and place it all in a cartage bin. These weren't pebbles or even patio stones, but large chunks of jack-hammered concrete. An hour in I say fuck this shit, and return for a face-to-face with the suit to find the guy absent. It was then the chief recording engineer invites me in to listen to a playback with Brazilian jazz singer Flora Purim and George Duke. I could not have asked the jazz gods for a grander moment of goodness and grace. Purim asked about me, what I thought of her music, and why I was there. I so needed that moment! Dispirited, without a job, and much like the vagrants up and down Sunset Strip, to be spoken to in such a kind loving voice was more than uplifting. It was damn invigorating! Nervously, I listened and thought to myself, how comforting her words, and how lovely the music. I'm then asked by the engineer what I thought of the track and mix. Seriously? Moments later, Duke walks in and back to business. Later that evening, I'm invited back to play and sing a number. I do just that. My main man listens, compliments, and

offers to call if a keyboardist ever needed. Hmmm — didn't I just
see George Duke?

During the '60s, Local 47 of the Los Angeles musicians' union
hosted a Thursday afternoon job fair each week. By that I mean
the main lobby was cleared, and musicians would assemble to
meet and greet and potentially hire. There was a post-it board
soliciting organ players who played that *greasy* funk, like organist supreme Jimmy Smith, or the psychedelic noodling of The
Doors. Rarely did talent of that magnitude present itself, but the
possibility of getting a paying gig spun in my mind. I'm hanging
around, and I see a black man dressed in a colourful dashiki and
pillbox hat, lift my card from the board, and ask, "Is Bill King
in the room?" I think "gig baby, gig!" I approach and introduce
myself, and told I'm speaking with Kent Sprague from Quincy,
Illinois, of Kent & the Candidates. We talk about the music and
songs we had in common, and I come to know I knew 75 percent
of the Candidates' repertoire from my time with The Boys From
Brooklyn and other dance clubs. Local 47 came with three performance rooms equipped with drums: one with a Hammond
B-3, the others with pianos and amps. We booked in for the day.

Kent brought that Black Panther vibe: militant, proud and
focused, yet when situated behind the drum kit, a relaxed Kent let
loose a big broad grin. A good 25 minutes pass when Candidates
bass player Reginald Douglas, arrives, sits down, and falls into
the groove playing what looked like a Hofner electric bass, and
not long after bandmate Pete Smith shows with his hollow-body
Gibson. In my young life, I have rarely experienced a groove like
this: uncomplicated, relaxed, and hot-wired to rhythm & blues. A
welcome change from the long-winded jams of psychedelic rock.
I kissed the ground, and proclaimed the room the sweet spot of
L.A. soul music.

After jamming, the players embrace me like a brother, and I
accept the gig. Up until then, I had performed in mostly all-white
bands, not of my choosing, but where the colour lines played out
musically. I was now stepping into the world of *all black*. This
outrageously dressed, long-haired white boy with few boundar-
ies was in for a righteous baptism in roots-soul music.

Sprague was not only a killer drummer, but a fantastic singer cut from the backside of Little Richard, Otis Redding, Bobby "Blue" Bland, and others. When Kent sang, the lyrics poured out as if stolen from a Sunday-morning Southern Baptist testimonial — Kent the "preacher man." Kent was also honest, hardworking, caring, and funny as hell. Committed to the Black Power movement, and clad in Black Panther trooper gear, Kent stood proud. Sprague would occasionally lay a "honky" joke on me, but never offend. If we were to become blood brothers and break the racial divide, we had to openly talk about race relations and get past the anxiety. What happened on the bandstand certified our unity. What happened off helped us understand our cultural differences and find common ground.

The Candidates played up and down the California coast, with two epic weeks in San Francisco. Once there, we settle into a rundown hotel on Geary Boulevard in the tenderloin district. Kent had big plans, and asked if I'd like to ride the backside of his motorcycle and drive to the black section of the Fillmore district to one of his favourite Black Panther bookstores. Kent was in search of new reading material by up-and-coming black authors, and historians of the movement. Inside, Kent talks me into buying Eldridge Cleaver's *Soul on Ice,* which I read cover to cover in one sitting. The book would have a profound impact on me, creating an awareness of the social inequities within the criminal justice system and the unjust incarceration of black men. Kent acted as a buffer between me and the most militant visitors in and out of the store.

The original Kent & the Candidates group made a name for itself playing the "bone-dry" regions of Kansas and Missouri. You've heard the band thousands of times on the Brenton Wood classic *Gimme Little Sign* on Double Shot Records, written by Wood, Joe Hooven and Jerry Winn. Kent mostly viewed former dishwasher and vocalist Wood as a "shot in the dark" artist with little upside, and stayed focused on his career. The world Kent was about to walk me into is still one of the most pivotal in my musical and cultural development.

The Candidates played nearly all the upscale black functions in Los Angeles, with Watts, South-Central Los Angeles, and Hollywood being crucial. We connected with an upscale fraternity of gorgeous young black women who billed themselves as the Astral Playmates. They would stage social events aimed at bringing upscale, young, professional black men and women together. The other side of the "we are black and we are proud" protest movement: "We are black and proud and in need of economic clout and a chance to be heard."

We played the Millionaires Club, Maverick Flats, and Ciro's on Sunset Strip. Great rooms with folks dressed to the nines and tens. We also played the after-hours clubs throughout Watts. It was a gig at Ciro's and a chance meeting with singer Clydie King. We are hired for a 2-week stand at the Californian Club on Santa Monica backing The Raelettes, then The Radiants.

Max Millard ("Mambo Maxi") opened the Californian Club in 1963. The audience was comprised of African-Americans and Mexicans, a good many in for the Wednesday night mambo contests. The Candidates arrived only months before the club closed, and the Buddy Rich Big Band was one of the last performing acts. We show for Monday's rehearsal, then are met by the three Raelettes: Clydie King, Merry Clayton, and Margie Hendrix, ready for a run-through of the planned night. First song up, *River Deep Mountain High*. Kent gave me advance warning of the setlist, for which I was able to chase down the 45s and learn the songs. One time through *River Deep* and my head spun; my jaw dropped, leaving me breathless. Towards rehearsal's end, Clydie King looks over at me and says, "White boy, you have something against black people?" I nearly collapse in my seat. She then grins, and says, "Cat got your tongue or something?" I smile back and say, "I'm listening, and awestruck by what I'm hearing. Secondly, you all are so damn beautiful." That was it! Big laughs, and then hugs all around.

The gig was outrageous, the most magnificent singing I had ever witnessed. Night after night, comedian Redd Foxx would step away from his comedy club, and drop in. Foxx would sit in the same section, halfway down a sidewall, night after night, and hold court. When they say, "The joint is jumpin'," this joint was high-steppin'. The following week, The Radiants' *Father Knows Best*, *Voice Your Choice*, and *It Ain't No Big Thing* — prominent gospel voices doing their best to bring in a crowd. But the room sat half-full. The music was superb; an education in bridging secular and spiritual music into something that could make a drinking crowd feel at ease.

When word came the Californian was closing, I visited Maxi and begged for the giant Buddy Rich mural gracing the club entrance, and Maxi says, "Give it a week boy, and if I can't sell it, it's yours." It sold!

Hollywood was decades ahead with the black and white thing, an oasis for music people. We shared the bandstand together, shot hoops together, went to ball games, watched championship boxing together, and hung out like family. None of that weird racially-charged Middle America shit. Coming from an integrated school system, it reminded me to never buy into that white-supremacy crap.

Kent hooks us up with an after-hours gig in Watts at the De La Soul Social Club, 1-4 a.m. He warned me to hang close to the bandstand, and that some brothers would be offended with me being there. The club stood near a large parking lot, much like an old-fashioned '50s banquet hall. It was a massive hang. In one corner of the building, a tight stage, the open areas arranged as a sprawling night club punctuated with folding tables and metal chairs. A cloud of toxic cigarette smoke, blended with body sweat and humidity, made it nearly impossible to breathe.

We opened playing Sam & Dave, Lowell Fulson, and James Brown, and then backing local darlings, The Younghearts: old-school smoothie stuff, slicked-back hair, tailored suits, and silky moves. Singing mostly ballads aimed at the beauties in the audience. Down front, the best-dressed men glared back, rattled shot glasses, eyed their dates, and dissed the singers. The band played on! Then a black comedian with a smart-looking dummy moves centrestage. The ventriloquist places the collegiate-looking puppet on his lap and shouts, "I'm black, and I'm proud." The crowd wildly repeats. The dummy again bellows, "I'm black, and I'm proud." The crowd chants back. The dummy then pauses, twists its neck, roll eyes, and looks directly at me and shouts,"He's white, and he's scared." The place goes batshit crazy with laughter. I take it as good fun and play along. Kent grabs the microphone and follows up, "He may be white and scared, but he sure does play the hell out of that organ," The place erupts in applause.

Soon after, the crooning troupe The Dells sing their hit, *Stay in My Corner*. My God was this ever epic. I caught a chill behind the organ that has never let go. End of the set, I stroll back to the bar. Along the way, folks shake hands and tease, "You some kind of brave, weird-looking white boy." Then confrontation. "Hey, hippie boy, you stepped on my shoes." I look back, and before me this angry pimp-styling guy is ready to punch me out. "Apologize for stepping on my shoe, psychedelic," he demands. My immediate thought was to tell the asshole to fuck off, but decide to tone down the rhetoric and address him straightfor-wardly. "Not a chance," I respond. "You calling me a liar, white boy? Let's take this shit outside." It worked. Well, maybe not. Just as Mr. Bad was about to have a go at me, the club owner intercedes and escorts me back towards the stage, waves the dude off, and insists I "stay in my corner." I hear you, Dells! Kent arrives, howling with laughter. "I told you, man, they are black, and they are proud. You? Not so cool. You might even get out of here alive tonight if you stay 'funky' on that organ. I'll get the drinks from now on. Damn, it's hotter than purgatory in here."

Kent gained us entry into the San Francisco topless-bar scene when it was red-hot. We worked Carol Doda's Condor Club, the Hungry I, and others up and down Broadway in North Beach. Afternoons we would cart the Hammond B-3 across the street, and set up for happy hour, and then back to Carol's for the long night's run. Doda was a topless stripper and entrepreneur who paraded her twin 44s like royalty.

Afternoons, tourists would drop in and gaze at half-naked college girls, down a beer, and occasionally ask to sit in with the band. That we could deal with, but dispensing with the singing doorman/bouncer who demanded we play *Georgia on My Mind*, took some clever maneuvering. At first, he seemed innocent and amusing, but after multiple trips and band jelling, we took a different stance. Kent bought a rubber chicken and tied a rope around its neck. If a tourist chirruped on too long, he would whip it the direction of the person and stun the offending warbler. I saved the chicken beating for the broad-shouldered doorman/bouncer. Somewhere in the middle of a long drawn-out episode, I fling the bird and snap the back of his head. At first, he looked amused, but on repetition, I could see the anger building inside. Instead of punching me out on the bandstand, he complains to the house manager who politely asks me to refrain. To counter, I began raising the key. "Bouncy" would walk over during a guitar solo, and ask Pete, "Are you sure you're in F?" Pete would grin and nod, and watch him struggle. Last words, "I think I'm losing my range." The poor sod sang in C. A year later, I returned to San Francisco and escorted Janis Joplin to Doda's, where she became a regular, befriending Doda and the house manager.

Kent's gigs were a constant source of hilarity and fun. We even played down the coast in Costa Mesa opening for East Los Angeles group, Cannibal and The Headhunters (*Land of 1000 Dances*), and ? and the Mysterians (*96 Tears*). In Watts, we played an inner-city park concert opening for comic Flip Wilson with *Hogan's Heroes'* Bob Crane emceeing in front of a flaming vehicle. As Crane and Wilson small-talk, the fire burns out of control, yet nobody seemed that concerned. I thought to myself, if this were Jeffersonville, every fireman from the Tri-City area would have been on the scene. Even with the park buried in soot and the stench of burning rubber, The Candidates put on a wicked soul-filled show. Next up, Las Vegas and after-hours club Duke's on Paradise Valley Road. More music and weightlifting.

Whenever we toured for an extended time, Kent would pack a set of dumbbells, the two of us all about physical fitness and working out together. No drugs or alcohol, only the healthiest of living.

The 270-mile ride through desert and mountains was a taxing affair. I chose to ride half-way backside of Kent's motorcycle, then shotgun in a van loaded with equipment, just long enough to catch sunrise and a bone-numbing chill. Kent and Pete Smith then motored ahead of the van, just out of view. That's when Reggie and I come upon the two being interrogated by a highway patrolman, pull off and wait. A second officer arrives, walks over, and orders us out of the van, then asks me, "What are you holding in that hand?" I respond, "Hostess cupcake—want half?" which sets him off. He barks, "Funny guy. Get the fuck out of the van. Step over here and put your hands on the hood." The guy then confiscates all IDs, and calls in. Nothing of a criminal nature comes up, so he escorts us to downtown Vegas police headquarters, and then fingerprints us. At the time, you couldn't work Vegas without an FBI clearance and cabaret card. We handled the questioning with ease.

Duke's was an entertainer's paradise, an after-hours club that opened at 10 p.m. and ran until 6 a.m., the lengthiest gig of my life. One hour on, one hour off, opposite the tap dance/singing group The Curtis Brothers. Night one, actor Andy Griffith and posse take over the joint; then a steady cast of show business greats arrive. We play only rhythm & blues classics, and the crowd loves it. Between breaks, Kent and the boys hang near the kitchen, and hound the black cook for left-over "steak-bits." Delicious and addictive! Then all hell breaks loose. Two days in, the police arrive and remove Reggie from the bandstand. Douglas had a previous conviction for robbery. The third day, Pete Smith is taken away and escorted to the outskirts of the city for a past misdemeanour. Night four, it's just Kent and me; Hammond B-3 and drums. We jam as if we're a complete band, until Harry James and his Orchestra drop in — James and orchestra a key draw along the strip. Then one of the greatest musical moments of my short life occurs.

I had seen the Count Basie band in Louisville with Jamey Aebersold and brother Wayne on a few occasions; eyes mostly fixated on drummer Sonny Payne, the most mesmerizing drummer I had ever witnessed. In walks Payne, who sits down front of Kent and me. Within minutes, Payne approaches Kent and says," Can I play with him?" I wasn't privy to the close talk, and thought he wanted to solo to impress some fine women in the audience. Payne, to my surprise, looks over and says, "Git it!" I quickly think what song should I call? Then it hit me: The Beatles' *Eleanor Rigby*! Over the past months, I had been working the song into a Jimmy Smith-style "funk it up" organ jam. Next to me, a used Wollensak reel-to-reel recorder, locked and loaded. I hit the record button. Payne digs in. We rip and roar. The power, the turbulence, the level of energy on the bandstand was electrifying. It just so happened that we rented a screaming B-3 organ, with a ferocious bite. The crowd joins in and foot-stomps their approval as we go about deconstructing, improvising, twisting, and reshaping the Paul McCartney song for a good 20 minutes. Then it was over. Payne slips by the organ, shakes hands, and offers words of encouragement. The night ends as the sun comes up, and we stroll outside into piercing morning light. A severe heat accompanies us on the ride back to the motor lodge, then a swim and playback of my epic jam. I rewind the tape, hit play, and nothing but a steady beat buried in subterranean distortion; my document of the night, a noxious mess. I cried real tears!

Mid-afternoon, the call comes: "Tell Bill to get out of town; the FBI is here looking for him — he's wanted for draft evasion," reported the owner of Duke's. Kent and I pack up the van and head back to Los Angeles. Before the band breaks up, we record two sides for Double Shot Records under a new name, Local Changes: *I Know You're Gonna Leave Me* and *Whatcha Trying to Do?* Whenever I hear those tracks, I listen to the intensity and integrity of our righteous four-piece unit. I also reflect on the joy and goodness, and lessons learned when one gives oneself over to another's culture and heritage — the desert, the casinos, the harsh light of morning, forever a Kodachrome interlude.

37

Steve Paul's Scene /
Fillmore East

After the stint in California, I find myself back in Manhattan and land a job with a band called the The Chicago Loop, who had a regional hit *(When She Needs Good Lovin')* *She Comes to Me*, #37 on the Billboard Magazine Top 100. The lead singer, Bob Slawson, was a frequent visitor to Steve Paul's Scene on 46th Street, an uptown nightspot where anyone who was anyone in the music business hung out. The Scene and its clientele stood in stark contrast to the chic patrons at Max's Kansas City, where Andy Warhol and his gang of "art warriors" bunkered. One humbling lunch, I was invited to the table and treated as if I was Hillbilly Bill. On closer inspection, the inhabitants appeared more drugged zombies than true artists, providing plenty of reason to escape the place.

After the featured band performed, all-night jam sessions kicked in — the Scene on 46th Street was the home of the monied elite and jetsetters. It was one of those two-stage entry clubs. First, get past maître d'hôtel Teddy, then bouncers. I'm introduced to the club by songwriter Bob Slawson and his partner Barbara Laszewski, friends of Elaine "Spanky" McFarlane of Spanky and Our Gang. A second visit solidified easy entry. Teddy mistook me for John Kay of Steppenwolf fame, and red-carpeted me. Inside, I would hide out until the main act finished and jam sessions started and await a chance to play. First call, I survive a jam session with a radical new group, the New York Rock & Roll Ensemble, and a line-up of dreaded unknown jammers. A second go-round I catch the Buddy Miles Express winding down. Miles was a member of the blues/soul ensemble, The Electric Flag, then Jimi Hendrix's Band of Gypsies, after drummer Mitch Mitchell's departure. This night, Mitchell played alongside Miles, bringing a high-level of thunder to an already storming band.

I waited until the group took a break, then slip within proximity of the Hammond B-3 organ. Herb Rich, Miles's organist, had the first crack at the drawn-out jam session, leaving me to wait in anticipation. Once Rich departs, I slide onto the bench and am abruptly met by Miles, who then pushes me aside. The front-line led by singer-guitarist Terry Reid and guitarists Larry Coryell and future Rolling Stone Ron Wood was in for the long haul. I wait patiently as Miles vamps a good 30 minutes between two chords, before retreating. When the opportunity arises, I light up the groove with my best sonic blasts. I twist and bend notes, pump the ritual comping patterns all organists learn when playing roots rhythm & blues. Flip the Leslie switch right to left for effect, pump volume pedal in time, and make the beast howl.

With little fanfare, a changing of the guard occurs behind me. A frilly cuff drops, from what looks to be an Edwardian garment, and brushes past my face. I whip around for a glimpse and do a double-take and recognize who it is; it is the man, Jimi Hendrix. Hendrix flips the bass upside down, strings facing the opposite direction. Twenty-plus minutes, I ride the pulse, toss in a few modal chord changes, and shift the tonal centre. Coryell and Wood one-up each other, even throwing in a few choice lines from guitarist Freddy King's blues anthem *Hideaway*. During one long exhilarating stretch, it is Larry Coryell, Mitch Mitchell, Hendrix, and me, deconstructing the blues. I played with such physical weight and excitement that I popped an organ key, sliced my index finger, blood spurting in all directions. The night ends with hand slaps, and Buddy Miles offering to hook me up with a rhythm & blues band in San Diego, one he once pushed.

The night replayed long into the dark embrace of night. I remembered each note, and every missed opportunity and tortured myself until dawn intervened, and morning wiped all evidence that I once "churned and burned" on one such starry night.

The Fillmore East, located at 105 Second Avenue at 6th Street, was my go-to spot for great music. Built 1925-1926 as a Yiddish theatre, it would become the church of rock 'n' roll under promoter Bill Graham, who presented two or three prime time bands on the same bill. Sometimes Graham would include a light show, or unusual stage theatrics. Only blocks from the Fillmore, my eyes focused perpetually on the changing marquee. Inside and onstage, and as bands played, a backlit screen projected splotches of colour, just enough to jack up the get-high crowd courtesy of the Joshua Light Show. Occasionally, an identifiable image would float past, earning a roar of approval. At times, I would drift by Graham's competitor, the Anderson Theater at 66 Second Avenue, for dollar Wednesdays. One opportune night I catch Simon & Garfunkel; another, the first edition of Blood Sweat & Tears — still a quartet. Those bookings were rare and far between.

February 10, 1968, a remarkable double bill at the Anderson caught my attention featuring San Francisco's Moby Grape and Britain's Procol Harum. Moby Grape was signed to Columbia Records and released five consecutive singles, all within weeks of each other. More a plea for attention than an astute business step. Procol Harum was riding high on the success of the radio-friendly single *A Whiter Shade of Pale*, and every bit as good live as their recordings. Lead man Gary Brooker's soulful voice spread to every region of the hall, at times brooding and melancholy. The band shared a preview of the soon to be classic *Salty Dog*, which Brooker supposedly played for Beach Boy Brian Wilson, who in response said it was the most beautiful song he had ever heard. Moby Grape was also electric. I mostly stay focused on drummer Don Stevenson and his soul-stirring vocals, which are most appealing.

April 26, 1968. A triple bill: Iron Butterfly, local band Blue Cheer, and closing, Traffic — with blues prodigy Stevie Winwood. Winwood was everything I wished I were in a vocalist. A guy musically rooted in the soil that birthed Ray Charles, and a voice so exquisite. *Rolling Stone* magazine ranks him #33 on their Top 100 list of Great Singers of All Time. In 1963, Winwood debuted as part of the The Spencer Davis Group. In the coming years, the band recorded *Somebody Help Me* and *Keep on Running*, written by reggae musician Jackie Edwards. Then *I'm a Man*, written by Winwood and producer Jimmy Miller, and followed by the smash hit, *Gimme Some Lovin'*, written by Winwood, Spencer Davis, and Stevie's brother Muff Winwood. The latter two songs would sell over a million copies each. *Keep on Running* rose to number one on the British charts, with Winwood 16-years-old at the time.

I would learn that, at 14, Winwood served time backing such blues greats as Muddy Waters, John Lee Hooker, T-Bone Walker, Howlin' Wolf, Sonny Boy Williamson II, Chuck Berry, Bo Diddley on United Kingdom tours. It was the golden age of pick-up bands. Whoever could learn the specifics of a song — the arrangement and parts — and play with feel, got the gig, as well as valuable experience. Winwood was already proficient on organ and guitar. Occasionally, I revisit the old film clips of Winwood from a variety of popular British music shows, and watch in awe. Winwood attributed Ray Charles's recording of *In Person* (from 1959) as being the blueprint for his vocal style. He copied Charles's inflections, rhythmic bounce, and the nuances in his vocal presentation — even recording Charles's number-one rhythm & blues hit from that session, *Drown in My Own Tears*, as a bonus track on the first Spencer Davis album. The 1956 blues classic, written by Henry Glover, was stylistically close to the original. Winwood accompanies himself on piano, in full command of the idiom.

The '60s were a time of great social upheaval, with Europe adapting at a faster pace than the U.S., still in the grip of '50s norms. There was the breaking down of the class system and the youth movement underway with music as the soundtrack of the impending revolution. One pitch-black moonless spring night, and inside the Fillmore East ballroom in April of 1968, something unusual was about to occur. Iron Butterfly, better known as a studio concoction, gaining traction through a twelve-minute drum solo by Ron Bushy on the recording *In-A-Gadda-Da-Vida*, shared the stage with Blue Cheer and Traffic. On this occasion,

Iron Butterfly was a messy unit. It was one of those opening acts you prayed was limited to a four-song set. Second up, the heavy metal trio Blue Cheer.

From Iron Butterfly to Blue Cheer, you heard the impending revolution and departure from psychedelic rock to hard rock — a movement afoot that would endure a good 40-plus years. Blue Cheer, managed by an ex-member of the Hell Angels named "Gut," paved the road for a new wave of British heavy-metal bands: Led Zeppelin, Deep Purple, and Black Sabbath, who mostly toyed with the blues, and would soon embrace progressive rock. Blue Cheer's setlist included Eddie Cochran's *Summertime Blues* as well as blues covers *Rock Me Baby* and Mose Allison's *Parchman Farm Blues*, all clocking in at a near 20 minutes each. Stage set up: 10 Marshall amplifiers, split between guitar and bass, and stacked horizontally. Enough firepower to collapse a city block. There was no escaping this relentless hour-long barrage. It was the first time I feared for my health, and sprinted towards the exit. As I cleared the front door, I was warned I would not be allowed back in if I left the building. Instead, I took up residency in the men's washroom, amongst other fearful patrons, all who had come for the soulful stirrings of Steve Winwood. Even at this distance, I was still not out of range of losing my hearing. Looking back, I must admit that this was the beginning of a new era. The guitar was no longer an instrument of subtle expression and complexity, borne in the electric hands of Charlie Christian. It was now a six-string assault weapon.

Winwood, drummer Jim Capaldi, and part-time reedman/keyboardist Chris Wood arrive and situate themselves behind an uncomplicated set-up: Hammond B-3 organ, one reasonably sized guitar amp, drums, and microphone for Chris Wood's horns. From the downbeat, the room lapsed into near-total silence. Compared to Blue Cheer, this was a controlled performance of supreme craftsmanship and superb technique. Not the finger-hustling exhibition that preceded it. Winwood picked up the guitar, and began playing the opening strains to *Dear Mr. Fantasy*. The move confused me. I thought of Winwood as primarily a keyboardist, and a guitarist secondarily — possibly a hobby.

Wood pumped the organ in support. Winwood's lead vocal referenced Ray Charles, the soulful mannerisms, but with a contemporary vibe. The Hammond B-3 was barely audible, buried under the weight of Winwood's rhythm guitar, Wood a victim of a weak left-hand at organ bass, leaving the band absent any bottom end. Then the group performs *Medicated Goo*, followed by the showstopper *Feelin' Good*, written by Anthony Newley and Leslie Bricusse, a song strongly associated with folk/jazz artist Nina Simone. Winwood then lays his guitar aside, and situates himself behind the B-3, allowing drummer Capaldi space to move front and centre. Capaldi proves himself to be an equally affecting vocalist and co-writer of the band's first single, *Paper Sun*. On this occasion, Capaldi took full advantage of the opportunity.

Winwood was still the central figure. All eyes viewed him with curiosity. A fully accomplished keyboardist, Winwood lifted the low-end organ notes to a reasonable volume, tying in nicely with the drums. Behind the microphone and seated comfortably on the organ bench, Winwood's expressive vocals sailed above and drifted throughout the cavernous hall. It was all pure tones, with just the right shades of blue-coloured empathy. These are the moments when a single soul-piercing phrase penetrates the psyche, and disperses a seemingly narcotic calmness. Winwood, in full control, staged arrangements built on short motifs and sustained crescendos. With Blue Cheer hinting at a future that would be heavy on guitar riffs and debilitating volume, Winwood and company carved space for future acts like Hall & Oates.

Amongst musicians in attendance, the concert was talked about for days until a double bill with British crazy Arthur Brown and San Francisco's Jefferson Airplane rocked the Fillmore only weeks later. It was the beginning of the big arena shows. The Fillmore acting as the entry point/stopover until big money began to flow, and 2,500 seat rooms were not large enough to answer the demand. The Fillmores, Andersons, Paramounts and Apollos — theatres of grand character and long history — quickly adapted, embracing artists of all persuasions.

38

She's the One

It is October 25, 1968, and The Chicago Loop is about to take the stage of the Bridle Path, West Hampton. On a previous visit to Long Island, with The Boys From Brooklyn, we played downtown Farmingdale in a golden-oldies club, backing The Dovells of *The Bristol Stomp* and *You Can't Sit Down* fame. The bandstand of the Bridle Path was off the main room in what seemed like a broad, poorly lit cavernous area — walls covered in dayglo paint, the trendy decor of the late '60s. Sitting to the left of the stage, a radiant, thin, sunny blonde in her late teens, perfectly tanned to a luscious amber tone, and wearing a most inviting smile, seemingly inter-connecting eyes and soul. Throughout the Loop's first set, I watch with curiosity, then lose sight of her as she vanished with a couple of my bandmates. On return, she positions herself behind a gearbox that controlled the multi-coloured revolving stage lights. So taken with her, I offer to buy her a drink, and we share a cola. As the conversation rolls, I soon realize how extraordinary this person is. "My name's Kristine, spelled with a K," she said. Back on stage, and behind the Hammond B-3, I closely monitor Kristine's every movement and make eye contact, periodically losing interest in the innocuous jams passed off as complete songs while focusing on this lovely person in hopes of arresting my loneliness. My greatest fear? She would exit without leaving me a way to contact her.

As the evening unfolds, time passes between us. I eventually hold her in my arms, then kiss her, wrap my fingers around her slender waist, and squeeze. We kissed long and passionately, uncovering that sacred province between where soul and heart intersect. I would soon learn Kristine was everything I longed for in a person: kind, compassionate, tender, effervescent, loyal, and rock-solid. Over the coming months, we shared numerous hours together. The occasional movie, mostly locked in one long loving embrace: *Cool Hand Luke, Wait Until Dark*. Paul Newman, Alan Arkin, big screen magic.

Each Sunday, Kris would arrive by train from Center Moriches, Long Island, and spend the day, then return at night. Occasionally, she would greet me at outside gigs. On one occasion, she joined me at Newburgh, New York, where a trusting bond developed between the two of us. That new partnership was soon tested when I landed the music-director position with vocalist Janis Joplin, causing me to relocate to San Francisco. Kris understood where opportunity lay. And it definitely wasn't hacking away with The Chicago Loop, which, for all concerned, had run its course. Before departure, we shared one last night: a night of intense soul-searching. I repeatedly asked myself if it were possible that anyone could love me, without expectations, a draft-dodger living station to station, one step from imprisonment. And could it be Kristine? Kristine understood the pressures and penalties. Five years in prison, and a $10,000 fine if convicted. I honestly did not want to hurt or involve her in something so troubling.

39

Janis Joplin: Memphis Meltdown

Word quickly spread among the musicians in Greenwich Village of Janis Joplin's departure from Big Brother and the Holding Company. I cannot say the announcement created the same impact as The Beatles' imminent break-up, or Bob Dylan converting to electric. Nevertheless, it did reverberate along Bleecker and Mac-Dougal streets, attracting more attention among working musicians than street buskers. I, for one, reacted swiftly to the rumour. It was another keyboardist from the Village streets Moogy Klingman of Todd Rundgren's band who told me of the opportunity, and that Janis was assembling a rhythm & blues band, much like those high-flying Memphis bands: somewhere between Sam & Dave and Otis Redding. A sound that originated in the Soulsville USA studios in Memphis, Tennessee, and reproduced on vinyl by Stax/Volt.

I wandered into a record store on 8th Avenue, one I frequented for its diversity and rarities, then scanned the cover jacket of *Cheap Thrills*, Joplin's most recent recording. I searched the backside, looking for information regarding her management team. Nearby, a clerk offers to assist, then points to a record by the The Electric Flag, who shared the same management. It happened to be Albert Grossman, noted for his successful campaigns on behalf of (and among others) Bob Dylan, Paul Butterfield, and Peter, Paul and Mary. I dialled Grossman's office, and reached associates Vinnie Fusco and Elliot Mazer, both intimately involved in Joplin's affairs. An audition was arranged at A-1 studios, the original home of Atlantic Records. Before the date, I was summoned for an informal meeting with Albert Grossman. I waited outside Grossman's office, and clutched the sole documented recording of my piano/organ playing: a B-side instrumental single released by California soul unit, Kent & The Candidates, entitled *Whatcha Trying to Do?*. The song was an ode to pianist Ramsey Lewis of *In-Crowd* fame; a mix of country blues licks and gospel piano. Upon entry to Grossman's office, I catch a glimpse of the man surrounded by massive stacks of papers positioned like a towering fortress. He then speaks in a near whisper, waves me forward, and advises me of his take on Joplin's radical new plan. I was taken by the flowing white locks tied into a ponytail, and small, wire-framed glasses — much like that of Ben Franklin, one of the original signatories on the *Declaration of Independence*. I can't recall anything specific of that conversation, but it landed me a plum gig: double duty as Joplin's keyboardist and music director for a new band about to be assembled: The Kozmic Blues Band. Rehearsals, $150 a week; touring, $300.

The first audition was little more than a formality meant to assess the compatibility of the players. The second audition involved recording the soulful number *Piece of My Heart* at A-1 Sound Studios with Herb Abramson. Herb was thrilled that I was bringing one of the giants of the business his way. Our trio made up of drummer Roy Markowitz and bassist Stu Woods (formerly Stu Wasserman) played it right down the middle, and a final mix was sent to Janis for her approval. Beforehand, I bought a 45 of the original, featuring New Orleans' Erma Franklin and did my research. From that session, drummer Roy Markowitz and I land the gig, and bassist Stu Woods goes on to work as a sideman for several Grossman projects; recording with Bob Dylan, Don McLean, the Pozo-Seco Singers, Tony Orlando and Dawn, Janis Ian, and others. In many ways, his career fared better.

After arriving at a financial agreement, management arranged a flight to San Francisco for Roy and me, no accommodations other than a few nights at a studio apartment, courtesy of Janis's road manager in North Beach. I had pretty much lived out of a suitcase the past couple of years anyway, so this was cool with me.

We soon connect with bassist Brad Campbell of The Last Words, the only Canadian in the group, at our temporary digs.

Rolling Stone magazine had announced the hiring of both Brad and drummer Skip Prokop from the Canadian band Lighthouse, but Prokop never showed. Just as well. The three of us had spent our young lives in the shadows beyond the glare of spotlights, and this was indeed Janis's show.

A day in, and Janis invites us to her Noe Street apartment for a get-to-know-you session. After dragging our bodies up San Francisco's impossibly steep terrain, we arrive at Joplin's front door, and are promptly greeted by a snarling dog. Joplin's live-in mate (and ex-wife of blues singer Nick Gravenites) Linda Gravenites collects her dog, then directs us to a small sitting room, resplendent in Salvation Army home furnishings. Joplin enters, laughing, from a side hallway with all the energy of a Texas dust devil. Joplin was the perfect host, serving up shots of Southern Comfort and reefer sticks. I pass on the refreshments, which causes her to exclaim, "Who's Albert sent me? Jesus Christ?" I assured her I wasn't one of those Bible-thumping Southerners sent to rescue her from a host of demons. Janis laughs, eases back into the conversation, then invites Brad, Roy, and me back for dinner later that evening, saying, "I've got a few friends I want you to meet."

The party was already in motion when we arrived. The soulful strains of Carla Thomas blared in the background, competing with the hearty laughter of six denim-clad men. From the dining area, Janis rushes in and steers us toward something that resembles a large stalagmite ripped from a cave. On closer inspection, it's a polished sculpture of a snow-white penis, a gift from a local Haight-Ashbury artist. The coveted centrepiece remained the focal point of conversation throughout the evening.

More guests arrive. With each rap at the door, another group of tattooed denim-jockeys enters, each grimier than the last; our threesome looking much like choirboys at a prison picnic. Janis journeyed from lap to lap, kissing and hugging each ratty biker. The room was now overflowing with party crazies; Janis quietens and introduces her new hand-picked band. First, the men in denim? The Oakland chapter of the Hell's Angels. As the drugs flowed, and music intensified, with alcohol splashing about, I coiled up into my safe zone. The bikers' romp bounced to a different rhythm than most musician get-togethers, and by calculating Janis's excitement, we recognized serious debauchery on the horizon. The three of us politely excuse ourselves, and promise to meet again at rehearsal. Those rehearsals on standby as we awaited the arrival of the two horn players who had just completed service in The Electric Flag.

Brad, Roy, and I scoured the pool halls of North Beach playing snooker long past midnight. We listened to jazz and traded road stories, accompanied by debilitating laughter, as we relived Janis's dinner-less dinner party. We also speculated about the future. Roy and I didn't consider rock music essential, even though I readily connected with the free-form improvisation of psychedelic jam bands. Miles and Coltrane were the most talked-about players in our sphere. Joplin was merely a quirky individualist with a wide following. For the two of us, it was a better gig than lounging about Grossinger's in the Catskills.

Rehearsals began early December 1968 at the old Fillmore Auditorium. A floor below us, Carlos Santana rehearses his band through final preparations for his Columbia recording debut, *Santana*. A level below him, It's a Beautiful Day, putting the finishing touches on material for their debut recording. Our band shared a great rapport with Carlos and company. During breaks, each would filter in, listen to one another restructure tunes, Santana miles ahead of our newly assembled unit. Santana was well-rehearsed, loved playing together, and did it with precision and commitment. We, on the other hand, had had barely enough time to acquaint ourselves with unfinished and untried material before pressing ahead.

Day one of rehearsals the horn players stroll in just past noon, and take their places. My job as leader was to bring order to the proceedings and act as a buffer between the band and Janis. This was a role I had played many times before, but never on such a grand scale. Eventually, Janis slips in, introduces herself, and trades hugs with the horn players before inching my way. She then slides along the organ bench and presents a modest list of tunes. The message? Janis is planning to bridge the raw elements of her persona with that of classic soul and rhythm & blues — the marriage arranged in her head, but yet to be consummated by the band. First up, Gershwin's *Summertime*, her signature wail. Guitarist Sam Andrews plays a fugue-like riff — an intro Joplin had grown accustomed to hearing. I then write a counterpoint line meant to embellish. It soon becomes apparent the organ didn't sonically mix with amplified guitar, causing Janis to rethink the intro. When the full band enters, Joplin all but forgets the incongruous colouring. I knew it would take some adjustment; her ears accustomed to Big Brother and the Holding Company's version.

During the rehearsal, I craft horn lines for the Bee Gees' *To Love Somebody*, which Joplin quickly transforms into a blues ballad, rife with guttural cries and evangelical testifying, a song chosen for its show potential and emotional temperature: great lyrics, moody, with a soulful melody. I then convince Janis to give a listen to the old Eddie Floyd soul hit *Raise Your Hand*, a crack staple from my days with Kent & The Candidates. The song had the same fat groove found in Wilson Pickett's *In the Midnight Hour* and *Mustang Sally*, with a memorable, gospel-style shout chorus. Joplin listens, smiles, then asks me to script an arrangement. Then the great implosion: *Ball and Chain*, another squealing testimonial. Too jazzy? Overdone?

By week's end the rehearsals began to lose their lustre. Gone were the rock celebrities and energized sessions. Trumpeter Marcus Doubleday starts showing up late. It seems Doubleday made a heroin connection, which eventually took precedence over scheduled rehearsals. Janis, agitated, begins scouring pool halls and nightspots on top of rehearsing and drinking heavily — evidenced by the swelling beneath her deep-set eyes and nearly every pore of Joplin's face covered in sores and scarred. I was starting to dread the daily sessions.

Around December 18, guitarist Mike Bloomfield noted for his ground-breaking work with the Blues Project, Paul Butterfield, and others, unexpectedly appears. Bloomfield's turf was Greenwich Village, which led me to question his presence. Janis arrives, introduces Bloomfield, then asks us to jam a few tunes with him. Before Janis showed up, we had already made the Bloomfield connection with a shuffle blues that lasted some 20 minutes. Janis then instructs us to play *Piece of My Heart*. Bloomfield plugs the holes with stinging blues lines and slashing chords as we stay reasonably close to the original. With the trial period complete, Janis confers in private with Bloomfield, then emerges, and delivers the verdict: "Mike likes the band." The momentary reprieve lasts until drummer Levon Helm of The Band fame arrives, and Janis instructs us to play. Levon listens, then awards the band a second vote of confidence.

I could sense the uncertainty in Janis's body language. This radical change is Janis's call, exposing her vulnerability. Gone was the certainty and comfort of Big Brother's blaring amps, plodding rhythms, and close relationships. I recalled a conversation I had had with then-producer John Simon, who confided that it had cost him six months of edit time just to give *Cheap Thrills* a consistent flow. Reliable tempos were foreign to Big Brother.

Nighttime was Janis's time to roar. Brad and I piled into the back seat of Janis's "psychedelic-embellished" Porsche and cruised the seedier pool halls around the Bay Area. Joplin knew every oddball and misfit on the circuit, and treated each much the same as her band members. To Janis, if you were a friend, you remained a friend. On one occasion, I accompanied her to the Kaleidoscope Club to hear Texas native Johnny Winter. Janis had caught up with fellow native of Port Arthur, Texas, the night before. Janis had also extorted a fur coat from Southern Comfort, payback for her personal campaign and preference for the beverage. Throughout the evening, the luxury fur served as a seat cushion, an impromptu floor covering, never a treasured garment. Afterwards, Joplin drags me backstage to greet the musicians before departing.

Late evening, we surface at the Fillmore to catch The Small Faces. Joplin again pulls me backstage, this time to meet Rod Stewart and Ron Wood and other members of the group. Joplin used her quick wit and undeniable charm to break through the indifference of the reticent British imports. She tried with little success to seduce with laughter and encourage genuine warmth. It was an uneasy meet-and-greet, one after which she walked away, commenting, "What a bunch of 'tight-asses' these British bands are."

After receiving an invite to play at the second annual Stax/ Volt Yuletide Thing at the Memphis Mid-South Coliseum, productive rehearsals became imperative. It was a night of stars, big soul stars: Isaac Hayes, Rufus and Carla Thomas, Johnnie Taylor, the Bar-Kays, Booker T and the MGs, and Eddie Floyd. Janis was eager to introduce her new band in an area rich in folk and blues history.

After landing, Janis asks to buy a bottle of Southern Comfort whiskey. The driver notifies her no liquor is sold in Tennessee on the Lord's Day. She then quizzes the driver about where to buy a drink. He says Mississippi. She orders him to redirect the limo and chart a path towards Jackson, Mississippi. The mission became more bewildering as the urgency in her voice increased. Tense words flared between the driver and Joplin, nearly escalating into a full-blown confrontation. He didn't accept driving out of the way for alcohol on the Lord's Day to be part of the job. A compromise was struck. Let the band off at the hotel, and Janis would hire an alternative driver willing to continue in pursuit of libations.

More lousy karma. We are booked into the Lorraine Motel, where only months earlier Dr. Martin Luther King Jr. is gunned down. Even creepier, in adjacent rooms on the same landing. The thought gave me chills. Little fanfare greeted our arrival, leaving Janis free to pursue her vices. As we strolled back to our rooms, Mike Bloomfield walks past toting a garbage bag filled with marijuana. Roy stops and asks for a joint. Bloomfield throws Roy a contemptuous look and says, "I don't have enough." A startled Roy looks back at me and busts a devious grin. The two of us howl our way back to the room.

Soulsville USA and the rehearsal. From the street, Soulsville looked much like a broken-down cinema — its marquee lettering cracked and shattered, most likely damaged by kids with rocks in hand. Nothing about the exterior spoke to its recent glorious history.

We set-up in the main studio with enough gear to run through an abbreviated set. Room to room, there was ample evidence of hit recordings, the many awards and citations. One room over, Booker T & the MG's rehearsing their hit, *Time Is Tight*. What a rush! The big-boom drum kit most prominent on those Sam & Dave recordings with big, deep military-style snare and oversized bass drum, the kind you see in marching bands, stood proudly in the open space. Further down the hall, the Bar-Keys laying down a smacking groove.

No sooner than taking a seat at the grand piano, singer/songwriter, Isaac Hayes squeezes in next to me, and smiles. I drop a couple of blues chords, and Hayes answers with a riff or two, then smiles. I thought to myself, "fucking Isaac Hayes, the hits he wrote"— *Soul Man, B-A-B-Y, Hold On I'm Comin'*. I truly needed his genius for songwriting to rub off on me. I have few memories of the rehearsal, other than it being disjointed, with people filtering in and out.

The Stax/Volt Yuletide Thing, held on December 20, 1968 at the Mid-South Coliseum, came with a good portion of the black population of Memphis's hometown heroes about to take the stage. Enter the The Staples Singers. Moments in I detect a flaw in the sound system, intermittent crackling and voices cutting in and out. A sound system borrowed from a local church, and barely suited for a room of 250 parishioners, but not capable of handling the volume and gospel pulse of the Staples or high-energy Bar-Kays. The locals did not refrain from expressing their displeasure, and sat idly by. They stood and shouted, "Fix the sound; I didn't pay good money for this."

We find ourselves wedged near the middle of the program between Memphis guitar giant Albert King and Carla Thomas. I remember standing in the vicinity of King, watching him tear at his guitar strings, and the piercing sound that accompanied. I also kept an eye on the organist and his set-up, and hoped everything would remain as is. Once on stage, I noticed the organ unplugged and nearly went into a panic. It needed to be rolled back into position, and switched on again. In doing so, I discover a plastic rod leading to one of my preferred drawbars bent upward topside the manual of the Hammond. I stalled until a stage technician arrived with a roll of electrician's tape and temporarily repaired it. I then held my breath. I knew the surrounding audience was not in the mood — or prepared — for equipment malfunctions. As soon as I flip on the Leslie cabinet, the switch plunges to the floor below. More tape, please.

The emcee gives Janis the "big-bump" intro, drawing muted applause. We roll with *Raise Your Hand*, *Piece of My Heart*, and *Summertime*, with the last song being the original I wrote and recorded with Herb Abramson at A-1 Sound in Manhattan, *Hurtin' World*. I introduced *Hurtin' World* to Janis from an acetate I cherished from singer Charlotte Stokes, and informed her Bernard Purdie and J.J. Johnson played on it. Janis loved it. Slow, 6/8, and "churchified."

The performance, with all of Joplin's antics and mad passion, passes with little response. She desperately tried to bridge the divide, with the odds stacked against her. I wrote it off as retaliation for the shit sound system. Even the band, which played with a hint of nervous energy, held it together. I would soon learn there was more in play.

Week's before the event, Janis's face was pasted all over Memphis. She took prominence over all the local heroes, her image blown up and more significant than that of Pops Staples, Carla Thomas, and the others. She was genuinely embarrassed. From one end of Memphis, to the other, her image penetrated the retail landscape. After the concert, a distraught Janis asked around and heard folks were pissed. She was devastated. The insensitive act came through the insistence of her management. Joplin's spirit was renewed later that evening at a party hosted by Stax/Volt president Jim Stewart.

Stewart's sprawling ranch-style house, situated among lush, tree-lined surroundings, was the social epicentre for invitation-only guests from both the black and white communities. Behind these doors, people could mingle without prejudice. The greats— the Memphis singers and musicians — were present. Stewart rigged the various rooms with monster-sized Voice of the Theater speakers. Throughout the night, he played unreleased tapes of Otis Redding, who had perished two years earlier, along with four of the original Bar-Kays, in a plane crash on December 10, 1967. Rivers of tears were shed. As much as it was an occasion to celebrate, it was nearing Christmas Eve, one to which everyone understood the ghost of the great singer would be unable to attend. Otis's music played and played, making the night a sombre, tender occasion. I walked about shaking hands and putting faces to album covers.

Janis calls for the band. We gather at a long table in an adjacent room with Stax president Jim Stewart at the helm. I recognize bassist Donald "Duck" Dunn, guitarist Steve Cropper, Booker T, and beyond that, the night goes dim. Janis introduces each member of the band by name, except me. To her, I'm Jesus. Then she says, "Can you believe, I hired Jesus Christ?" with great warmth and humour. The place erupts in laughter.

The following morning, the band meets for a final get-together. It was indeed one of the saddest moments of my entire life. After returning from the gig, we hear that Janis and Marcus Doubleday had shot up heroin and passed out on top of each other, both found lying in a fetal position. Several days prior, Janis had stopped briefly in Dallas and encountered a young band she recently befriended who bestowed on her a gift box of twelve syringes. Janis remarked that she and Doubleday fought over the distribution of the prize. The thought sickened me. I was ready to move on.

Kristine and I would catch up with Janis in 1970, backstage at the Festival Express in Toronto, when I was opening with my band, Homestead. The first person I recognize from the Kozmic Blues Band was bassist Brad Campbell, then the road manager Mark Bronstein who eventually escorts Janis over. Janis was all laughter and hugs and utterly optimistic. She told us of a new boyfriend, and spoke passionately about detoxing from drugs and sipping a bit of wine. She also appeared happier than anticipated and loved her new group, the Full Tilt Boogie Band, and now in control of where she wanted to go with her career. Blues, folk, rock, and soul music congealed in her heart as she found a genuine medium for expression with the Full Tilt Boogie Band as the perfect conduit. Janis and company came on just before midnight, and from reports, intoxicated and performing a forget-table set.

Janis Joplin died later that year, at age 27. The time I spent in her company covered barely a month, yet so much transpired during that eventful period. Her open-hearted kindness, as well as her naked insecurities, linger in my mind. Above all, I will remember and cherish the sincerity and joy she brought to the music she loved.

40

The Army –
Ft. Knox/Ft. Campbell, KY

The Memphis gig with Janis in the past, I considered reconciling with family. With a return flight to San Francisco booked, I decided on a detour and drop-in for Christmas. I was close to my younger sister Karen, and understood we needed to see each other. Three years apart was an exceptionally long time. Karen was my joy, that loving spirit who could initiate compromise and bring calmness to an otherwise stressful atmosphere. I dialled home, and informed Mom I was visiting over Christmas, and received one of her warm greetings. "But, what are you going to do about the draft?" she asked. I told her I would decide once I thought it over.

I land at Standiford Field, Louisville's then-airport, built by the Army Corps of Engineers in 1941 and neutral ground for repatriation. Cloaked in silence, the pickup and drive home was a sober affair. Few questions were asked about Memphis, and there was relatively little interest in Joplin. Occasionally, Karen would look over at me, squeeze my hand and smile that smile of absolute joy. That evening, the subject of the draft moved to the foreground. I explained why I was debating entering the military, and needed a night to think it over. Both Dad and Mom remained stoic, knowing their son was home, gone for three years, and not the same boy who left by packing up at 19 years of age, living in fear, and sheltering too much anger.

Eight a.m. the following morning, Mom shouts up the stairs and summons me to the living room. I dress, shuffle down past the pine-walled staircase, and am immediately greeted by a man in a dark gray suit, balancing a stack of papers in his hands, "Son, this is so-and-so from the FBI," says Dad. "We've been talking about your situation, and he says he can assure us if you go with him now and stand before a county commissioner, he can get all charges dropped, and you into the army." My first thought? "Holy shit! Did I just hear that? What the hell is going down? Did I just get turned in? It's fucking Christmas, people!"

Dad goes into a story about the FBI guy being the same one who located his stolen Ford in 1949, retrieving it with bullet holes sprinkled back and front. How does one inhale and take a deep breath and not pass out from this weird intervention? Dad and Mom soon abandon the living room, and leave the FBI and me to sort things out. The guy opens a thick dossier and begins, "You know you're in big trouble, and I can resolve this for you. We have been following you for two years across the States, and I know you are a good kid. No trouble here. We could have seized you sooner, but between you and me, the places you went to were hot spots: New York City, L.A., San Francisco, and most enjoyable. Hey, what the hell was this crap about Seattle?" he asks. I thought for a moment, and remembered Scooby, Chuck Berry and drummer Roy Burns at the musician's union in L.A. How Scooby received visitors all the time.

Scooby had set me up with a clinic playing alongside drummer Roy Burns, an absolute monster behind the kit. After which, I walked upstairs to his office. He hand-signals me away from the door; the FBI are camped inside. The G-Men flash photos of suspected draft-evaders as if they were playing cards from a freak deck, and my face appears on one. Scooby excuses himself, pushes past and escorts me down a hallway and asks what he should say. I say, "Tell him I'm living on a commune in Seattle. I moved there months ago."

The guy continues, unveiling a photo of me — a surveillance capture taken along the way. He then says he had spoken with higher-ups at Capitol Records in Hollywood, and insisted they get a message to Linda Ronstadt: if caught in my company, she could be arrested too. Damn! The longer he spoke, I began to see this guy as just a guy, and not a bad one. He then opens a dossier, and retrieves a stack of photos snapped of me walking the streets of various locales across America: in crowds, and just hanging out, as well as pages of accompanying notes. While taking all of this in, he suddenly pops the big question, "Shall we leave and get this over?" I pause long enough to think ahead. I had no beef with the military beyond the war in Vietnam. The long bout living in poverty would now be over. I would have a routine and security, with the heroin queens, junkies, street urchins and pimps all in the rear-view window. I thought about Janis, the slow descent into addiction purgatory, life on the road, and constant fear of the government arresting me, and imprisonment. I agree to his terms.

Other than contracting mononucleosis in college, I had never undergone body trembles of this magnitude. It was one of those "to the bone" icy shivers. Frigid January temperatures in Indiana mixed with high humidity is much like a swim in the wintry Lake Superior. The body shakes for days.

A half-hour passes, when I find myself standing down front of a county commissioner and Mr. FBI, my defense counsel. Working now as my protector, he retells the story of my dad's stolen car, with a bit of embellishment, vouches for my character, and assures the judge I'm not a "runner."

"We've had runners come in here; are you sure you've made up your mind?" asks the commissioner. As quickly as I arrive, the case is settled, and a date arranged for my pick-up and induction into the army: January 2, 1969. I'm to show on that day at Fort Knox, Kentucky, and begin basic training. But beforehand, I'm assigned a session with a psychiatrist in Louisville. Just a formality, I am told.

The session was suspicious. It was as if the outcome was predetermined. I filled out the forms, and checked off box after box of human disease and mental illness, then meet with a military psychiatrist. He questions me about the health mishaps and my mental state, and asks me if I am gay. I thought to myself, why not say yes? I respond in an awkward, unconvincing voice in the affirmative, to which he says, "Great! You'll love the army — so many men to get to know." I had been had!

With the holidays in full swing, I'm shipped to a detention / holding facility, and told I would spend two weeks in custody before being transported to Fort Knox and basic training. Minutes after check-in, I'm assigned a bunk and wall locker. My arrival draws a crowd — the scene resembling something out of one of those *Scared Straight* prison documentaries. Trapped in stage clothes from Janis's gig — brown velour pants, frilly white shirt, brown suede vest, and shoulder-length hair — the odd wardrobe drew a crowd. A gang of certified criminals look me over as if I'm a meat sandwich. Then one speaks up, "You know I could seriously fuck you up." I heard that. "What are you in for?" asks another. I slip past the ringleader and request a call home. I speak with Dad, and advise him of the complicated situation I am facing, and ask him to make every effort to get me out of this place before civil war breaks out. Within an hour, Dad's back, and a deal struck, and me in his custody.

Back home all is quiet, other than Dad raging at protesters: "Commies, commies, commies; send them all to Vietnam." I get a call from jazz educator Jamey Aebersold asking, "I need a pianist for New Year's Eve, you up for it?" That was the best news I had heard since playing Memphis. Music was back in my life, and I am about to be $125 richer.

On the morning of January 2, Dad drives me to a waiting bus. I soon discover I'm the only person in for the ride. Even the driver could not grasp this picture. "You must be someone really important to get a solo ride to Fort Knox," he says. Beyond the window, I examine homes partially hidden by tall grass, watch street signs blow by, and bare-naked trees undressed by seasonal change, and imagine what awaits only a short hour or two down the road. No longer pursued, the slate clean, I thought about the future: the remaining miles deep in thought about the woman I had only recently met and fallen in love with.

Military police greet me at the front gates of Fort Knox, peruse my documents, then escort me to orientation. Along the way, I am yelled at and dressed down for wearing flashy clothing and excessive hair length, yet never felt physically threatened, unlike at the holding centre. A physical follows, including a heart exam. I'm then cautioned of electrical irregularities surrounding the heart, a blocked main artery, courtesy of a birth defect. A medical officer warns me, "By your 50s, you'll likely face open-heart surgery." Initially, I thought it was the army fucking with me; then I remembered our medical history: my mother's side, the heart attacks, strokes, loss of life, and I decided to heed the warning, and always take care of my body.

In my new digs, beyond the ground-floor window, and nestled somewhere between numerous rectangular buildings all the same character and size, I look out the window and count 40 horizontal white planks all similar in width and distance from each other. At least that is how they appear through the modest-sized window angled a few feet above my assigned bunk. The following morning, I'm greeted with insults, compliments of a moronic corporal. I'm informed that a plan had been hatched to trolley me to the post barber, summon the post newspaper and a photographer, then record and bear witness to the shaving of a draft-dodging hippie head.

Late night and on fire-watch, I kept an eye on sleeping recruits throughout the 3 a.m. to 4 a.m. shift. Moments earlier, I had swiped a razor blade and slipped it into a shirt pocket. Halfway through duty time, I disappear into a back washroom, face a long mirror, and begin shredding the long locks. I give myself one of those JFK Ivy league haircuts then slide back into bed. Early the next morning, I hear my name echo over the house sound system, ordered to stand at attention next to a footlocker, and introduced to my appointed guardians, two grizzled looking drill instructors. "I was told we had ourselves a hippie," one says to the other? The corporal arrives. "You fucking asshole motherfucker! Where'd that long hair go?" Drill instructor number two: "You are a hippie, aren't you?" I respond, "No, sir, I'm a piano player."

"We had fucking great plans for you, you know. Why did you fuck this up?" I pause, then say, "Sir, I grew tired of the look and was thinking about something different." That did not play well. From under the brim of his wide hat, the older of the two stares back at me, coughs, spits what looks like a half-infected slug onto the tiled floor, and starts laughing. The other throws me a stinging eye-to-eye rebuke, then threatens to bury me in the woods. "I reserve the right to shoot you later; now, get the fuck out of my sight," he says. I watched as the two exit the hallway and poke fun at one another.

The next morning, our company is called upon to give blood. Lined up in a dimly lit hallway, and about to be frog-marched, I hear my name come blasting from an overhead speaker, "Private King, come to the office!" I'm thinking, here it comes, the stockade. The same pissed-off corporal walks me down a corridor barking in my ear, "You are so fucked, trainee." I must admit to harbouring overwhelming fear. "Private King, have a seat," says this black drill instructor. "I want to welcome you to basic training, and if you keep your nose clean, you'll be all right." Seriously? Is this real? "I've been looking through your papers, and it says you studied with Oscar Peterson and Ray Brown. Is that true?" "Yes, sir," I say. "Ray Brown is my hero. I have his bass method book and play like him. What's he like?" I go about explaining my time at the Advanced School of Contemporary Music and how Brown would lug his bass in my practice room, and we would play. "Good God almighty, you played with Ray Brown. Sergeant, King here played with Ray Brown, and now he's the new piano player in our jazz trio. Ain't that right, King? Why don't we take off and jam awhile?" That moment I quickly advanced from a failed poster boy to a celebrated piano man. The jam session was decent; the sergeant could play and walk a rock-bottom groove. The drummer, passable. From that moment on, I had me a guardian angel!

It was the next encounter that gave me a clear view of the men who made a career of training soldiers. Marines had it much worse. We heard the stories and were warned of the conditions and the brutality many were subjected to during basic training at Parris Island, South Carolina. If you harmed a recruit at Fort Knox, you could face a court-martial. The scenario played out during boot camp when a rumour circulated of a drill instructor, long after training hours, forcing a recruit to crawl through freezing mud in wet clothing, abused, and humiliated. He was eventually reprimanded and dismissed.

The next six weeks were spent mostly crawling belly-down through slippery mud and across frozen earth, hands trembling from the wet and cold. It was the depths of frigid January, with rarely a day of golden sunlight. Up at 5 a.m., five minutes to down a plateful of eggs and "shit on a stick" as it was fondly identified, then marched in cadence to some remote wooded area. We jogged, climbed, stabbed, and attacked dummies with a bayonet. Cleaned rifles, scrubbed floors — things you do to prepare for combat. Our platoon was a mix of college draftees, hillbillies, and guys who just wanted to kill something. I got on well with most everybody, and soon realized I was somewhat of a legend: the guy who beat the system by chopping off his locks — nothing to do with music. I was also in far better physical shape than most. I regularly played basketball on one of the world's most prestigious testing grounds, 3rd Avenue in Greenwich Village, next to the legends of the game at that time. There were days I would show up barefoot, run the asphalt and blister the soles of my feet. I would start mornings lifting weights, and continue throughout the day. Friends would drop by the flat and I would converse while twisting arm curls. One crazy obsession! Whenever possible, I would swim lengths. By day, I walked and walked and walked — the body one long, toned muscle.

Then the conversation turns to the war in Vietnam. I asked each non-commissioned officer the same question throughout orientation, "Why are we in Vietnam?" Most would say, "To stop communism from coming to our shores." I would respond, "But the Vietnamese are mostly farmers, and don't have enough money to buy an airplane ticket here." This line of questioning played out during my six weeks in boot camp until the older of my two drill instructors, Sergeant Fruehauf, calls me to his office and says, "King, I can't answer your question. I just want to do my time, and get the fuck out of here without seeing Vietnam ever again, then collect my pension. You've got to end that line of questioning. I get you, and understand where you are coming from. Just do the time!" That was the second-most human contact I had with my custodians. Another sergeant pulled me aside during bayonet drills and asked, "Have you ever done acid?" I just laughed. "You know," he says, "We had a guy here last year who had these flash-backs, and he wanted to stab everything that moved. He was an acid head, you know. You sure you're alright?" I asked him why he thought that. He responds, "We've read your psychiatric records. Damn, you've had every disease, did every drug, and completely insane, right?" I just smiled. "I knew it, knew it; you were bullshitting," he says with a grin.

Mail arrived every other day like clockwork. A young recruit would yell "mail call," and a letter would magically appear from Kristine. I would curl the precious envelope, retreat from sight, read and re-read, spread the stack of letters across my bed, memorize my favourite passages, and count the days when we would see each other again. Kristine's words were sincere and clothed in affection, and as difficult as life had become, I was fully prepared for the days ahead. The years roaming the side-streets of America—at times homeless, at times on the run and most times consumed with music—made this interlude seem almost bearable, the next chapter about to be written. I had the security of a bed, food, no serious worries, great guys around me, a world outside squeezing politicians to bring an end to war, and a beautiful woman who cared about me. I prayed the war would cease before my two years were up.

Alabama Fred, a black recruit from Birmingham, and a couple of his friends and I would gather in the men's room and sing, "*I was born in a bunk, mama died, and my daddy got drunk, left me here to die alone, in the middle of Tobacco Road.*" We were sons of tobacco farmers. I'd retell stories my dad told me of running moonshine through the backwoods of Tennessee and Kentucky; Fred and his pals would speak of their folks, the sharecroppers and the ones who hid those moonshine stills in the foothills of the Deep South. The guys questioned me about my musical life. I said little or revealed much of my former self, not intentionally, but out of humility. There was no reason to address the hillbillies or even my instructors of my profession, until I felt confident there would not be any bitterness or suspicion. I would eventually tell them about Janis, the finale in Memphis, and let it go.

The weeks ahead were all about physicality and bonding. I gained a good 40 pounds of muscle. I left New York weighing 165 pounds, now pushing 210, and excelling at every athletic demand. I understood my body and endurance. I also kept in mind the hardships and uncertainty of living without. Three decent meals, brotherhood and security have a way of muzzling doubt.

Only days in, a first altercation flares. It started with a black recruit from Detroit who decides a change of scenery is needed, and moves his duffel bag loaded with personal effects to a bed presently occupied by some poor clucking farm boy. I heard, "What chu doin' n.......," a pause, then "Whack!" A body meets the floor. I'm serious. A "farm boy" spouts the N-word then swallows Detroit's fist in one gulp. The incident came fast, few words spoken. Most recruits quietly circled the victim and stared. Detroit then flings himself on a bunk of his choice, nonchalantly wraps his thick fingers around the back of the head and eyeballs the pack. Two guys lift farm boy upright, and then escort him to his new digs a level above.

A momentary hush smothers the room as another farm boy goes about plugging in a radio. We were forbidden to have any conveniences, and certainly not any entertainment device during training. I wondered what the hell the guy was thinking. You could hear the frantic movement of the radio dial shift left to right, and then familiar twanging guitars and sad yarns. Fiddle, steel guitar and the melancholy voice of Eddy Arnold singing *Make the World Go Away*. I wasn't prepared for this, maybe some Bob Wills and a little Texas swing, but not one of those sobbing middle-of-the-road hillbilly ballads. Just as the music settles, I spot Detroit unwind to the size of a tall redwood, walk over, rip the cord from the wall, and coolly walk away with the radio. He placed it bedside, and then plugged it in — an invitation for punishment. Detroit fumbles the dial, then locates a rhythm & blues show out of Louisville. Farm boy number two makes a play at retrieving the stolen item, when Detroit leaps from a crouched position, and smacks him dead centre in the face, causing farm boy to topple and kiss a half dozen dirt-soiled planks. A crowd gathers, passively watches, whispers between themselves. One brave soul says, "I'll get the MPs."

"Bring your sorry ass over here, milk boy," bellows Detroit. I couldn't believe I heard the remark, not that that kind of trash talk did not occur on most basketball courts. Detroit simply did not care. I couldn't figure for the life of me why anyone would put himself in such a tenuous position with what I perceived to be a genuinely punitive military system. We were just numbers to be memorized; no more, no less. Why serve more time than necessary, was my mantra.

"No motherfucker ever sending me to Vietnam, so fuck all of you," a voice comes booming off the walls. The ominous declaration freezes activity, suppressing all conversation. Two MPs and a drill sergeant arrive and work their way into Detroit's company. "Get up, soldier, and come with us," the drill sergeant commands. "Fuck you, motherfuckers! They should send every one of you cracker-ass hillbillies to Vietnam where you belong." A good 30-second interval passes when I hear, "Get up, soldier!" We all leave the security of our bunks to witness the standoff. "You corn-husking goat fucker — there ain't no way you gonna send me to Vietnam; it's a white-boy fight and nothing to do with us black folk. I told them when they picked me up and brought me here; you weren't sending me to that shithole." Detroit reclines, stares back at the three men standing in a uniformed circle. They quickly lunge forward, overpower and cuff him. Detroit offered little resistance. I watch as they drag him away, trying to make sense of the ordeal. You would never mistake the guy for an anti-war protester or Martin Luther King Jr. disciple. The guy lived by street code, not military. With only a few blacks out of 200 men in our company, many Southern recruits freely spouted racial slurs. Guys would "tough talk" miles from the safety of their neighbourhood, pool hall or girlfriend, absent any threat to themselves. That is sort of the way the barracks transformed itself in Detroit's absence.

As calm was about to set in. A voice from behind spoke, "You should have taken that guy, hippie. You some kind of coward or something?" Here it comes, friends of John Wayne riding tall in the saddle. I'd heard those lines a thousand times before, and in no need of reviewing any of my recent travels. "I didn't see any of you big peckerheads stand up for either one of us so-called farm boys," says the second victim, whose nose by now is swollen to the size of a well-fed pig's snout. "Whose radio was it? Punks like that back down when you show some spine," spouts another. Right! I thought about those somewhat naive remarks, and the kind of men they most likely face in an environment much like Detroit's hometown. I know for a fact, nine out of ten times, farm boys talk the talk but run even faster.

Three days pass, and we're just getting back from a second day of physicals when I see Detroit stretched horizontal on his bunk. I could not believe my eyes and then he says to me in a menacing tone, "What the fuck you looking at, you fish-eyed fool?" I quickly drop my head, and tend to personal matters before the room fills with more trainees, each within view of the company bully. "I told you motherfuckers, I ain't going to no Vietnam. That's a tourist destination for dumb-ass white boys. Where is that shit-digger that called the police on me? I'm going to fuck him up good." Everybody froze in position. "Where's the little shit who called the cops?' No one muttered a sound until one large white boy says, 'Nobody holding you here, why don't you just take off?' Detroit pauses then replies, "If I leave here right now, they come for me. If I stay, I get to fuck you up. Which do you prefer?" Detroit was wired to the same current that managed undue pain. "I tell you, bring five of your baddest white boys, and I'll fight all of you — right here, right now. I swear I'll stuff your lungs up in your brains before you land a punch. Any of you pussies ever see Sonny Liston fight?" The room falls silent. "No, I guess not. You white boys been waiting for Roy Rogers to slug it out with Tonto, haven't you? I'm the baddest dude in Detroit. I bet you white boys fuck goats and chickens. The hell with all of you pussies." Just as I thought, no takers. The room silenced. Detroit sleeps.

It was now 19:00 hours, and lights out. I've never in my life climbed in bed at seven in the evening. Even the thought seemed absurd. The same could be said for the rest of the room. Lights dimmed, but sexual fantasies spread. Plenty cheap talk about fondling a pair of large orgasmic female breasts, and the ever-popular elusive snapping pussy, described in gruesome detail. The narrative evoked this visual image of a large turtle's head covered in a thin membrane lurking about in search of piping hot male genitalia. Twenty minutes pass when I hear, "Fuck this shit, I'm getting a beer and something to eat. Which one of you fools going with me to the PX?" At this stage, we weren't allowed to even possess a candy bar, let alone leave the barracks in pursuit of sustenance. "Anyone with me? Come on, white boys; I'll buy two of you chicken-humpers a beer." I look up and see Detroit's immense black silhouette blocking the firelight. "Yeah, I'll go," shouts a voice from back of the hall. "Hey, me too, just as long as you buy me a cold Bud and not any of that near-beer piss they try to pass off." I liked the cockiness in the room, the disregard for authority.

As the party exits, the room buzzes. "Who's got the balls to do the same? I've got five dollars for anyone who'll buy me a chocolate bar and a beer." "I'll match that," yells this grunt they called Mishap. (Don't ask me why Mishap.) A bidding war ensues. I thought about it and made a play. "Over here. I'll do it." Suddenly, I'm swamped with orders, "Two Baby Ruths, a bag of salted pretzels. Over here! I'll have five Clark bars and some licorice twists." On and on and on. By the time I was prepped to leave, I'd collected over $25 dollars, a quarter of that profit. Since we only made $52 the first month, I had myself spending money. Why $52? The army kept the other $40 for the basics given on entry, namely clothes, toothpaste, brush, comb, boots, etc.

While everyone keeps a lookout, I slip out the back door, stumble past a dozen or so poorly lit barracks, and remind myself to remember where my tracks lay. Unfortunately, the PX, located in an area a great distance from our quarters, and out of our designated zone, challenged my sense of direction. With mind focused on the mission, and aware of military police, I invent a host of excuses, each designed to bluff my way past security. "Yes sir, I'm just out of basic training and awaiting assignment to my next

company. Just dropped in for a nightcap and a couple of apples."
Fortunately, I never had to deliver the speech.

As I cracked open the PX doors, I could not help noticing
Detroit and the two farm recruits inhaling beers and downing
hot dogs. "Fuck, look who's here? It's motherfucking fish-eyes.
Let me buy you a beer before I toss your smelly ass back in the
creek." Knowing full well something unexpected could erupt in
Detroit's presence, I pass on the offer and go about the business
of collecting samples.

While cashing out, I notice this MP come face to face with
Detroit, then words fly. I quickly secure the goods, slip past the
conversation, and then sprint out the exit ahead of both. To avoid
conflict, I decide to try an alternate route back to the barracks.
Two blocks out, a voice yells from behind, "Trainee, what the
hell are you doing in my neighbourhood?" I slow down, and face
the broad-brimmed hat. "I'll ask you again. What the hell are
you doing in my neighbourhood?" I hesitate, then reply, "Sir, I
think I'm lost." "I'll ask you again, soldier, what are you doing
on my property?" I straighten up, then answer, "Sir, just waiting
for my new assignment." With a keen eye, the man inspects then
squeezes his chin. "It looks to me like you haven't learned much
in basic training. I can't for the life of me see how they'd accept
such a pathetic-looking mistake as you.' He pauses, looks downward, tilts the brim of his hat, "You know, they'll take anyone in
the army. Fucking Westmoreland!" I prayed the sergeant would
not insist on inspecting my laundry bag. The guy just stood
there, massaging a patch of morning stubble, before looking up.
"I ought to ram a boot right up your ass; get the hell out of here."
I turn to veer left, then hear, "Hold it!" He laughs. "Tell them
when they measure you for your next uniform to fit you with an
extra-large body bag,"

I ignore him, and quickly sprint past row after row of undistin-
guished buildings bathed in precisely the same quality of light,
until I see a familiar face hanging out a side window. "Over here,
King. You've got to climb through the window — the sergeant's
awake. You know the MPs are out looking for that black dude
from Detroit." I climbed through with all the goods, and am

greeted like a butcher in a lion's den.

While savouring the catch, the barracks door springs open, and two MPs bust through. "Have any of you seen so-and-so?" No one recognized the name, until one of the farm boys walks forward and asks, "You mean that black troublemaker from Detroit?" "That's right. Where is he? " "Sorry sir, none of us have seen him all night; we've been sleeping." The reply was unacceptable. The MP says, "My ass, you haven't been sleeping. Look at all those candy wrappers around your bed and that chocolate smeared about your nose?" The time of reckoning had arrived. "You know I could pop your ass for that contraband. I could search every one of you pissants and lock your sorry asses behind bars." That's when the crazy talk starts. "Every one of you could do five years in Leavenworth for disobeying a company ordinance. Do I smell beer farts?" Five years in Leavenworth, I thought. You've got to kill a soldier, steal a tank, or drown someone in the kitchen grease pit to earn that amount of time.

Just as things were about to get more heated, two additional MPs bust into the room and march upstairs. The next moment I see Detroit in cuffs. It was spooky and totally disturbing. I was anticipating another tirade about black men in Vietnam, but not a sound. Detroit left gently, like someone who'd been injected with morphine or clubbed over the head.

I spent the next two weeks sloshing about with rifle and pack deep in snow — hands numb, half-frozen from mud and sleet, my brain disoriented from instruction and standard military ridicule. "Trainee, if your girlfriend saw you now, she'd think you were a circus clown." At first, the words felt a bit demoralizing, but once you get a feel for the game, you put pride on remote, and count down the days and forget the nonsense.

The rumours flourished about Detroit: he was accused of beating a half dozen MPs, a couple of drill sergeants, and a full-bird colonel. I suspected they had packed him away in a dingy cell, hoping he'd plead for mercy. It is 16:00 hours when we arrive safely back in the barracks. I notice a tight group of about 15 soldiers huddled in conversation. One soldier spots me, and gestures me over. "Did you hear? Detroit's coming back to our unit tomorrow." I thought to myself, someone's bullshitting. "They want him to finish up so they can dump his black ass in Vietnam," one of the farm boys proudly states. "Aw, the shit's gonna get wild." Farm boy was on the money. At 18:00 hours, Detroit strolls in a free man. "Fuck all of you white motherfuckers. Nobody can keep me down a hole for long." At that moment, I sensed things were about to get worse, and even more unpredictable. I could read the rage and anger, from his eyes to his heart. Detroit, I surmised, had no recourse other than a significant act of defiance or worse to save his ass from Vietnam.

This lanky jerk from Arkansas kept goading another recruit, questioning his masculinity, earning him a surprise night visit. It was nearing 3 a.m. when I hear this loud smack, a blood-curdling scream, then a crashing sound. I spring to the edge of the bed, and spy someone fleeing the room, then hear a plea for help and cries of agonizing pain the length of the building. Someone then switches the overhead light on, and I recognize Arkansas trying to cover eyes, nose spurting blood through cupped fingers. At first, I thought it was a minor cut, but on close inspection, I could see the volume of blood. It was apparent that Arkansas had accidentally fallen from the top bunk to the floor, but we would soon learn he was a victim of a "boot to the face," a popular army scheme for settling scores. You fill a combat boot with water, catch a guy napping, then whack him dead centre to the nose. That will get you a quick trip to the emergency room — blurred vision, and a nose the size of a ripe pear. No charges laid.

Detroit continued to hang around the barracks like a foul smell, refusing to participate in any formal instruction. Orders were to leave him alone, and let war own him. Every time we'd return from training sessions, Detroit would be yelling, "Look at the white boys, gonna kill some yellow boys while I'm here fucking your white girlfriends — now ain't that a bitch." Those were not exactly the most encouraging words, but we'd gotten used to the profanity and daily pronouncements.

Week five began with me submerged in a foxhole firing an M1 rifle locked on a target a hundred or so yards away. They could have pasted a 50-foot bullseye on a nearby building, and I'd still have planted more slugs in a nearby tree. I have no talent for marksmanship. Every time I hoist the clumsy firearm, condensation would engulf my glasses. I'd try cleaning with a rag or palm of my glove, but it only made matters worse. I could not concentrate, and would fire at targets three rows over for the hell of it. I still hadn't made up my mind about Vietnam, or the army, other than cracking up at these buffed drill sergeants swaggering around like 5-star generals. The army was the army; war was a different matter.

I thought about what Detroit had to say, and watched a lot of nightly news reports, with all the casualties we'd been suffering, and hippies out there acting like we could win the war smoking pot, passing out daffodils and dropping hits of acid. I couldn't make up my mind. Some days I think this place was not so wrong; at others, I think my brain was about to explode.

We were returning to the barracks, and look at an ambulance and several military police officers rushing about; the area cordoned off from spectators and not allowed near the barracks. Some 15 minutes pass before I see this stretcher come out — six men in white holding bottles and tubing all around. I heard there was a tourniquet placed around a soldier's neck and blood spilled all over. Everyone was frantically trying to maneuver the wounded soldier into the back of the ambulance. I had this morbid sense that death had already spoken. My intuition was unfounded. There was much bloodshed, but the soldier survived the attack, thanks to the quick actions of another recruit who applied a tourniquet. It was a sickening moment, one forever etched in the soul. It was a prelude to war, and possibly my future.

None of us knew for sure who cut who. Some thought it was the work of Detroit. I surmised it would take nothing short of murder to save him from Vietnam. I could not for the life of me get a handle this. Why he cut this young man's throat, no one knew for sure. The memory will always haunt me. Graduation day, the army awarded a soldier from our company a medal for assisting the wounded soldier as we paused for a moment in silence. Later, it was rumoured Detroit was shipped off to Fort Leavenworth and held in a facility for dangerous offenders, then shipped on to Vietnam.

Six weeks of basic training ended, and it was time to figure out a military occupation. I was told music auditions were coming, and I should sign up. I knew I wasn't equipped to service tanks or become an officer candidate. An interview is arranged, me hoping to hook up with an army band. The test took all of 10 minutes. I sight read, soloed, and easily passed the exam. Within days, I learned I would be on my way to Fort Campbell, Kentucky, and the 82nd Army Band. It seemed the post required a pianist. Then someone higher up in the military food chain decides to give the ex-hippie one last slap upside the head.

I find myself assigned to a spinal meningitis ward for two weeks. A severe outbreak plagued the post, and I am charged with overseeing hygiene for two buildings. I worked out schedules, washed and cleaned rooms, and tried to keep a distance from the contagious disease. It is the middle of May, with temperatures pushing the high 90s, and I'm now trapped in a scene out of one of those art films I caught at the Waverly Theater on 6th Avenue in the Village. A film where soldiers are stationed in some remote malaria-infected jungle; each bed partitioned with a thick, white see-through scrim, and promises of a sweat-soaked nightmare. Next stop, Fort Campbell, Kentucky, and the 81st Army Band and 101st Airborne Division.

Fort Campbell, Kentucky, only a 3-hour drive from Abraham Lincoln's cabin, had much in common with its proximity to the Tennessee border. It was not like I was entering unfamiliar territory. May 2, 1966, Third Army General Order 161 directed the activation of a Basic Combat Training Center at Fort Campbell, Kentucky. The post was built in 1941.

Moments after my arrival, I'm in new housing connected to the 81st Army Band, a far cry and more welcoming than the intimidating atmosphere of boot camp at Fort Knox, Kentucky. A refrigerated Coca-Cola vending machine with 12 oz. bottles of Coca-Cola at a nickel a snap stood just inside the doorway, in what was called the day room of my new barracks. It was something familiar and calming to see. High above, a television blared soap operas and games of chance. A pool table with soldiers arranged about like marionettes, each taking a turn sinking the one surviving eight ball — other service members lounging about, smoking everything from Camels to Winstons, and all dodging the oppressive temperatures outside.

I'm the new guy in motion, shaking hands and soaking up the warm reception. Then a voice from the wilderness shouts, "You're that draft dodger, ain't you?" I pause, then reply, "I'm a soldier like everyone in this room." The voice responds, "No offence, man, that's cool. Sergeant Rowe says you are a celebrity of sorts. You played with all of those stars. He read your files."

First up, a meet-and-greet with Staff Sergeant Rowe, second in command, and his band of merry men. I assumed Rowe was "well-oiled" the moment I caught a view of his closely cropped, brush-cut hair, swollen face, and "heart-attack red" skin; quite possibly a victim of one too many 40-ouncers. Rowe extends his big mitt for a handshake. "I guess you know what your job is?" he asks. "Not exactly," I respond. Rowe shuffles a few papers. "It says here of your MOS (military occupational specialty) that you're the new post pianist. That is one coveted occupation, don't you think?" I'm thinking how cool this is. No marching or concert band, a few gigs here and there, then back to civilian life. "So, what does the post pianist do," I ask? "Whatever the man in charge decides." The man in charge happens to be Chief Warrant Officer "Iggy" Ignacio, from Honolulu, Hawaii, a former band-master at the Naval School of Music, and one clever/cunning survivor. "He'll see you now," says Rowe.

Ignacio lays the hard-ass, no-nonsense bullshit talk on me, then asks, "Have you ever played for bigwigs?" I tell him plenty, some more notable than others. "If you keep your nose clean, you'll be playing in the homes of the most important people on this base: generals, colonels, and majors. And all I have to say to you is, don't fuck up." Ignacio pauses, then looks directly at me. "Get rid of those civilian glasses, and switch to army issue. You hear me?" All through basic training, I wore aviator glasses, and drew a fair amount of grief for doing so. It was my only fashion connection with my diminished rebel self. Ignacio arranges a visit to the post optometrist for an examination. Not long after, a new pair of geeky-looking glasses arrive, which did nothing to enhance my look. My best defense against wearing them? "Sir, the prescription is fucked up. I can't even see my hands." This scenario played out the entire time I was in the military. Ignacio would catch a glimpse of me coming and going, and yell "Kinggggggggg," a bellowing howl rattling the building. "Didn't I tell you to change those glasses? Are you ignoring me, soldier?" Patience and persistence guaranteed victory in this stand-off.

Television then, as today, played a prickly roll in illuminating our differences. From the day room, we watched actress Lucille Ball mock longhairs, and perform some mindless skits about hippies. Vice-President Spiro Agnew stamped longhairs and anti-war protesters as the enemies of America, and subversives. Not far behind, evangelical Christians took the lead in condemning and playing the patriot card, a far different mindset than the anti-war Catholics. Life was unreasonably complicated. You were either a draft dodger, unrepentant radical, or possibly a commie. I gained a decent read on the region and people caught behind political battle lines.

Down south, men were men; some good ole boys, others children born of neighbours, uncles and aunts, and dirt miserable. Some spent hours collecting hubcaps, snoozing in lawn chairs, locked to the bleachers of a ball diamond, lost in a backroom card game, or inside a pickup truck crammed with other gun-toting crazies. Back then, men's desires were as complicated as the contents of canned soup, and easy prey for parasitic politicians. Most wished someone would just say they looked good, and recognize them as the breadwinner in the household.

After being assigned a bunk, room, and locker, I calmly greet my fellow bandmates. One who called himself Gettier, from San Diego, took an interest in me. Steve Gettier was counting down the final days of service as a member of the concert band, then processed and released. Steve served a year in Vietnam. You want to know about war, what it was like on the ground and all around, just hang with someone only days back from the theatre of war. Gettier was somewhat crazy, sometimes in a good way, and at others, in need of psychiatric care. He hated

Ignacio — called him Pineapple. Initially, I thought he meant that as a term of affection, but decades later when we reconnected on Facebook, I surmised he was an avowed racist with a terrible habit of calling the Obamas "monkeys." That's when the block feature came in handy.

Gettier escorted me everywhere, and when the urge struck, laughed insanely. I diagnosed the strange affliction as "mind debris" left behind from Vietnam. Steve played trumpet and talked Miles Davis, more a fan than a player. Gettier also spoke endlessly of his own experiences in Vietnam and those episodes that found him in perpetual conflict with commanding officers. For a brief period, he was a driver for those designing offensive strategies, there to escort polished brass from one command post to another. After being shot at, Gettier purposely ingratiated himself with everyone. That got himself unceremoniously dropped in rice patties amongst tall grass for up to six weeks at a time, with a collection of paperback books, a rifle, supplies and surrounded by fields of "get high" pot. Gettier saw the war mostly stoned. His passion? Kung Fu.

My closest pal was a draftee high school teacher named Ron Sullivan, an educator from Aliquippa, Pennsylvania. Ron played sax, and had a monstrous sense of humour and high intellect. We talked a bit of music, but the heart of our conversations were current affairs: Lyndon Johnson, Kissinger, Nixon, and the most pressing issue — war! Ron and I theorized how and when the endgame would play out. Would the North Vietnamese come to the table and engage, trust negotiator Henry Kissinger, and call an end to war? Or carry on another decade or so? We had heard rumours of peace treaties in play, yet recognized the manipulative games politicians' pushed for political gain.

The politics of war is very much a sinister chess game and, for most, ends in a stalemate. An uninformed public follows order. Toying with the lives of the extremely poor and minorities, the draftees and committed men and women in uniform, was, from where we stood, a privately negotiated scam between the well-heeled and the well-connected. Ron and I, and those around us with life experience and acquired knowledge of the charade, debated the course each should take to defend our own lives. We were aware politicians serving in Washington and throughout the country, in statehouses, and on Capitol Hill, could easily shield a son or relative: place a call to the well-connected, and have a child either reassigned a sweet desk job in Germany or removed from the draft entirely. Big-money deferments were the game. Vietnam was a numbers game. General Westmoreland commanded American forces in Vietnam from 1964-1968, and talked small victories and body count. It was as if he operated his own neon "death scoreboard," designed for political gain and news-hungry Americans. There was always confusion about whether we were fighting to discourage the Vietnamese from surfacing in America and turning Rhode Island into a communist foothold or nation-building. An NCO I grew to knew as an administrative assistant to our company commander retold his experiences in Vietnam to me.

"There were nine army bands deployed throughout Vietnam. Much of the duty time as a musician was spent cleaning a rifle, burying bodies, and fighting off a variety of jungle-related diseases, a fair portion of that time spent getting high. I lived with an open wound. One that would not heal no matter the treatment. The open sore leaked a pus-like substance, and never closed. While serving in the band, I was sent ahead of doctors and nurses under the guise of inoculating villagers from diseases. When marching, clarinets were pushed upfront, saxophones, then trumpets, heavy brass, and far behind, percussion marched forward, playing patriotic songs; then, all hell would break loose. On occasion, the front line was ambushed, leaving the clarinetists either dead or injured." It was much like a scene out of Francis Ford Coppola's 1979 movie *Apocalypse Now.* Our company, connected to the 101st Cavalry Airborne Division, expected results. More bodies to count. Each month we would rotate housekeeping duty, a component of that assignment: mopping and waxing the front offices. I'm sweeping and sloshing near the gentleman's desk, and inadvertently notice a trash can filled with discarded Benylin bottles. I open a lower desk drawer, and recognize a collection of 30 or more capped bottles of codeine cough syrup, and knew this guy was hurting!

The next while, music was my focus. I played private parties, banged brass cymbals during marching and concert band, and copped a few paying gigs off the post. During my stay, it was revealed I played clarinet, an instrument I excelled at in high school— one for which I collected numerous awards in state and regional competitions. I purposely hid that fact, knowing I would be called on to march, something I did with less skill than a man with two broken legs. When word leaked out, Ignacio auditioned me, and then awarded me first chair, within striking distance of his baton and observant eye. The consolation prize: playing the same arrangements from *The Sound of Music* that I played in the high-school band.

Beyond the front gates, a long row of pawnshops and shady drinking holes, a region where Jimi Hendrix and bassist Bill Cox, later of the Band of Gypsies, jammed. Hendrix was part of the 101st Airborne Division, and, from what was said on the base, injured himself during a parachute jump. Hendrix reportedly snapped an ankle and was let go. The records say otherwise: that Hendrix had been forced to serve, and was mostly incorrigible, then was released. Hendrix played the same row of bars, leaving a trail of women awaiting his return.

There was a lifer, an older African-American sergeant named Frank, who liked to talk jazz and blues with me. Frank played the bars, and would occasionally hire me to swing some blues on the organ. He was comfortable with the routine, and secure in his job with the military, and there until retirement. A lot of Lou Donaldson, Jazz Crusaders, and old rhythm & blues in his setlist: *Honky-Tonk* and *Kansas City*, which were crowd favourites. Frank and I would sit around the day room and talk albums. Big jazz recordings like Gene Ammons, Miles and Coltrane — mostly soul-jazz. There wasn't too much that could rile or disturb Frank. The army was his day job, and at night he'd completely vanish.

I am hanging near the front door of one of these roadside beer halls, and chatting with this seemingly 9-foot-tall bouncer sporting a cowboy hat and menacing scowl, when this brush-cut paratrooper blows past, and refuses to show ID. The legal age for drinking then was 21. The big guy shouts him down. Then the two converge in front of a table thick with empty beer bottles. They exchange obscenities, prompting the cocky trooper to take a swipe at the doorman. In one move, the big guy lifts and drops the paratrooper on his head, then stomps dead centre on the guy's chest. Out cold! He then lifts the guy over his right shoulder, carries him outside, and tosses him on a pile of gravel near a row of motorcycles. The guy comes to, jumps on a motorbike, and accelerates into oncoming traffic, where he's hit dead-on, and thrown violently into the middle the road. The last scene was a half-dozen military police and an ambulance blocking the highway, and the poor sod loaded into the back of the medical vehicle.

Kristine arrives from Long Island, and finds herself in the middle of thousands of sex-starved servicemen. The episode could have been the makings of a World War III, or maybe an Italian cinema classic. Kristine came with intentions of staying. Her appearance was so overwhelming that the guy who drove us back from the airport refused to make eye contact. The two of us agreed to give it one year, and see where the relationship landed. I failed to notify my superiors of our intentions.

A first walk around the base drew a posse of soldiers. The crew marched alongside, laughing, smiling, curious, with plenty of questions from post library to PX (Post Exchange), focused mostly on Kristine. The coolest thing about this scenario: Kristine knew how to manage, entertain, keep the men off-guard and on good behaviour. Only days in, our company of men became protective of her. Most had never met a woman as liberated, one from New York who spoke openly about anything that came to mind, and without being condescending or demeaning. Kristine became one of the boys, the company mascot! As the weeks and months passed, Kristine assumed a position of rank. She was invited everywhere, and expected to show. Most southern women took a back seat to their spouses, and usually agreed with whatever the man cooked up. Not Kristine! There was no debating her views on the Vietnam War. When face to face in those encounters, one must come fully equipped with answers.

You could sense May was a prelude to a long hot summer, and

Kristine and I were invited to share apartment #103 at 507 Greenwood Avenue in Clarksville, Tennessee, with Gettier. At first, we occupied a cot stuffed in a far corner of a room, where the two of us wildly entertain ourselves until Gettier offers to swap his bed for the folding cot. Our schedules were as such that Kristine and I would spend off-duty hours together.

I had PX privileges, and could purchase most supplies at a discount. The PX also had the best collection of vinyl recordings, and it was the most up-to-date selection I had seen since relieving Tower Records in San Francisco of nearly all monaural Blue Note jazz sides during my short time with Janis. Our base store had copies of Crosby, Stills, & Nash, Blood, Sweat, & Tears (*Child Is Father to the Man*), jazzman Gary Bartz (*Libra*), and Richard Harris (*MacArthur Park*). Kris brought with her several well-played Laura Nyro sides, a Jefferson Airplane, The Temptations, and Smokey Robinson. The apartment blared sweet soul music from the rooftop to the street below.

We shared the rustic Greenwood Avenue house with an eclectic mix of service members who stayed mostly out of sight and huddled with their girlfriends. Kristine and I had the upstairs to ourselves. The walls to our room papered floor to ceiling in a floral print, from vines to fading greens. The bed? A wrought-iron implement of torture. The space? Expansive, sunny, and inviting. The nearest window looked down on trees thick with the leaves of summer, shading the children at play in a nearby schoolyard.

In the ensuing months, Kristine and I would hitchhike away from the base, travelling the back roads and towns farther south, engaging with everyone. Hitchhiking for us was much like summoning a taxi. Kristine would stand roadside with thumb extended. Me? Off-road and out of sight. A car would pull near, Kristine would climb halfway in and ask whoever was steering to wait and say, "Hold it, my husband is just behind me." Hilarious, but it worked.

A 3-day pass arrives, and Kristine and I agree to visit my Aunt Marjorie, now married for the first time at age 63 to a blind man, 70 years of age. Marjorie, who had been a servant and spinster most of her adult life, moved to the small southern hamlet of

Dresden, Tennessee, only 83 miles south of Clarksville, Tennessee. We quickly hitch a ride with a lovely woman decked in a sunbonnet, who says, "You can get in, but please don't rob or hurt me." We assure her we have no such intentions, and laugh our way further south. The two of us did little preparation for the occasional hour or two intervals between rides, no canister of water or sun-shielding hats.

On arrival, I notice Marjorie still wore the same turn-of-the-century fashions I remembered from my youth. She was friendly, yet overtly reserved. Our first outing around what we perceived to be a town was a quick walk, only to find everything closed, including the feed mill and a general store. The only sign of life was a few weather-beaten men, who, by the looks of it, had been in the same positions on similar seed bags a good portion of their lives. Later, a short chat around the kitchen table and a walk around the backyard frog pond. Not long after, Marjorie feeds us, then orders all house occupants to bed by 7 p.m. Seriously?

Our assigned quarters came with a spring-loaded bed, protected by a white sheet encased in slippery plastic. I wondered if Marjorie had been pre-warned that hippies carried with them the "love bug." After lights out, the room boils up to a stifling 100-plus degrees—a suffocating strongbox with no air flow. The only sounds came from the two of us, naughty sounds — the two of us twisting one way or another atop a rustling casing. We spent a good portion of the night trying to contain the laughter. In the still darkness, we whispered and speculated what was going down in the adjacent room. There were times we nearly choked from laughter and quietly opined for an alternate plan. The next morning, Marjorie comes knocking before sunrise. She admits having difficulty sleeping with all that ruckus outside her room. It was apparent she was curious about what young folks do, and lay awake studying our practices. The new husband mostly rocked in his rocker, and smiled.

The trip back was a classic, the backroads empty of traffic, the sun a murderous constant. Coming up the road and partially hidden in a heat-spilling asphalt mirage, a duotone, blue-and-white, 1958 Ford sedan. The car slows to pick us up. Through the

driver's window I can make out the tan brim of a straw hat fram-
ing the face of an aged man draped in denim overalls, suspenders
looped down to his waist. Next to him, a young woman, her white
blouse open and holding a small child. I can also see the outline
of what looks to be a boy of 12 years or younger, sitting tall in the
back seat. "Where you folks going?" asks the young woman in
a cordial tone. "Heading back to Clarksville, Tennessee and Fort
Campbell," I say. She looks over at us and says, "You-all can sit
backside with my children if you want. It's plenty cramped back
there if you don't mind. I hope you can make it work." I then
spot two or three smaller beings packed tightly in. "I'm sure we
can get you up the road," she goes on to say.

The woman then informs us of her new husband nearing 70
years of age, the family en route to lay a wreath at the grave of
a dead son in Paducah, Kentucky— *Grapes of Wrath* poor. Dead
centre of the spare tire, a young boy sitting up high, and, when
spoken to, could barely form an intelligible answer. The grieving
woman went on to describe the hardships and recent marriage
to the "good man." I catch a glimpse of her newborn. The sweet
young face covered in flies and open sores, the flies buzzing
about the cheeks and forehead.

The "good man" never pushed the speedometer past 20 miles
an hour, making the trip an excruciating affair. Kristine and I
would look back and forth at each other, squeeze hands, and
pretend we weren't dying of asphyxiation. An hour or so in, we
notice a sign affirming the mileage distance to Kentucky Lake,
and held tight. We carried on conversation, spoke of our relatives and recent marriage. The older man never moved his head,
eyes always focused on the road ahead. It was certainly a strange
marriage, one of convenience and survival. It's the South, and
people marry for various reasons. At times, extreme poverty
decides for you.

Eventually, the tree-lined roads gave way to a clearing, revealing a large body of water, Kentucky Lake. Shrouded in sweat,
grime, and short on breathable air, we asked to be dropped on
the right side of the road. Seconds after waving goodbye, Kristine and I sprint down a short embankment, and dive headfirst

into the murky lake — clothes and all. Baptism and rebirth.

As the weeks play out, Kristine would accompany me to most every solo piano gig, army functions, and even the most mundane military assignments. Ignacio never missed an opportunity to direct me to multiple "point-scoring" gigs, as he pushed for the rank of Chief Warrant Officer; my evenings reserved for unanticipated army functions, a good portion of them without pay. Off post, we struggled to pay rent and cover basic food costs. Any dollars earned from gigging made the sacrifice plausible.

I would soon join the military theatrical production of *How to Succeed in Business Without Really Trying*, on orders from Ignacio. I had never worked on a mainstream musical before, and found myself trapped five nights a week in rehearsal. Kristine would hang near the piano, and sing along, "*No coffee, no coffee, no coffee?*" In my mind, I had already decided I was ready to marry her. I had few doubts she was gifted to me, and we would soon spend future decades loving and living side by side. Between tunes, I began to practice a charismatic drop to one knee and proposal. Kristine played along and reminded me we agreed to wait a year and then we'd consider. Late May, I informed my unit I was marrying Kristine with no intention of letting her escape. So much goodness and joy poured from every region of her soul; I couldn't envision sharing her with another. A bit selfish, I guess, but that was it! Word got back to Kristine, and I was exposed. June 30th, 1969, we were married at my parents' home in Jeffersonville, Indiana. To say the wedding was a bit unusual would be understating it.

The two of us took the mandatory blood test, walked into downtown Jeffersonville to the courthouse, and signed the necessary documents. Neither of us possessed wedding rings, so we purchased one at a pawnshop, with the other gifted from my parents. The ceremony was held in my parents' living room. Most of the guests were friends of Mom from church, in fact preacher man, Brother Beard as they called him, officiated at the ceremony. My best man, Charlie Craig, and his wife, Vicky, were there to support Kristine. Anyone daring to assume that military couples have money better rethink. Mom cut and stitched a hand-me-down white dress from my sister Rhonda, and walked me to J.C. Penney, and purchased a pair of $11 Haggar slacks. Big weddings? The hell with that. The two of us beamed nothing but happiness and joy.

That evening, we celebrated at Eddie Donaldson's jazz joint at 118 Washington Street, across the river in Louisville. It so happened the Billy Paul Trio was in the house. Kristine and I cruised through the first set wearing big smiles. We then meet Paul's drummer, Sherman Ferguson, who invites us one floor below to the catacombs for a pipe of hashish. Second set, Bill Paul begins with these lines: *"Me and Mrs. King, we got a thing goin' on, we both know that it's wrong, but it's much too strong, to let it go now."* How could one top a night like that? Night two, we catch the remarkable Little Jimmy Scott.

Independence Day rolls around, July 4, 1969, and a knock comes at my parent's door. After celebrating five days of marriage, a military officer inquires of my whereabouts, and then passes an envelope with orders for Vietnam, a sober, heart-wrenching reversal of emotions. My feelings about war, especially this war, had evolved; from a young man scarred by Dad's war experiences, to a grown man about to face his own. Kristine and I had learned first-hand about the so-called enemy, the Vietnamese people, and took offence when we heard others call them "gooks" and "slant-eyes." Kristine started talking about Canada. I thought back to those Thursday afternoons I played piano at a veterans' facility at Fort Campbell. It was there I gained a first-hand understanding of the casualties of the Kennedy, Johnson, Nixon, and Kissinger administrations, left to suffer out of sight of the American public. Men arrived in gowns, some missing limbs, others hooked up to IV machines, most lost in distant thought. I walked the back rooms, the recovery areas, where the untreatable lay for weeks and months in virtual isolation. I played whatever was requested, and listened to their experiences — a place where truth and reality intersected. We would congregate in a neutral zone, sometimes talk, but mostly sit in silence.

We investigated other options from "Conscientious Objector" status to "Compassionate Reassignment." I applied through the appropriate channels, and was first interviewed by the post chaplain, before working my way up the chain of command. Kristine debated with the clergyman, who ended with this rebuttal: "Wouldn't you rather have an honourable husband than dishonourable?" Kristine: "Honourable and alive." Meanwhile, there was no let-up from Ignacio. As my rank grew, the extra duty mounted. I was promoted from Private 1st Class on arrival to Specialist 4th Class only weeks before departure — all within the first in six months, Ignacio assuring me Specialist E-5 on arrival in Vietnam.

41

Goodbye America, Hello Canada

Two military officers I got to know from hanging out nights away from the base filled me in on what to expect once in Vietnam. United in their opinion, they vowed never to return, and swore they would quit the army before returning to a land that smelled and tasted of death to them. They saw the war much the same as Kristine and me, a political struggle — soldiers pawns of political and corporate interests. Both had encountered and known the Vietnamese first-hand, and found them humble and mostly an agrarian society: giving and most forgiving. They also understood the U.S. had a long history of overthrowing governments deemed hostile to its interests, and would not hesitate to assassinate a head of state or obliterate a nation refusing to abide. The two invite us over for party night — that being a night of soul and jazz sounds. They also cooked up an exit plan for me. "Here's what you do, Bill. Carry that clarinet with you everywhere. Never speak a word again. If anyone asks something of you, blow the horn in response, and never change expression. Remember you're crazy. Just do it for a month, and you're gone." I thought about the prospect of walking among the guys whose company I enjoyed, the silliness of doing so, and declined. Both swore they would quit the military if ordered to return.

September arrives, and I'm about to be released for a month-long vacation, enough time to get personal matters in order. But Ignacio won't sign my papers, and steals two weeks of my vacation. Iggy was dead-set on scoring additional merit points, sending me on a slew of bullshit gigs. I file charges against him with the post Adjutant-General. The two of us are then interviewed, and I win the case and am gone by September 16, 1969. I also walk away with a Letter of Accommodation from the Army in recognition of superior performance and service.

On return to Indiana, Kristine and I unload and store our possessions, then spend time visiting friends, catch a bit of jazz, and pack what's needed. Before departing Louisville and on to Erie, Pennsylvania, we watch the Count Basie Orchestra on the 21st of September at Club 118 on Washington Street, music of this calibre hard to come by in the military. In Erie, we visit both Kristine's great-grandmother and grandmother, then fly on to Manhattan and a lay-over at the cockroach-infested Hotel Earle. Memories!

October 12th, we leave Manhattan for Fort Dix, New Jersey, board a train from Long Island to Manhattan, then hitchhike on to New Jersey. Just beyond the front gates of Fort Dix, we hail a taxi. It just happens the day 10,000 antiwar protesters gather to protest the war and encourage soldiers like me to refuse Vietnam. It was the biggest moratorium against the war, and Kris and I had to navigate our way past the unruly crowd. We check in at a military police booth, where I am questioned and then threatened. I wore two weeks' sideburn growth, which somehow offended one officer, who demanded I immediately shave. He then warns if seen again, he'd willingly administer a beating on me. Bizarre, but true. We drive on. Next up and close by my final stop, Kristine and I are once again waved off the main road by a military police cruiser, and threatened with violence. I lose it and tell the police officer, "I'm being sent to some foreign land to possibly die, and you are threatening me over sideburns?" He waves us ahead.

I then navigate my way past a multitude of service members going and coming from orientation, into a room with 200-plus soldiers, all destined for Vietnam. Then a First Lieutenant delivers the bad news. It is decided we are to be separated from spouses, and transported to the far side of the base and quartered until flown to San Francisco. Then on to Vietnam. Several protestors had breached the presumed secure gates, climbed fences, then fanned out through the tall grass, down side streets, screaming for an end to the war. I cannot express the level of nausea that overcame me. It was comparable to that ride with the FBI agent to the courthouse in New Albany, Indiana. First body tremours, the heart nearly ceases, then an unwelcome wave of depression consumes me. I envisioned saying goodbye to Kristine, and never returning; a good life wasted on a bullshit war, then determine I should bargain with the man in charge. I approach him, and talk of our recent marriage and my bride outside waiting, and that saying goodbye was near impossible. Despondent, I wave a hand, and am then called forward. I express my concerns having my new bride along, and the sudden change of plans, to which he replies, "I'll give you a pass for the night at a post guest house. But if fully occupied, I expect you back here." I take the offer to rejoin Kristine, and find accommodations.

As we search the side streets for the three designated family units, we turn a corner near a military barracks, and are confronted by a platoon of returning veterans dressed in battle fatigues and sporting beards. One notices my uniform and rank, and shouts, "Hey asshole, you're going to Vietnam?" Caught off guard by the question, I watch as he whispers something to a group, laughs and mumbles. As we close in, he again turns and shouts, "You're a fucking moron if you go, you know that?" Still laughing, the group slow-marches around the corner, then fades from view.

Kristine and I arrive at the post guest house, and find it wholly occupied. She then asks, "What are we going to do?" In what becomes the most significant decision of our lives, I pause, then say, "We are going to do what you suggested months back: going to Canada." Done!

I have replayed that moment so many times in my head, and it remains preserved as a movie still from a classic film. It was the tears, the depth of love and goodness I saw in her eyes, the fearlessness and willingness to follow through. If there was a juncture in my life when someone I deeply loved could have simply replied, "Enough of this. I'm not leaving friends, family and country for a guy I hardly know and move to a foreign country," it was this moment.

We returned to the orientation centre, I undressed and placed all my military apparel on a bunk, snatched a T-shirt, pants, and pair of shoes, leaving the rest of my possessions in a duffle bag atop an assigned bunk, and began looking for a clear path away from the post. We stride cautiously past incoming recruits, ignore the numerous non-commissioned officers milling about, and slow-walk towards the tree-lined lanes leading to the front gates. Just ahead, a military cruiser is policing the roads. We leave the road, and hide amongst the tall weeds just beyond the main thoroughfare. Once out of view, Kristine moves back on to the main road, and begins thumbing a ride only moments before a car pulls alongside. Kristine waves it down, and explains our intentions to a young man who himself appeared to be full-blown military. He directs us to the back seat, and suggests I cover myself with a blanket, and squeeze onto the floorboards, then confesses to being the son of a military officer, and against the war. With much confusion and military police driving left and right lanes, he salutes the police stationed at the front gate's booth, navigates us out the entrance, past guards, and down the main highway to the first gas station within range. Then a short thank you and goodbye, a quick change into civilian clothes, and the last remnants of military apparel banished.

We soon notice a long-haired couple coming up the road, and flag them down. Both are protesting outside the gates, and then we are asked, "Where are you two going?" The answer? "Canada, but first, New York City and a visit with our best friends, Bob and Barbara, as they have some fine hashish," I say. "Well, get in." We call ahead, and Bob Slawson answers and informs us he has the best Lebanese hash known to man, and upon arrival, we are all getting stoned. I had never smoked good hash before, and Bob made it sound like a cause for celebration and most inviting. During the ride, I was overcome by paranoia. Would the lieutenant send a fleet of armoured personnel in search, or would it be an old-fashioned throng of hound dogs? How many hours' leeway did I have?

Our hippie escorts proved to be a godsend, both compassionate and generous. After hellos, Bob smokes us up, and we get seriously stoned. A few bowls of hashish did the job, and our ride was on their way. Bob had other plans, and wanted us to sample the best soul food in Manhattan. Bob, Barbara, Kristine and I hit the streets. Until now, the only thrill of being stoned I'd experienced came from the cheap weed that band sergeant sold from his Benylin cough drawer, and the old matchbox of stems and seeds that wasn't so magical. The intensity of Bob's get-high struck with a Force 10. On the walk there, I paused to look up at a street sign, and suddenly realized the strength and power of the high. I shared that epiphany with Bob, Barbara, and Kristine and kept repeating, "I'm so fucking stoned, I'm really fucking stoned," knowing full well I'm only a short distance from capture. To keep nerves from fraying, that evening it was decided catching a movie was mandatory. Barbara thumbs through the *What's Playing* section of *The Village Voice*, hands it to me for a run-through, and I discover *Night of the Living Dead* showing nearby. I told everyone of the creepy zombie "flesh-eating" bonanza, and recounted an afternoon viewing with a half-terrified Gettier.

Gettier and I had escaped the blistering Tennessee heat, and checked into a post-movie house. Popcorn, colas, and air conditioning, and before us, scary stuff. Or that's what the billboard advertised. From the opening scene, it was apparent this was no ordinary horror flick, but one that grabbed the gut and squeezed. Gettier laughed out loud at every bizarre killing, the bouts of on-screen panic, and bloodshed. Although filmed in black-and-white outside Pittsburgh, Pennsylvania, the film bled red just the same. The two of us screamed, gagged, covered eyes, and left the theatre with one mission in mind — get every soldier to watch this absurd mental and physical disembowelment. I sold Bob and Barbara on the experience, then find out the two had dropped acid. The film rolls with the four of us wholly engrossed and mesmerized by the platoons of ghouls jabbing and stabbing, when Bob taps me on the shoulder and says, "I think I'm going to throw up. You know, you weren't bullshitting; this is the scariest flick I've ever seen." As Barbara laughed nervously, Bob's face said it all: "Fuck me! Thank God, this wasn't in colour."

The next morning, we begin the journey to Canada. Kristine and I make our way to the Triborough Bridge in Brooklyn, and did what we have always done, hitchhike. Minutes in, a motorcycle policeman approaches, questions us, then warns he'd arrest us if caught hitchhiking anywhere near the bridge. We circle back, and move a fair distance from view to see what looks like a milk truck rolling in our direction, so we flag it down. Once inside, we discover the van is carrying a full load of sauerkraut. Before entering, we agree between ourselves not to speak of the military or anything anti-war.

I sit below on the floorboards, Kristine high above on oval-shaped sauerkraut containers. The ride for me is uncomfortable, but seeing Kristine high above, legs dangling, brought smiles and big joy. The driver, mostly disinterested, spoke little. There was something about him that said "don't engage." He then drives us to White Plains, New York, and drops us on a side road.

An hour passes before we catch the eye of "Mr. Straight," a clean-cut gentleman who pulls over, and invites us in, then announces he was on the way to Springfield, Massachusetts, to visit the Baseball Hall of Fame. Over the next hundred miles or so, he attempts to extract information from us — he could not get a handle on two young people, alone, and hitchhiking, one sporting a military-style haircut, the other an extremely attractive young woman. To him, it seemed bold, dangerous, and suspicious. We resisted his questions, and mostly ignored his compulsive follow-ups. I talked baseball: Ruth, Maris, Mays, and Mantle. Yankee greats enshrined in the hallowed hall. He'd occasionally smile and play along, then try to steer conversation back to our being alone, rain falling all around and why? In a heavy drizzle, the guy eventually drops us the far side of Rochester, New York, near an off-ramp. We weren't prepared for the change in temperature, and huddle beneath an overpass, shivering and waiting for a next ride. No easy feat.

Until now, everything seemed possible and under our control. Rides came in batches. The overpass provided a fair amount of cover, but did nothing to alleviate the fear of being caught by a highway patrol officer, or tame the bone-chilling tremors. Another hour passes when an elderly gentleman wearing a tweed overcoat and short-brimmed hat signals us over. He quizzes us, and asks the reason for us being there. Then he says he is not about to pick us up, and slams the car door as if driving off. He then hesitates, flings open the door, and asks for some assurance we are not going to rob him. Kristine and I turn to him and say, "We don't rob people; we're heading to Canada." He notices the one suitcase, a reel-to-reel tape recorder, and relents, invites us in, drives a few miles down the highway, then quickly changes his mind, and drops us at the next off-ramp, stops, and insists we exit the car. This was fucked up! I couldn't get a handle on this guy. From the downbeat he was edgy, and in no way hospitable. I assumed he'd never picked up a hitchhiker before, and was uncertain of the outcome.

With darkness approaching, and facing an unrelenting downpour, we stumble down an off-ramp, and away from the highway. Just beyond the roar of trucks and away from speeding cars and about to earn a moment of solitude, we are promptly intercepted by a state trooper, who grills us about being alone and without an umbrella and what he assumes is no destination. We explain ourselves and our plans. He warns us to stay away from the main highway, or he'd return, arrest us and take us into custody.

Not far from the off-ramp, and down the road, two occupants sit in an idling sedan. Kristine approaches, taps at a window, and then asks if the driver was going anywhere near the Canadian border. The guy responds, "Why not?"

Hair slicked back, and with an edge to him, the guy behind the steering wheel was a fair bit older than his travelling companion, who looked to be in her mid-teens and talked a mean streak. We had yet to learn the two had been living in the car, and welcomed the diversion. All that was needed was gas money. With tank filled, he agrees to drive us to Toronto, saying, "It's been years since I've been there — a great party town — maybe we could stay the night." There was something uncomfortable about the guy, and from her looks, I doubted the young girl had ever ventured far beyond the surrounding trees.

As we approached the border and crossing at Niagara Falls, I understood there would be no turning back, and would possibly face five years in prison. Customs and Immigration loomed up ahead — heart-pumping scary. After stating our intentions to visit Canada, two customs officers wave the car to a holding area, separate us, and then question the driver and his young companion. Immigration isolates and interrogates the guy, who, upon his return, approaches Kristine and asks if she had extra ID. Kristine had a photo taken when she had brown hair, and she shows him. He then grabs it, says thanks, and hands it to the girl. Next up, the girl. She disappears into a backroom, and quickly returns. Then it's Kristine and me. We show ID, express our intent to visit Toronto and the fact I had been a music student a few years back, and wanted to show my new bride what a great city Toronto is. All is quiet until border police arrive from New York State, blow past us into a side room, cuff our driver, and rescue the girl. Nothing is said to either Kris or me.

Time passes. We await the verdict in silence. An hour or so in, I decide to make a play, and approach the counter, behind which is a uniformed officer. I ask, "Sir, what happened to the guy and girl who drove us here?" The officer answers, "I thought you were friends; he's heading back to New York and jail. Parole violator. The girl's only 14 and underage. If you have any property with them, you should retrieve it now." We had our only possessions: a few clothes and a Sony tape recorder. Then a moment of clarity. "Sir, we don't know those people, we were hitchhiking, and they picked us up in the rain and gave us a ride." He pauses, then asks, "What are you doing here?" I knew then I had one shot at this. "Kristine and I were recently married, and we haven't had a honeymoon yet, and we thought Niagara Falls was the most exciting trip we could afford. I was here with my parents years ago, but Kristine has never seen the Canadian side of the falls. Besides, I went to music school in Toronto a few summers ago." He steps away from the front desk and disappears into a backroom, returns, and waves me down the front. "We have no criminal record of you two, no arrest warrants, so we can't hold you; so, I'm assuming you've committed no crimes, right? I see no reason to hold you here, but first, where are you staying in Niagara Falls?" I look beyond a broad window, and point to a motel up the hill. "The Rainbow Inn, sir!" He smiles and says,

"Well, you two young folks have a great time, and remember you can only spend a night in Canada, you understand?"

I cannot remember a time in my life like this. Kristine and I holed up in a sleazy, border-town motel, secure in a coin-operated vibrating bed, windows covered in grungy orange drapes, a blinking TV, and shag carpet. And then the capper. Kristine pulls out a matchbox packed with beautiful weed. Lights out!

42

The Arrival

From the moment we met, I soft-sold Canada. Kristine imagined a pastoral land, much like the German countryside, with long stretches of carefully manicured rolling hills; absent those intrusive Burma-Shave signs witnessed on roadside billboards and painted barn tops throughout the South. I assured her there were no ghettoes or districts given to poverty or derelicts, and one could ride streetcars between quaint European-style neighbourhoods, much like San Francisco, and people-watch from sidewalk cafés. It was an idyllic new world I planned for her.

The roar of Niagara Falls played tricks on the mind. It was as if we were suspended a foot above the rapids. We shower away the previous day, and prepare for the road ahead. Even after an intense grilling at Customs and Immigration, we hadn't lost the will to hitchhike, and now it was imperative. We move far out of sight of our interrogators, and locate a highway leading to Toronto. With thumbs extended, we quickly hitch a ride with a well-dressed businessman who offers to drop us close to the city. There was nothing exceptional about the drive, other than the both of us grinned a lot and poked each other in the ribs. Near the Jameson Avenue exit, the gentleman pulls over, lets us out, and wishes us well.

A welcoming October sun backlit the early morning hour. Poorly dressed, the two of us were in for an eventful day. Kristine wore a light sweater, jeans, and sandals. Me? Desert boots, jeans, and light denim jacket, and nothing to combat a brisk autumn wind which was not playing favours. I often think of this moment and how other immigrants must feel when they

first arrive in a new land, the walk along Jameson Avenue forever etched in my memory. There were feelings of helplessness,
moments of laughter, fear, anxiety, and curiosity. The surrounding apartments looked familiar, much like 1960s austerity housing. We could not help but ask ourselves what it would be like to
live in one of those places, absent money worries, rent paid, food,
and employment. Or how grand it must be to sleep in a heated
room in one's bed. To read a book or watch an old movie, and
know that the following morning, you were not facing eviction,
being pressured or stalked.

Before leaving the States, I called Albert Grossman's office.
Though I mysteriously disappeared after Janis's gig in Memphis,
there were no hard feelings, and was told I should have asked for
help. The agency had been successful in dealing with artists with
draft problems. I requested agent Vinnie Fusco, who had kindly
steered me through the mechanics of copping the Janis gig and a
big supporter. Vinnie was not available. I then patched through
to his partner, Elliot Mazer, and explained what had happened
following Memphis and the fact I had just served 10 months in
the military, and was heading to Canada. Instead of hanging up,
Elliot suggested I hook up with folk singer Adam Mitchell. He
felt Adam would be sympathetic to our situation. Elliot gave
me a phone number and street address. I clutched a small suitcase with our few possessions in one hand and that Sony tape
recorder in the other. Only steps away from Parkdale Village,
we witnessed a radical change from the colourless 1960s style
housing of Jameson to large, ornate, brick-laden houses, the city
I had promised Kristine. The walk from Jameson Avenue to 10
Hazelton Avenue in Yorkville was an exhausting 17 kilometres.

One can assume the unannounced arrival would be shocking,
yet Adam and his young wife Carolyn warmly invited us in. We
appear just as the dinner table is being set, and invited company
situated all around. After a bit of small talk, Adam invites us to
spend the night, and sleep between the living-room couch and
floor until the following morning. He also invites us to stay for
dinner. The menu? Chicken à l'orange. Entertainment? A night
of euchre, the card game. There is no way an encounter such as

this didn't come with a level of uncertainty. We understood we were outsiders, and Carolyn went out of her way to afford us a night of normalcy, free from worry and doubt.

Early morning October 17th, Kristine and I canvass the nearby neighbourhoods in search of permanent shelter. After a couple of failed attempts, we locate a vacant front room at 43 Chicora Avenue, just off Avenue Road, south of Dupont. It is three days out from Kristine's 20th birthday, and we are still getting our bearings. We pay a week's rent. On October 20th, we celebrate Kristine's birthday, secure in a warm bed, divide a lemon-meringue birthday pie, and revel in the joy of the moment. The following morning, rebirth! Welcome to Canada!

Epilogue

Dad passed away June 17, 2005. On the final day, the family gathered around as families do.

Wayne and I took turns applying morphine candy swabs under his tongue. Leukemia proved to be a far greater opponent than the many operations that slowed (but never sidetracked) his passion for music and sport fishing.

In one last attempt to communicate, Dad whispered to Mom and me, "They are here, and I'm going to travel." I got goosebumps. It was as if the unseen world was looking on.

Mom interpreted his words to suit her understanding. I took it to mean that all those young men who perished all around Dad, the boys and girls who skipped lightly through the backwoods of Kentucky and Tennessee with Dad, those many men who sat on the banks of small ponds and swampy lakes who had passed before him and their ancestors, were there to walk him into the hereafter.

It was October 1969 when Kristine and I confronted our past and decided to flee to Toronto.

Thirty-one years later, in May of 2000, we received an invitation to the 39th Contact (Photography) Festival and showing in Toronto by curator Lesley Sparks.

Sparks insisted we be part of this historic event and meet the girl in the photo — the young south Vietnamese child napalmed while fleeing war — a photo that Nick Ut captured that brought home the horrors of the war.

Phan Thi Kim Phuc spoke of that day, the hundreds of skin grafts and operations, and the fact she was now a Canadian citizen. Kristine and I cried throughout.

After the ceremony, Lesley walked Phuc over. Kris and I embraced Kim Phuc and cried, cried, cried.

To this day we have never questioned the moment we crossed over into Canada or ever taken for granted the renewed life that was awarded us. The scars of war remain, but our hearts sing on.

About Bill King

William (Bill) King's recording career began in 1965 with a cover recording of jazz great Bobby Timmon's classic soul-jazz hymnal "Moanin'" by the southern band The Chateaus, in Louisville, KY. King arranged and played piano on the top 50 Billboard hit.

King arrived in Canada in late 1969 and scored a record deal with legendary producer Jack Richardson and his Nimbus 9 label, who then recorded and released *Every Living Thing* by Homestead, King's band. Then came two solo projects for Capitol Records, *Goodbye Superdad* and *Dixie Peach*, under the helm of producer Paul Hoffert and H.P.& Bell.

Through the years King has been nominated for three Junos, won New Artist of the Year with his Rockit 88 Band at the 2003 *Maple Blues Awards;* was a two-time recipient of Producer and Photographer of the Year from the *National Jazz Awards;* received four nominations for Jazz Journalist of the Year; and was twice nominated for Jazz Photo of the Year by the *International Jazz Journalist Association.*

King has played on numerous recordings from Stan Rodgers, John Allan Cameron, The Rockit 88 Band, The Rhythm Express,

OKAN, Dubmatix, and The Saturday Nite Fish Fry to hundreds of tracks with an array of accomplished singers. His keyboard work comes with a distinctive style, rooted in American jazz and blues. King produced vocalists Liberty Silver, top-selling Sophie Milman, Shakura S'Aida, June Garber, Cornelia Luna, Kinga Heming, among others. King was also the music director for Janis Joplin, Linda Ronstadt, Martha Reeves, Craig Russell, The Pointer Sisters, and others. Bill's latest recording projects include the celebrated J&B Kings with son Jesse and a companion recording to *Coming Through the '60s*, *Mondo Jumbo*, a mix of funk, soul, and rhythm & blues.

King's career in radio began at Q-107 in 1985, eventually building a national network, *The Jazz Report Radio Network* (1988-91), heard in 26 Canadian cities. Currently, King hosts the *Bill King Show* at CIUT 89.5 FM and is music director/cohost of the *Saturdays with Ted* at Newstalk 1010 and *Soul Nation* at Jazz.FM91 with son Jesse King.

Along with these endeavors, King published the *Jazz Report Magazine* from 1988-2006; produced the *Jazz Report* and *National Jazz Awards*; curated *Jazz at the ROM*; was music director for *Director's Guild Awards*; contributed five years as Artistic Director of the *Children's Aid Gala*; and has been artistic director of the *Beaches International Jazz Festival* since its inception in 1988.

King has also published four books of concert and travel photography. In 2020, Bill published *Volume 1: Talk! Conversations in All Keys*, 72 interviews with the icons of Canadian music. Coming in 2021: *Talk! Volume 2: The Business*.

www.ingramcontent.com/pod-product-compliance
Lightning Source LLC
Chambersburg PA
CBHW031945090426
42739CB00006B/88